The City Natural

HISTORY OF THE URBAN ENVIRONMENT
Martin V. Melosi and Joel A. Tarr, Editors

THE CITY NATURAL

Garden and Forest Magazine
and the Rise of American
Environmentalism

SHEN HOU

Foreword by Donald Worster

University of Pittsburgh Press

Published by the University of Pittsburgh Press, Pittsburgh, Pa., 15260
Copyright © 2013, University of Pittsburgh Press
All rights reserved
Manufactured in the United States of America
Printed on acid-free paper
10 9 8 7 6 5 4 3 2 1

ISBN 13: 978-0-8229-4423-2
ISBN 10: 0-8229-4423-5

Cataloging-in-Publication data is on file with the Library of Congress.

To my parents

献给我的父母

CONTENTS

FOREWORD

Donald Worster

In his *Principles of Psychology* (1890), the scientist and philosopher of pragmatism William James asserted that an infant feels the world "as one great blooming, buzzing confusion." Growing older, we learn to see it as an orderly succession of discrete objects, but that order may or may not conform to reality. Confronted by bewildering complexity, we tend to look for a few simple categories and organize everything into them. Sometimes the categories work, sometimes they don't. Pragmatic wisdom consists in staying flexible, constantly making revisions, and testing new ways of ordering the confusion that surrounds us. But that is hard work, and it is always easier to cling to what we have learned to perceive and expect. Worse, we let our categories harden into fixed ideas.

This perceptive, elegant, and important book by Shen Hou is about a group of American environmental thinkers who practiced the pragmatism that James taught. I like to think he would have found them soul mates, for like them he was drawn to nature but in an open, inclusive, and experimental way. That nature was not a fixed idea but a powerful organic force in the universe that humans did not create but was always changing in shape and meaning. With that philosophy of nature in mind, those environmental thinkers created a magazine, *Garden and Forest*, that James might well have read, for it was established in his home city of Boston and published there while he was on the faculty at Harvard University. We owe a great debt to Hou for her efforts to bring those thinkers back into the light, giving us a chance to read them anew and providing environmentalists with an important set of predecessors whose pragmatism is more needed than ever.

While asking us to appreciate the achievement and point of view of those turn-of-the century thinkers, Hou also asks historians to rethink some familiar categories and fixed ideas. Like nature itself, our traditions of environmental thought and action are a great blooming, buzzing confusion, full of names and places that do not reduce readily to neatly defined types like "wilderness lover" or "seeker of justice." We must always remind ourselves that past thinkers were a lot more complicated than we remember and that their efforts do not fit neatly into any set of simple positions or pattern of change.

As they moved westward, Americans repeatedly fell in love with the color, diversity, richness, and possibilities of nature. Excitedly, they began writing and painting about what they saw and experienced. By the late nineteenth century, they had created a powerful tradition of environmental thought. It is one of the most distinctive contributions of American civilization, and over time it has made a global impact. Think of the multitudes around the world who have read Henry David Thoreau, George Perkins Marsh, John Muir, Aldo Leopold, and Rachel Carson or of those who have been moved by the artistry of American outdoor photographers, landscape painters, and wilderness film makers and by the political consequences of their art and writing. Without them, the world landscape we know today would be very different from what it is: Walden Pond might be a real-estate development, the African elephant and the bison might have completely disappeared, and institutions like the National Park Service in the United States or China's Friends of Nature (an organization of concerned citizens) might not exist.

Historians have traced the development of that thinking and organized it into categories. Environmental concern, they explain, divided people into rival camps of "conservation" versus "preservation." Some environmental thinkers, it is frequently noted, cared only for wilderness, while others cared only for cities and their problems. As always, we tend to reduce complexity into two, or at most three, discrete objects or ideas vying for influence, when the reality has been more tangled and fused.

America's environmental thought, to be sure, has included diverse voices, often conflicting with one another. That diversity comes from another demographic movement, besides that of the frontier, in which people left their rural way of life and moved to the city (and to factory jobs). The backyard privy and the urban park drew as much attention from reformers as did western plains or mountains. From privies came infection, stench, and contagious diseases, threatening human lives. Environmental reformers found in the polluted slums of Chicago, New York, and Boston a challenge to their ideas of cleanliness, justice, and humanity. At the same time, urban environmentalists tried to create and preserve green spaces within reach of city dwellers, rich and poor. Together, whether they were green-space advocates or landscape architects, doctors or industrial hygienists, those urban reformers have inspired the United States and other nations to save cities as well as the land.

Wilderness versus city, frontier versus industry, sanitation versus sustainability: these have become the organizing dichotomies of American environmental thought. But historical reality has been messier than that. In this book, Hou shows how oversimplified and false such pairings are. The different mobilities were intertwined, the ideas overlapped, and many people believed the battle to safeguard the environment should be fought on many fronts at once—in the city, yes, but also on the margins of society. Some might concentrate their energies on one front rather than another, but, like the environment itself, thinking about the American environment was always eclectic and pragmatic, not easily divided into rigid categories.

Hou's strategy for getting beyond worn-out dichotomies and recovering that pragmatic spirit is to examine closely the pages of a single magazine, *Garden and Forest*, whose very title called for an ecumenical spirit. Despite its short run of publication, it was a significant influence on American public opinion. Ostensibly, the magazine was aimed at anyone who wanted to put in a backyard garden or to landscape a house site in the city, or anyone who loved plants, wild or domesticated. It was full of practical advice on which plants to grow and where to obtain them. But along with the green plants came a more comprehensive, wide-ranging approach to the human environment. The magazine stood squarely in the midst of the emerging metropolis, with its sewers, factories, crowded tenements, and sprawling suburbs. Unmistakably, this was a magazine by and for city people. But for more than a decade it also encouraged city people to care about far more than their private gardens or even their urban neighborhoods. The whole environment of America, including places that were hundreds and even thousands of miles away, appeared in the magazine's pages. Nothing less than integrating the modern city into the natural world—creating the "city natural"—was the magazine's theme.

And what a magnificent magazine it was! Its pages enticed the eye with appealing images of flowers, trees, gardens, parks, and houses carefully adapted to the landscape. Its authors, more than six hundred of them, coming from many walks of life and professions, wrote with wonderful insight and style. Their contributions suggest that many more individuals became engaged in environmental improvement than we have realized—some of them remaining famous down to our own day, but most of them now obscure and forgotten. Reading their words deepens our knowledge of the breadth and talent, the variety and sophistication that flourished at the grassroots of American environmentalism in its formative years.

This book, explains its author, is a "collective biography" of that magazine and its contributors. Although much of the information on the business side of the magazine, including data on circulation and distribution, has been lost, its words and images survive and can be tracked over time. Biographers commonly conclude that, after all their efforts to penetrate and understand the innermost thoughts of their subjects, they cannot reduce them to a simple profile. Any individual is full of conflicting ideas and inexplicable impulses. So it was with this magazine: it did not present a unified formula, ideology, or worldview. Hou wisely lets its voices speak for themselves and does not try to impose any uniformity on the magazine. But she makes clear that there was a common vision—an urban society in which all residents would enjoy a measure of health and beauty through the continuing presence of nature in their lives—and a common ethic of taking responsibility far beyond the limits of the city.

This book by a rising young international talent in environmental history is a major contribution to our understanding of the rise of American environmentalism. It will give historians a deeper and more complete picture of the foundations of environmental thinking than we have grasped. It will give today's environmentalists a new appreciation for the multitudes who have gone before and created a legacy of constructive solutions. Readers all over the world, whether they live in Beijing or Boston, Mumbai or Berlin, will find in these pages a wealth of ideas about problems still confronting us. Above all, they will discover here an astonishing array of men and women who, in the spirit of William James and American pragmatism, faced the future with open minds, with a wide outlook, free of confining categories and narrow interests, and with persistent optimism.

ACKNOWLEDGMENTS

A decade ago, I undertook a big life adventure, heading toward the Great Plains of the United States to study environmental history with Donald Worster at the University of Kansas. Bewildered, I was almost lost in this completely new cultural and natural landscape, but fortunately, Don became my adviser, and his guidance was one of the most valuable things in my life. No one could expect a better guide. He has opened a window, leading me to appreciate another culture and use another language. He has taught me to cross national boundaries to see an entire planet and to break the cultural restraints to discover a natural realm. Without him, I would have never finished this book and never been able to find such a colorfully animated world in history and in life.

My equally deep gratitude goes to Professor Susan Flader of the University of Missouri. I have known her for more than two decades as a family friend. For many years, she has supported my pursuit of environmental history with her insightful understanding of both American and Chinese cultures and societies and enriched my experience in the United States and other countries with many field trips and activities.

I am also very grateful to my editors, Cynthia Miller and Maureen Bemko, and the anonymous reviewers for their constructive questions and suggestions. I will always remember the professional help from many libraries and librarians in the United States. At the top of that list is the Library of Congress, which digitized the run of the magazine *Garden and Forest*, thus enabling me to have full access to the basic source of this book when I was not in the United States. There were other archival libraries to which I owe a great debt:

the Arnold Arboretum Library, the Francis Loeb Library, and the Herbaria Library, all at Harvard, along with the library of New York City's Department of Parks and Recreation, the New York Public Library, and others. Those libraries and their staffs carry on the same "public spirit" that *Garden and Forest* was searching for.

My home institution, Renmin University of China in Beijing, provided me with a generous academic environment after I came back to China. The completion of the book was funded by the university's Special Funds of the Third Term of 985 Project. Also, I owe much to a generous fellowship at the Rachel Carson Center (RCC) in Munich, Germany. Life at the RCC was always culturally and academically exciting.

I also want to take this opportunity to thank many teachers in my life whom I had the great honor and pleasure to work with, especially Judith Major, Karl Brooks, and Greg Cushman, whose advice and comments have inspired me in many ways. And those professors I had when I was studying ancient Chinese history in China helped build a strong foundation of diverse knowledge. My friends and colleagues Guorong Gao, Xueqin Mei, and Mingfang Xia, although never my formal teachers, have done much to help me launch a new career in my home country. Meanwhile, an affectionate acknowledgment is also owed to many friends on various continents, especially my "sister" Yin, who was always there, listening when I needed to talk and cheering me up when I felt frustrated.

Finally, I want to thank my family. My brother Chen, his wife, Sara, and his son, Han, created a warm home for me in another country. Most important, I want to dedicate this book to my parents. They are not only the ones who brought me into this world but also the ones who led me to a career as a historian and teacher; I am following in their footsteps. Indulging me with unlimited love, they have always been the best teachers and friends. They make me know how beautiful life is!

The City Natural

INTRODUCTION

‿‿‿‿‿‿‿‿‿‿‿‿‿‿‿

A NOVEL PUBLISHED in the late nineteenth century, *Looking Backward, 2000–1887*, offered a highly influential glimpse into America's urban future. The whole nation would move into cities reorganized into a socialistic paradise where everyone received the same income and lived together in harmony. Science and technology would meet every human need and enhance happiness and freedom. The novel's hero, Julian West, recalled an older America where an elite few had monopolized the wealth, where cities had been plagued by strikes, crimes, and poverty, and where residents had lived lives filled with unrest, anxiety, and bewilderment. To the hero, that old urban world was only a dark memory.

Looking Backward quickly jumped to the top of the best-seller list. By the end of 1891, it had sold almost half a million copies, a success suggesting that fin-de-siècle Americans were eager to hear remedies for the problems they sensed around them. While the majority might not have agreed with author Edward Bellamy's socialist vision, they did like his confident promise of a stable and prosperous urban future free of social ills.[1]

There was, however, one highly desirable feature hardly mentioned in that utopia: the presence of nature. Only once in 470 pages did Bellamy envision some sort of nature inside the city: "Miles of broad streets, shaded by trees and lined with fine buildings, for the most part not in continuous blocks but set in larger or smaller enclosures, stretched in every direction. Every quarter contained large open squares filled with trees, among which statues glistened and fountains flashed in the late afternoon sun."[2] The twenty-first-century Boston in Bellamy's fantasy was rich, clean, healthy, organized, and comfortable, full of human-constructed majesty and technical miracles, but he did not give many details about the future relationship of city people to nature.

For contemporary environmental reformers like Frederick Law Olmsted, Charles S. Sargent, and Charles Eliot, all of whom wanted to bring nature into the American city, the future Bellamy depicted must have seemed a little pale and vague, lacking the vitality of nature and the charm of the native landscape. In the wrenching upheaval brought by economic forces, these reformers all worried more than the novelist did about the deleterious impact on the natural world caused by modern civilization, the alienation of urban residents from nature, and the dull artificiality of much of urban life. In contrast to Bellamy, they set out to ease not merely the social tensions of an urban, capitalistic age but also the tensions between human beings and nature.[3]

This vision of a greener future for America's cities was not merely the dream of a few isolated individuals. It was also the project of an extraordinary weekly magazine called *Garden and Forest: A Journal of Horticulture, Landscape Art, and Forestry*. The magazine came into being on 29 February 1888, only one month after the thunderous appearance of *Looking Backward*, and it ceased publication on 29 December 1897. Among its voices were Olmsted, Sargent, and Eliot, along with many other contributors. Like Bellamy's novel, the magazine *Garden and Forest* criticized the social system and aimed to improve it, but, unlike the "fanciful romance" (as Bellamy called his novel), *Garden and Forest* argued strenuously that nature's presence, with its beauty and resources, was not only necessary but also desirable for an urban age. In other words, for Bellamy, whose design of a future urban society found favor among many of his contemporaries, a clean, tidy, but faceless urban landscape was merely the setting for social, political, and economic reforms; such a landscape was merely a backdrop rather than the focus of reformers' attention. For many others, nature needed plenty of space, and well-protected space, in an urban civilization.

The magazine's central focus was how to civilize the nation by creating a more harmonious fit of cities into their natural habitat. The founders of *Garden and Forest* offered no succinctly expressed philosophy or programmatic vision, nor any label for their effort. Yet it is possible to distill their core ideas and to give a name to their common environmental philosophy—the "city natural"— and see the magazine as the founders' principal organ of thought and influence. Although related to the later City Beautiful movement, the "city natural" ideal promoted a unique aesthetic and cultural vision for America.

Influenced by the contemporary Beaux-Arts movement, the City Beautiful movement originated in the last few years of the nineteenth century and reached its peak in the first decade of the new century. Its most spectacular statement was the White City, built in Chicago for the World's Columbian Exposition in 1893. The chief architect and planner of that famed architectural expression, with its Venice-inspired Court of Honor and Grand Basin, was Daniel Burnham, and he followed his triumph of the White City with his 1909 Plan of Chicago, perhaps the most influential document in the history of American urban planning. The scale of the plan, like the White City, was monumental, and both were meant to suggest the very antithesis of the wild beauty of nature.[4]

In 1901, Charles Mulford Robinson, the most articulate proponent of the City Beautiful movement, published a manifesto, *The Improvement of Towns and Cities*; two years later, he wrote *Modern Civic Art, or, the City Made Beautiful*, and thus gave the movement an official name. In the latter work, Robinson claimed that a new age of the city was coming, an age of cities made beautiful by large-scale planning. The ideal urban appearance Robinson envisioned looked very much like Bellamy's projection for Boston in 2000, with colossal buildings, grand plazas, and wide road systems. Although, unlike *Looking Backward*, Robinson's plan of beautification emphasized parks, parkways, and a park system, these elements were "ornaments" for the city and their purpose was to decorate a constructed elegance, not to reestablish a connection between urban people and nature in the new age.[5]

Although distinct in time and ideal, the City Beautiful movement and the "city natural" vision had many overlapping projects and shared leaders. The key figure in the latter, for example, was Olmsted, who, William Wilson points out, made three major contributions to the City Beautiful movement. First, Olmsted transformed the idea of a park from an isolated, single urban space to a more ambitious park and boulevard system with multiple functions inside cities. Second, he taught Americans to see the social and moral values of parks and helped make natural beauty a central theme of the movement. Third, his insistence on professional planning helped legitimatize the role of expertise in urban planning.[6]

But the main emphasis among City Beautiful advocates was on promoting architectural grandeur. Transforming America's cities into splendid statements of empire, improving the built environment, and impressing the world with the nation's vision and enterprise was their main project, not integrating nature into the city. The city, those advocates said, should manifest order, harmony, and dignity through imposing clusters of artifacts—grandiose structures arranged along wide avenues, as Baron Georges-Eugène Haussmann had done in modernizing Paris in the 1860s. The fundamental ethos underlying the City Beautiful movement was a celebration of the nation's scientific, artistic, economic, and technological power.

In contrast, what we can call the "city natural" ideal was focused on bringing nature into the city and the city into nature. Even though this ideal also endorsed scientific and artistic intervention and implied some control over natural processes, it maintained a deep love and respect for nature and its laws. Instead of transforming the city into "a vast desert of houses, factories, and stores, spreading over and overwhelming the natural features of the landscape, as lines of sand dunes, advancing from the seashore, overwhelm and obliterate the woods and fields," in the words of Sylvester Baxter, secretary of the commission of the Boston Metropolitan Park System and one of the major contributors to *Garden and Forest*, this urban ideal intended to make the city more natural and thus more deeply humanizing and civilizing. The appearance of the city was only part of the concern. Beyond that, the city natural movement saw urban society as a whole and addressed the interdependence and interaction among various natural and cultural forces.

Four themes dominated the magazine's environmental focus over its decade-long publishing history. First was the belief that all people, whatever their class or gender, need nature—its resources and its beauty—in their lives, although this need may vary some from group to group and individual to individual. It should be the obligation of a civilized society to acknowledge, defend, and cultivate everyone's ability and right to satisfy that need in his or her life. The second belief was that urbanization threatened to deny people the means of satisfying that need for nature, and it was up to planners and architects to design cities in better ways to overcome this threat and make cities fulfilling places to live. Third was the idea that nature can be experienced in gardens as well as wilderness. Within the confines of the city, the experience of natural gardens is most appropriate, with "gardens" ranging from the potted plant on the window ledge to the grand urban park of carefully organized but still naturalistic beauty. The fourth idea was that city people should take an interest in the fate of nature far away, doing things to support national forests and parks and to protect natural resources for present and future generations. In its essence, the magazine envisioned inclusive environmental planning that centered on the city but reached out to rural areas and wild places.[7]

This book examines that "city natural" vision through a close analysis of *Garden and Forest*. It presents a careful reading of all its contributors, many of whom are not well known today or have not been recognized as important figures in the nation's environmental tradition. Charles S. Sargent, founder and director of the Arnold Arboretum at Harvard, and William A. Stiles, a *New York Tribune* editorial writer, were the magazine's editors and are central to this work. But the magazine had hundreds of other contributors, including landscape architects Olmsted and Eliot, foresters Bernhard Fernow and Gifford Pinchot, botanists Charles E. Bessey and Sereno Watson, nursery experts Thomas Meehan and Edward Orpet, journalists Sylvester Baxter and Jonathan B. Harrison, the art critic Mariana Van Rensselaer, the horticulturist Liberty Hyde Bailey, and many amateur nature lovers. Although these people came from diverse social and educational backgrounds, they shared a set of common values: a firm belief in democracy, a commitment to scientific progress, and a devotion to nature.

By weaving together its twin images—gardens (representing a tamed nature) and forests (representing a wilder nature)—*Garden and Forest* was a unifying voice among environmental reformers. Like others of the period, the magazine called on government to protect the country's natural heritage and manage its natural resources, especially forests, through scientific and efficient methods. Thus, the magazine anticipated an important aspect of the Progressive Era of the first decade or two of the twentieth century: the conservation movement. At the same time, the magazine expressed a "back-to-nature" attitude that sought a more natural life through preserving nature in, around, and even far away from cities. Some contributors were concerned about modern industrial society encroaching on spiritual freedom, while others were more concerned with the physical health and well-being of urban residents or with restoring masculinity to what they perceived to be a more effete generation.

Thus, the magazine's topics spanned a wide spectrum, from the discovery of new plant species to the cultivation of a single kind of ornamental plant, from the introduction of new techniques in horticulture and agriculture to theoretical discussions of botany, from the defense of urban parks to the preservation of wild primeval scenery, from aesthetics to utilitarian values. Rather than providing a single utopian blueprint, as Bellamy had done, the intention of *Garden and Forest* was to spur practical reforms in government policy, urban design, planning processes, and public opinion.

The magazine had only a "modest circulation," according to its editor, and it ceased publication partly due to financial difficulties.[8] But its influence was not confined to its limited number of subscribers or short lifespan. Other newspapers and magazines, such as the *New York Times*, the *New York Tribune*, and the *Century*, reprinted many of its articles. The magazine's arguments and schemes were frequently quoted as authority or provided stimulus for further discussions in meetings, conferences, and college classrooms. *Garden and Forest* helped redefine two traditional fields, botany and horticulture, and shape two fledgling professions, landscape architecture and forestry. But above all, in its brief life the magazine helped lay the foundations for a broad and diverse environmental movement that would far outlive it. That movement, like the magazine, represented an important intellectual synthesis—on the one hand, romanticism's celebration of natural beauty and, on the other, the modern scientific spirit. Finding no necessary conflict between aesthetic sentiment and scientific practice, the magazine and its contributors attempted to integrate nature into civilization as a progressive social value.[9]

Any magazine has what might be termed its own unique soul, mind, belief, and impact. Compared to an individual person, it might have more inner conflicts, but a magazine can also reflect the ethos of a society better than any single man or woman. A single writer can deviate from his or her society's norms or be otherwise unrepresentative, but a magazine must recruit an audience and must mirror common sentiments. Editors play a pivotal role in a magazine, for they are responsible for recruiting that audience and giving it what it wants. Meanwhile, contributors, who may come from different social and educational backgrounds, are at least motivated by similar interests and purposes when they write for the same magazine. Thus, compared to a biography of an individual person, a biography of a magazine displays a wider and fuller picture.[10]

To study the biography and ideas of a magazine, one needs to pay attention to its social, cultural, and political context. One must also learn about those individuals who constitute its collective voice: what is their social status, education, professional identity, or interaction, and what is their motivation for writing? One must then identify and analyze the major themes that recur in its pages. Finally, the historian of a magazine should explore the relationship between the magazine and its readers, especially its influence on the development of thought in a particular time period.[11]

The collective voice of *Garden and Forest* in environmental history has already been recognized to some extent. All its issues, for example, have been digitized by the Library of Congress, which provides free online access. Although the magazine has not heretofore been the subject of a comprehensive study, in 2000 the Arnold Arboretum published a special issue on *Garden and Forest* in its magazine *Arnoldia*, which collected six short essays discussing the magazine from different perspectives. Sheila Connor gave a brief introduction to the magazine, its connection with the Arnold Arboretum, main contents, and major contributors. Char Miller focused on its relation to American forestry and pointed out that it was in *Garden and Forest* that the ethos of the modern conservation movement, "this assertion of professional specialization, . . . linked to the slow but significant growth of public support for an increased federal intervention in forestry management," was first expressed. Ethan Carr analyzed how the magazine elevated landscape architecture to the status of a fine art and argued that, "in an era before a professional organization or academic instruction existed in the field of landscape architecture," *Garden and Forest* "took on aspects of both." Phyllis Andersen evaluated William Stiles's role in editing the magazine and sketched his career as an urban park advocate. Stephen Spongberg explored the magazine's contribution to botany and its close relationship with the notable botanists in the nation. Mac Griswold reviewed its influence in horticulture and argued that the stance taken by the editors and contributors of *Garden and Forest* in American horticulture was democratic and balanced, one that intended to make farmers and growers "actively involved in and the beneficiaries of, scientific horticulture."

This book has been greatly informed by the arguments made in those *Arnoldia* essays and tries to expand their analysis into a more full and complex picture of the magazine.[12]

Garden and Forest has also been mentioned or discussed in various environmental histories. For example, in *Forest and Garden: Traces of Wildness in a Modernizing Land, 1897–1949*, Melanie Simo borrows her title from the magazine; however, she deliberately starts her book when the magazine ceased publication because she thinks that the demise of the magazine signaled the end of a unified era in American environmental thinking. She makes the useful point that *Garden and Forest* was a unique attempt to gather professionals from various fields, along with amateurs, to discuss nature's role in American civilization. Its legacy continued through the first half of the twentieth century, when people from different disciplines were still trying to talk to one another and when overlapping concerns with both cultivated landscapes and wilderness could still be found. But Simo indicates that the post–*Garden and Forest* era was a time when the conflicts and tensions among different environmental groups grew deeper and more intense. As part of that fragmentation, professionalization and specialization became increasingly distinct and separate from amateur environmental concern. Some of the important contributors to *Garden and Forest*, such as Frederick Law Olmsted and his sons, as well as Charles Eliot and Gifford Pinchot, still play important roles in Simo's story, but she is less interested in the contents of the magazine than how the issues it raised progressed in later years.[13]

Some of the magazine's more prominent contributors have attracted the attention of historians and other scholars. For instance, there are biographies of Sargent, Olmsted, Bailey, and Pinchot. But aside from these famous names, most of the magazine's contributors remain unknown or forgotten today. Famous or not, the contributors were all "environmentalists" before "environmentalism" had a name. They all had an intimate acquaintance with nature, a sincere love of natural beauty, and a genuine commitment to constructing a new harmony between nature and culture.

Furthermore, by examining this magazine, we discover a more complicated foundation for American environmental thought than we have fully realized. Earlier syntheses, by ignoring the magazine, have diminished our understanding of how large a place the city occupied among early environmental thought and how rich, diverse, and wide-ranging was its understanding of urban people's relation to nature. In his still-influential essay "From Conservation to Environment: Environmental Politics in the United States since World War Two," Samuel Hays drastically foreshortens the appearance of urban concerns in the American environmental movement. Even while admitting that there were other aspects to the country's first wave of reform, Hays argues that "the theme of management efficiency in physical resource development dominated the scene prior to World War II and natural environment programs continued to play a subordinate role." After World War II, however, when consumption replaced production as the focus of the economy, the movement was transformed. Conservation, he argues, gave way to environmentalism, which aimed at improving the quality of life, especially urban life. Later, in his important book on postwar environmentalism, Hays uses the phrase "beauty, health, and permanence" to summarize the characteristics of the later movement, implying that these were not important themes in the late nineteenth or early twentieth centuries.[14]

Other historians, in contrast, have argued that this interpretation is too simple and does not give enough attention to early urban activists. Perhaps the most prominent challenge to Hays's interpretation of change has been Robert Gottlieb's *Forcing the Spring*, which aims to provide "a broader, more inclusive way to interpret the environmentalism of the past as well as the nature of the contemporary movement." An impressive galaxy of diverse faces and causes finally get their due in Gottlieb's account, but he shifts attention too radically from "protection or management of the natural environment" to "the environmental consequences of industrial activity." A concern for "beauty" and "permanence" almost disappears from his book, leaving mainly the issue of "health," and a purely medical idea of health at that, as the core of American environmentalism. He virtually ignores another group of urban reformers who conceived of "health" in broader terms, following William Stiles's argument that "open spaces are quite as essential to health and comfort" as buildings (or hospitals). For urban environmentalists of the late nineteenth century like Stiles, the health of nature and the health of people were intertwined, and human health required green spaces and natural beauty as much as unpolluted air and water.[15]

Thus, a study of the magazine challenges the standard distinction historians have made between urban environmental issues and wilderness enthusiasm, between preserving natural beauty and conserving natural resources, and between reformers interested in urban beauty and those interested in urban health. By showing that the main contributors to *Garden and Forest* formed a collectivity, a mutually supportive group, the present book argues that this national campaign, launched in the last two decades of the nineteenth century, was not so fragmented in the beginning as it became later. Similar to the integrated landscape these early environmentalists hoped to construct, the American environmental movement was before 1900 a multifaceted one, unifying urban and rural spheres and joining together both aesthetic and utilitarian approaches.[16]

Finally, this study sheds light on modern controversies over what nature means to Americans. Rather than seeing nature as a single place or a single object, the magazine's contributors regarded it as a primeval force of many dimensions, functioning at different levels in human life. Nature as wilderness implied an area where nature was the predominant power, where human traces might be found but where their influence did not overwhelm the natural order or change the trajectory of evolution. The city stood at the other end of that spectrum of places: an environment where built elements predominated but where nature still existed and was essential for human development. The magazine argued that people needed all these aspects of nature in their lives.

Therefore, the magazine raised questions that endure to this day and that are still relevant to environmental thinking. To what extent and in what forms should nature exist in cities? Should we try to integrate more trees, grass, clean air, and fresh water into cities, or is doing so merely a fantasy of the American middle class imposed on other urban dwellers? Is a need for nature shared by all people in all times and places? Since urbanization is still an ongoing process across the world, it becomes more urgent than ever to answer these questions.

More than ever, the United States is a highly urbanized country, and most of its citizens do not live close to the earth or get their living from working directly in nature. They buy and consume the products of nature, but for most citizens the natural world is an abstraction or a distant place that is difficult to know or understand. Few seem aware that cities, like farms, are part of the natural world and must follow the laws of nature and respect its limits. For an urbanized society, the place and meaning of nature in human life remains uncertain but vital and critical. We cannot get "out of nature" and live somewhere else. But as the magazine and its contributors understood, we can choose whether our city homes and jobs will allow nature and humans to thrive as one, or we can turn our cities into bleak, dispiriting, and ultimately unsustainable places.

1   THE ORIGINS OF ENVIRONMENTAL REFORM

THE UNITED STATES in the late nineteenth century was at the crucial milestone of entering a new urban industrial age. Immigrants from abroad and migrants from the countryside flooded into cities, looking for jobs and housing in the changing economy. Right before the Civil War, the US urban population constituted only 19.8 percent of the total population. In 1880, it reached 28.2 percent. Ten years later, 35.1 percent of the American people were living in cities, a percentage that would increase to 39.7 over the next decade. The building of local, regional, and transcontinental railroads accelerated this city-ward motion. In 1850, there were only 9,000 miles of railroad track, but, by 1900, there were 193,000 miles. The spreading railroad system made transporting raw materials and finished products to and from the city increasingly simple and inexpensive. Along with the leading European nations, the United States was undergoing a transformation, from laissez-faire capitalism to a monopoly-prone economy. No place could escape the intricately organized web of the new American economy, not even the remotest village or the wildest forest. While forests vanished, skyscrapers rose; while prairies retreated, cultivated fields expanded; while rivers rolled, mills roared;

while bison disappeared, cattle proliferated; while nature yielded, human beings marched forward.[1]

Material wealth was not the only product of an urban industrial society. Cities were also celebrated for their cultural wealth—for offering a higher level of civilization with more sophisticated and diverse arts and ideas. Yet in the American mind there lingered much suspicion of the city as a source of national degeneration and decay. Since the Jeffersonian period, many Americans had associated their national identity with their rural traditions. They believed that the best representative of their national virtue was a farmer, as Thomas Jefferson taught in *Notes on the State of Virginia*: "Those who labor in the earth are the chosen people of God." In this view, the foundation of American democracy should be an agrarian society, made secure by the abundance of land. The wide continent promised that the traditional Arcadian ideal long ingrained in Western literature would become material reality. Yet even in the antebellum period, some insightful American intellectuals already sensed the collapse of this rural ideal and the conquest of industrialism. The whistle of the train abruptly entered the natural scene and broke the tranquility and harmony in that mythic American place called "Sleepy Hollow."[2]

In "Public Parks and the Enlargement of Towns," an essay presented at the meeting of the American Social Science Association in 1870, Frederick Law Olmsted decried that old resentment toward cities and the accompanying celebration of rural virtue. He countered that urbanization (or, in his own words, "a strong drift townward") was infused with "elements of human progress," including "the dying out of slavery and feudal customs, of priestcraft and government by divine right." He exalted the educational, technological, and social benefits brought by urbanization and pointed out that "no nation has yet begun to give up schools or newspapers, railroads or telegraphs, to restore feudal rights or advance rates of postage. King-craft and priestcraft are nowhere gaining any solid ground." Therefore, Olmsted concluded, it was "more rational to prepare for a continued rising of the townward flood than to count upon its subsidence."[3]

Desirable or not, urbanization was a powerful social force that had to be reckoned with. Environmentally, it showed four basic characteristics. First, the formation of an urban-based market and transportation network turned the remotest and wildest places into subordinate hinterlands, forcing nature's economy to serve the human economy and leading to the collapse of ecological systems in many regions. Second, expertise, which cities promoted, became the major means for people to manage nature. Before urbanization, people's activities within the natural world had relied mainly on personal experience and local knowledge. By the late nineteenth century, however, many new professions had arisen, thus filling the new America with professional spirit and respect for expertise. Third, federal, state, and municipal governments intervened in the management of nature by passing laws and establishing special agencies. To control the older laissez-faire economy, urban society began to emphasize government's responsibility for the regulation and preservation of natural resources and scenery. Fourth, as people left the land and entered factories and cities, they cut themselves off from a direct connection with the sources of subsistence. This change not only reflected the transformation of social relationships in production but also meant the subversion of the traditional relationship between humans and land.[4]

Urbanization may have been a positive step forward, but it generated many complaints and problems. Behind the affluence of cities, there were slums, crimes, and poorly designed infrastructure. Underneath the prosperity of the industrial mode of production, there were strikes, frequent bankruptcies of small businesses and industries, and severe depressions that could last for years, forcing millions into unemployment. And then there was the daily experience of living in a dull, gray place far from any contact with nature.[5]

People wanted to escape their often-stressful new conditions, and the refuge they sought was in "nature" or, in many cases, an illusion of nature. Historian Peter Schmitt shows how in the last decades of the nineteenth century America's urban middle class began a "back-to-nature" movement. Schmitt draws a distinction between this "back-to-nature" movement and the "back-to-the-land" movement; the first was motivated by the Arcadian myth, or the belief in a long-lost paradise, while the second came from notions held in the late nineteenth century by farmers who advocated a return to an agrarian society. The former movement emphasized spiritual inspiration derived from natural beauty, while the latter idealized a living made from agriculture.[6]

Along with nostalgia for vanishing nature there appeared late in the nineteenth century a growing dissatisfaction with the relentless rationalization of society that cities promoted. Dissenters believed that "real life" was being lost in an "overcivilized" and abstract way of living and that a more genuine physical, emotional, and spiritual experience was disappearing. Some began to seek "authentic" alternatives to "unreal" urban life in medieval craftsmanship, a materially simple life, Asian culture, the martial or warrior ideal, or Catholic mysticism, art, and rituals. The central theme of that fin-de-siècle antimodernism, according to historian Jackson Lears, stemmed from "revulsion against the process of rationalization first described by Max Weber—the systematic organization of economic life for maximum productivity and of individual life for maximum personal achievement, the drive for efficient control of nature under the banner of improving human welfare; the reduction of the world to a disenchanted object to be manipulated by rational technique." Antimodernists to some extent also questioned the principles of modern science. A nature free of scientific control became a cultural goal for many, for the alienation of humans from nature was seen as the root cause of "unreal" urban life. After all, what could be more real or authentic than living with nature and instinctively following its laws?[7]

All the same, among most Americans science was still enshrined as the means to the good life, and economic growth was highly desired. The urban middle classes may have grumbled about the new economic system, a more intrusive government, a deteriorating environment, and their pressured existence, but they called for more and better progress, not rejection of the modern. This was the view underlying the emergence of various strands of social, political, and environmental reform. Such reform marched forward in the vanguard of progress (or Progressivism), beginning in the 1880s and growing until it became a national movement, culminating during and after the presidential administration of Theodore Roosevelt (1901–9). The same spirit of reform was often reflected in the pages of *Garden and Forest*.[8]

Progressives intended to professionalize society, strengthen government, clean up the slums, restrict the monopoly power of corporations, widen the rights of women, Americanize the new immigrants, raise the living conditions of the working class, and at the same time make more efficient and careful use of nature. Above all, progressives emphasized the responsibility of government to address social and environmental problems. In the period when the relationship between nature and human beings was undergoing substantial change, many progressives considered it urgent to find a more secure and carefully protected position for nature in the new social order. Thus, one of the most important expressions of progressive reform was the conservation movement, which began to emerge on the national scene in the 1880s and reached maturity during Theodore Roosevelt's presidential administration.[9]

Since the nation's founding, many Americans had believed that although their new nation lacked a long history and a long tradition of architecture, painting, and literature, it enjoyed an unsurpassed natural environment—unspoiled landscapes of sublime beauty, suggesting freedom and challenge. Furthermore, much of that environment was held in public hands, which meant that common people could enjoy it. But the growth in population and technology eroded that celebrated natural beauty. An effort arose to defend the remaining unspoiled landscapes from defacement. In the last three decades of the nineteenth century, Yosemite Valley, Yellowstone, and Niagara Falls were established as national or state parks, and hundreds of urban natural parks were built inside cities and served as important markers of a national movement to protect the nation's priceless heritage of natural beauty.[10]

Another set of environmental reformers challenged the old belief in the land's inexhaustibility, which prevailed until the end of the nineteenth century and the closing of the frontier. After the Civil War, a fear of "forest famine," stirred by the increasing need for timber with which to build cities and provide energy, began to spread. But even before the war a warning had come from George B. Emerson, president of the Boston Society of Natural History. In 1846, the first edition of Emerson's *Report on the Trees and Shrubs Growing Naturally in the Forests of Massachusetts* was published as part of a state survey of natural resources. Emerson described the state's tree species as well as their habitats and economic value, but then he went on to criticize the "wanton and terrible havoc" caused by overactive axes and to suggest that these forests "would be better kept in reserve for his [the farmer's] grandchildren."[11]

Later observations showed that Emerson had been too optimistic when he observed that "this profuse waste [of forest] is checked, but it has not entirely ceased." Both in the East and the West, the forest resource was still considered inexhaustible by many farmers and timber companies, while simultaneously new and more serious dangers began coming from industrial demands. The construction of railroads required a huge amount of timber for fuel and crossties and radically increased access to the remotest forests. Millions of wandering sheep, which supplied raw wool for the textile industry, were another fatal intrusion into the forest, especially in the West. Industrial mining commonly destroyed the vegetation protecting hills and mountains. In the two decades after the Civil War, "forest famine" was no longer a vague anxiety among a minuscule portion of the public. In 1876, the US Department of Agriculture (USDA) appointed Franklin B. Hough, a physician and natural historian from New York, as special agent to investigate the situation of the nation's forests, and, in 1881, Hough became the first chief of the newly founded Division of Forestry in the USDA. Together with those advocating the preservation of natural beauty, the forest conservationists launched a reform drive.[12]

The themes of environmental reformers were multifaceted, and their tenets were complicated. Their goals were both utilitarian and aesthetic. They looked to government intervention at all levels, from local to federal, to manage more effectively the nation's natural resources and treasures. Their major projects ranged from establishing federal forest reserves for efficient and wise use of endangered timber resources, setting up national parks to preserve primitive beauty, building urban parks to enhance the physical and moral environment of cities, and constructing and renovating sewer and water systems and cleaning the air in cities for the health of their residents.[13]

Expressing the reform ideal were several new environmental festivals, publications, and organizations appearing in the two decades after the Civil War. Activity burgeoned with exceptional energy in the 1880s and 1890s, as the relationship between humans and nature was growing intensely problematic. Along with *Garden and Forest*, the new nature-oriented entities helped shape a reform campaign to improve the public's environmental awareness.

One of the earliest environmental festivals was Arbor Day, established by J. Sterling Morton, who had been governor of Nebraska and the secretary of agriculture during Grover Cleveland's presidential administration. For the first Arbor Day, in 1872, urban and rural residents participated in what was simply a tree-planting festival. It soon spread throughout the nation, and by the time that Nathaniel Egleston, the second chief of the Division of Forestry, was writing his pamphlet *Arbor Day Leaves* in 1893, forty-four states and territories had adopted this annual festival. The concept of Arbor Day evolved as it spread, and it became a part of nature education programs in schools. According to Egleston, "The teachers and pupils of the schools were invited to unite in its observance, and instead of trees merely being planted as screens from winds, they were also planted for ornamental purposes and as memorials of important historical events and of celebrated persons, authors, statesmen, and others." Thus, this festival functioned as a means for learning not only about trees and their uses but also about conservation.[14]

Then there were the magazines that appeared to promote new environmental awareness and concern. In 1873, *Forest and Stream* was introduced, focusing on recreational aspects of the natural environment. Quite different from *Garden and Forest*, which featured plants and activities related to plants, *Forest and Stream* mainly focused on hunting, fishing, and other outdoor activities related to wild animals. In 1876, George Bird Grinnell was appointed the editor of *Forest and Stream*. In 1887 he, with Theodore Roosevelt, helped establish the Boone and Crockett Club, which had a significant influence on the early conservation movement.[15]

The pioneer ethos of heightened masculinity, forged by the nation's frontier experience, was the inspiration behind both the magazine and the club. The frontier was the symbol of rugged America, supposedly engendering a spirit of liberty, equality, and self-reliance and making Americans different from Europeans. Many people were afraid that the old spirit of the frontier was disappearing among the younger generation. They warned that, on the one hand, American society would be made weak, feminine, and mentally feeble by the comfort and luxury of urban life; on the other hand, wild game would be driven to extinction by market hunting, the invasion of millions of domesticated animals, and the disappearance of natural habitats. People believed that, even though the frontier was vanishing, the American pioneer character could be maintained by encouraging such activities as recreational hunting and fishing. They advocated a more refined hunting ethic—the so-called "fair chase" ideal, which was "the ethical, sportsmanlike, and lawful pursuit and taking of free-ranging wild game animals in a manner that does not give the hunter an improper or unfair advantage over the animal." They argued that the person upholding this ethic was both truly masculine and truly civilized.[16]

Grinnell's attitude toward wildlife was not confined to big game. He also saw the need and urgency to protect other forms of wildlife, especially birds. Under his inspiration, the first Audubon Society was established in 1886, and, in 1905, the National Audubon Society was formed. Slightly different from Grinnell's original concern, the Audubon Society groups successfully challenged the fashion industry, which was decorating women's hats with stuffed birds or feathers. Unlike the Boone and Crockett Club, infused with a masculine spirit, the Audubon Society emphasized female activism and a nurturing ethos in the conservation movement. The first issue of *Audubon Magazine* was published in 1905, and it focused mainly on the preservation of wildfowl habitats and species.[17]

Still another environmental organization and magazine that appeared during the time when *Garden and Forest* began publishing was the Sierra Club, founded in 1892, and its print organ, the *Sierra Club Bulletin*. The club's first president was the celebrated naturalist and writer John Muir. Its establishment was inspired by the Appalachian Mountain Club, which came into being in 1876 and was the nation's earliest club promoting outdoor recreation. But the Sierra Club was more engaged in preserving the beauty of wilderness, especially in California. Its spirit of nature conservation may be gathered from the words of its president, extolling the beauty of the mountains of California:

> Every rock seems to glow with life. Some lean back in majestic repose;
> others, absolutely sheer, or nearly so, for thousands of feet, advance their
> brows in thoughtful attitudes beyond their companions, giving welcome
> to storms and calms alike, seemingly conscious yet heedless of everything
> going on about them, awful in stern majesty, types of permanence, yet
> associated with beauty of the frailest and the most fleeting forms; their feet
> set in pine-groves and gay emerald meadows, their brows in the sky; bathed
> in light, bathed in singing water; while snow-clouds, avalanches, and the
> winds shine and surge and wreathe about them as the years go by, as if into
> these mountain mansions Nature had taken pains to gather her choicest
> treasures to draw her lovers into close and confiding communion with her.[18]

To preserve and appreciate that natural beauty, in its most sublime forms, was the mission of the Sierra Club and its *Bulletin*.

Whether emphasizing practicality or sentiment, forests or birds, these new conservation organizations and magazines reflected intellectual trends that had deep roots in the Western intellectual tradition. One of the most profound influences came from European and American romanticism, behind which lay a naturalistic tradition. Historian Donald Worster points out that the romantics "were the first great subversives of modern times." Their targets included "the accepted notion of what science does; the values and institutions of expansionary capitalism; the bias against nature in western religion." In the United States, the New England transcendentalists echoed the romantic vision of nature as an interdependent unity and a necessity for the human imagination. Their leader, Ralph Waldo Emerson, called for liberating the individual from conformity to society while preaching the significance of linking humans and nature. Among the majority of the new generation of American intellectuals, especially in New England, Emerson's views became definitive. The editors of and most contributors to *Garden and Forest* were rooted in the transcendentalist soil, and their vision of nature and the human world was shaped by this legacy.[19]

For the magazine, however, these older and broader influences were less immediate than the influence of two New England men: George Perkins Marsh and Frederick Law Olmsted. One cannot understand the magazine without understanding what these two men contributed intellectually to its many authors. They were its chief guiding lights, as they were for the new environmental reform movement in general. Both Marsh and Olmsted were at once heirs to romanticism and New England transcendentalism, as well as the Victorian-era faith in science and progress. Both believed that a higher civilization in America could be built by learning to get along with nature in a more respectful and careful way. Like Ralph Waldo Emerson, they emphasized the positive human role in transforming nature and were committed to the development of modern civilization guided by the power of reform. Although they cherished the natural world, neither denied that humans had a special destiny.[20]

Marsh made it clear that humans were "above nature," not "of nature," even though it was crucial to learn the laws of nature and respect them. In Olmsted's case, the perspective was still more complicated. His underlying philosophy was romantic, and all his major works manifested the appeal of natural beauty. He was critical of the alienation of modern society from nature and devoted his career to restoring the public's physical and spiritual contact with the natural world. Ultimately, however, like Marsh, he was anthropocentric in outlook, concerned with humanity's welfare, not nature for its own sake.

Sharing much, these men also diverged in important ways. Marsh asked how the interaction between humans and the natural environment had affected the material development of society, and his fundamental goal was to find a more sustainable way to use the earth. Olmsted, however, was mainly concerned with noneconomic needs. His major purpose was to harmonize and civilize people by applying the balm of nature. Although Marsh died before the magazine was established and Olmsted only backed it from behind the curtain, these two men could have written many of the essays and articles in its pages.

George Perkins Marsh was born in 1801, in Woodstock, Vermont. At age forty-eight, after a career in law and politics, he was appointed US envoy to Turkey. Firmly believing in the spread of democracy, he was sympathetic toward Europe's revolutionaries and supported them. Meanwhile, he traveled to Egypt, Palestine, Central Europe, and Italy, collecting flora and fauna for the Smithsonian Institution in Washington. In 1854, he went back to the United States, but, after seven years, the newly elected president, Abraham Lincoln, returned him to the old continent. For the next two decades, he served as US ambassador to Italy, living in various cities. His duties enabled him to see much of the Old World, not as a tourist skimming over the surface but as a scholar closely observing and contemplating the history of humans and nature.[21]

However, in the decades before he went abroad, Marsh had already witnessed the radical transformation of the Vermont landscape from infinite-seeming forests to denuded fields and pastures, the result of reckless and wasteful cutting:

> The changes, which these causes have wrought in the physical geography of Vermont, within a single generation, are too striking to have escaped the attention of any observing person, and every middle-aged man, who revisits his birth-place after a few years of absence, looks upon another landscape than that which formed the theatre of his youthful toils and pleasures. The signs of artificial improvement are mingled with the tokens of improvident waste, and the bald and barren hills, the dry beds of the smaller streams, the ravines furrowed out by the torrents of spring, and the diminished thread of interval that skirts the widened channel of the rivers, seem sad substitutes for the pleasant groves and brooks and broad meadows of his ancient paternal domain.[22]

Being an "observing person," Marsh was sensitive to all those environmental changes. His feelings were not completely negative but mixed criticism, regret, patriotic pride in the nation's growth, and celebration of human power.

In 1847, Marsh delivered an address before the Agricultural Society of Rutland County, Vermont, which summarized his views as they had been shaped in rural New England. He was full of enthusiasm for the victory of his country in the struggle between "civilized man and barbarous uncultivated nature. . . . This marvelous change," he wrote, "which has converted unproductive wastes into fertile fields, and filled with light and life, the dark and silent recesses of our aboriginal forests and mountains, has been accomplished through the instrumentality of those arts, whose triumphs you are this day met to celebrate, and your country is the field, where the stimulus of necessity has spurned them on to their most glorious achievements." And like most of his contemporaries, he believed that the exploitation and cultivation of wild nature was a divine right endowed by the Creator.[23]

Nevertheless, Marsh's enthusiasm for civilization did not blind him to the approaching dangers created by thoughtless behavior. Although his address sounded very much in tune with the triumphant temper of the era, his views were edged with unease. He indicated that, while cutting down trees had been necessary and wise to a point, forests were no longer the encumbrance they had once been. He warned that there had been "undoubtedly already a larger proportion of cleared land in Vermont than would be required," and if people did not cease their reckless cutting, they would deprive their descendants of valuable resources. He called for "a better economy in the management of our forest lands."[24]

Later, after five years of living and traveling around the Mediterranean, Marsh could still marvel at the awesome changes in the landscape forged by human beings but also gasp at the catastrophic destruction they wrought. He saw that environmental degradation was always followed by the ruin of civilization, which led him to an even more critical scrutiny of the human-nature relationship in his home country.

Marsh began writing his most important book, *Man and Nature*, a classic text for the conservation movement, in 1862 and finished it in 1864. As his original working title, "Man the Disturber of Nature's Harmonies," suggested, the theme of the book was that humans are not part of nature and that their actions can intentionally or unintentionally upset the economy of nature in a fundamental way. He opened the book with a striking picture of the decline of ancient Rome and the desolation of its natural environment. Throughout the book he described similar decline around the Mediterranean coasts and across Europe and Asia, but his ultimate concern was his own nation, where natural resources had wrongly been thought boundless by his fellow citizens.

In *Man and Nature*, Marsh was more pessimistic than in his 1847 address. Rather than thinking that "her [nature's] fruitfulness increases with the numbers of civilized beings who draw their nutriment and clothing from the stores of her abundant harvests," he argued that, as man "advanced in civilization, he gradually eradicates or transforms every spontaneous product of the soil he occupies." Marsh pointed out that human achievement could not balance the loss of nature, nor could the domesticated animals and plants keep the balance of the economy of nature in the way the more purely natural species did.[25]

The question for Marsh, however, was not whether human beings should or should not modify nature for their progress. He acknowledged that there must be "a certain measure of transformation of terrestrial surface, of suppression of natural, and stimulation of artificially modified productivity." The common failing in civilization was that humans exceeded this measure. Marsh argued that in nature the destruction of one vital element, like the forest, usually led to a chain of calamities. What disappeared were not only trees but also water stored by trees and soil held by them. The result would be not only a timber famine but also an increase in drought, flood, and erosion. Humans were too often engaged not in making the world more suitable for their lives but in changing the earth into a barren and chaotic place. Thus, Marsh warned, "it is evidently a matter of great moment, . . . to the general interests of humanity, that this decay should be arrested."[26]

The second key figure in the environmental thinking of the editors of and contributors to *Garden and Forest* magazine was Olmsted. He was not only the most famous urban park designer in the nation but also a leader in the struggle to preserve Yosemite Valley and Niagara Falls. At the same time, his interest in practical forestry brought him into close cooperation with several important figures, including Charles Sargent and Gifford Pinchot, who were promoting this new profession in the United States. Olmsted's passion for beauty did not conflict with his concern for improving health and sanitation.[27]

Olmsted was born in 1822 in Hartford, Connecticut. Experiencing the outdoors formed his intellectual and mental world far more than did strictly indoor academic training. Wandering in the woods and fields of picturesque

New England, he was intrigued by everything he saw. As he grew older, the scope of his roaming expanded. In 1848, he persuaded his indulgent father to buy a farm for him on Staten Island, where he undertook a career in scientific farming, absorbing knowledge of agriculture and horticulture. An unsatisfied curiosity about the world distracted him, however, and, in 1850, he and his brother, along with another friend, left on an extended trip to the rural shires of England. That six-month trip enabled him to witness both poverty and prosperity in the world's most powerful empire and to learn new ideas about how to bring the city and countryside into harmony. In 1852, he compiled his journals and articles written during the trip into his first book, *Walks and Talks of an American Farmer in England.*[28]

Although calling himself a farmer, Olmsted was not interested in agriculture so much as in the social aspects of British life. He observed the creation of some of the world's first public parks and studied their function in an emerging urban society. A park built on an abandoned farm in the city of Birkenhead and designed by Joseph Paxton, one of the most prominent British landscape architects, inspired his imagination. What impressed Olmsted about this park were two things: its picturesque scenery and free access to everyone. In this "thick, luxuriant, diversified garden," Olmsted experienced "five minutes of admiration, and a few more spent in studying the manner in which art had been employed to obtain from nature so much beauty." But it was how people used the place that most intrigued him. "In democratic America," he admitted, "there was nothing to be thought of as comparable with this People's Garden." Delighted by both the scenery and people in the park, Olmsted declared, "The poorest British peasant is as free to enjoy it in all its parts as the British queen. More than that, the baker of Birkenhead [who insisted that Olmsted and his companions had to visit the park before they left the town] has the pride of an owner in it."[29]

The second volume of Olmsted's book came out several months later and was dedicated to Andrew Jackson Downing, an early American practitioner of what became known as landscape architecture. Born in 1815, Downing was the son of a nursery expert in Newburgh, New York.[30] Although living in a period in which the majority of the population still inhabited rural areas, Downing early on discerned the powerful trend of urbanization and wrote about it in editorials for *The Horticulturist* magazine (a predecessor of *Garden and Forest*) in the early 1850s. In an editorial published in 1851, Downing wrote that "it is needful in civilized life for men to live in cities," but "it is not . . . needful for them to be so miserly as to live utterly divorced from all pleasant and health-ful intercourse with gardens and green fields." He made it clear that public parks were as important as libraries, art galleries, or outdoor sculptures, espe-cially for republican America.[31]

In 1857, the lessons of Birkenhead's park and Downing's ideas came to fruition for Olmsted and changed American urban thinking profoundly. That year he became the superintendent of the new Central Park that was to be built in New York City. It was the first big urban park in the United States, standing right in the center of the metropolis. Earlier he had accepted an in-vitation from Calvert Vaux, a former partner of Downing, to collaborate in the design competition for the park. Their "Greensward" plan won first prize, and the two partners set out to use nature's materials to compose a living landscape for what was then a 780-acre wasteland and a wretched home for the poor.

Central Park became far more than a beautiful design at the heart of the nation's largest city. It was intended to begin a larger process of healing and improving the entire urban environment. Although Olmsted believed that ur-banization led to better life, he, like many of his contemporaries, was con-cerned about the "disease and misery" and the "vice and crime" of urban life. "This would be a very dark prospect for civilization," he wrote, "if it were not that modern science has beyond all question determined many of the causes of the special evils by which men are afflicted in towns, and placed means in our hands for guarding against them." Science provided the means for curing physical ills that came with urbanization; however, it lacked po-tency to uplift urban people's moral and spiritual well-being. What worried Olmsted the most was the loss of "communicativeness" caused by commercial competition, factory discipline, and crowded urban conditions. When people walked along a narrow, crowded urban street, "to merely avoid collision with those we meet and pass upon the sidewalks, we have constantly to watch, to foresee, and to guard against their movements. . . . Our minds are thus brought into close dealings with other minds without any friendly flowing toward them, but rather a drawing from them." That was what he meant by a loss of communicativeness. What he wanted to construct was a city where people could be drawn together in cooperation and harmony, sharing some common experience without any sort of competition.[32]

Central Park, from every angle, was the masterpiece illustrating Olmsted's integration of nature, art, city, and civilization. Here was a peaceful green space re-created inside the city, giving urban residents visual enjoyment and physical relaxation, providing temporary freedom from restraint and stress, and serving as a source of refreshment. Twelve years after the park's construction, Olmsted proudly asked reformers and social thinkers to see the park as a means to reform society:

> Consider that the New York Park and the Brooklyn Park [Prospect Park, another major urban place designed by Olmsted and Vaux] are the only place in those associated cities where, in this eighteen hundred and seventieth year after Christ, you will find a body of Christians coming together, and with an evident glee in the prospect of coming together, all classes largely represented, with a common purpose, not at all intellectual, competitive with none, disposing to jealousy and spiritual or intellectual pride toward none, each individual adding by his mere presence to the pleasure of all others, all helping to the greater happiness of each. You may thus often see vast numbers of persons brought closely together, poor and rich, young and old, Jew and Gentile.[33]

To create such social interaction was the motive driving Olmsted to build urban parks, and it became the underlying goal of *Garden and Forest*.

The explosion of the Civil War interrupted the construction of Central Park and drove nearly everyone into the conflict, including Olmsted. He performed his duty in the war by cofounding the Sanitary Commission (the predecessor of the Red Cross) in 1861, and he served as its executive secretary until 1863. When he became exhausted by the work of the commission, he resigned and accepted a job as superintendent of California's Mariposa Estate, a mining company in the Sierra Nevada foothills. There, he found himself near some of the grandest natural scenery in the world but also immersed in the harsh reality of frontier life. It was a world, in Olmsted's eyes, yet to be civilized.

In 1864, President Lincoln approved the grant of the Yosemite Valley and the Big Tree Grove of redwoods to the state of California as a park for public use, the first such grant in American history. Olmsted was appointed to be one of the commissioners who would manage the grant, and, in August 1865, after traveling through the region, he presented a report to his fellow commissioners. It was the first report to explain systematically why it was the government's responsibility to take care of wild natural beauty and to suggest how to protect and manage such beauty. Olmsted argued that "it is the main duty of government, if it is not the sole duty of government, to provide means of protection for all its citizens in the pursuit of happiness against the obstacles, otherwise insurmountable, which the selfishness of individuals or combinations of individuals is liable to interpose to that pursuit." And the right of enjoying nature was part of the pursuit of happiness.[34]

Olmsted never doubted the potency of natural scenery in strengthening people's bodies and morals. "It is unquestionably true," he wrote, "that excessive and persistent devotion to sordid interests cramp and distort the power of appreciating natural beauty and destroy the love of it which the Almighty has implanted in every human being, and which is so intimately and mysteriously associated with the moral perceptions and intuitions, but it is not true that exemption from toil, much leisure, much study, much wealth, is necessary to the exercise of the esthetic and contemplative faculties." He quoted Downing's words that the "destinies of the New World" would not only make reading and writing universal but would also bring "common enjoyments for all classes in the higher realms of art, letters, science, social recreations and enjoyments." Throughout the rest of his career, Olmsted kept up a persistent call for governmental action in preserving and managing the nation's natural heritage for everybody.[35]

In 1865, Vaux urged Olmsted to come back to the East Coast and complete their unfinished Central Park and, across the East River, to build Prospect Park in Brooklyn. His return to New York City signaled the beginning of the "Age of Olmsted" in the nation's urban history. America's cities from east to west would be dramatically changed by him and his followers. His influence went far beyond the profession of landscape architecture, however. His long formative period had enabled him to understand the emerging society in a more profound way than did most of his contemporaries.

Garden and Forest magazine was the legacy of both Marsh and Olmsted. It was part of an environmental reform movement that had begun much earlier in time but came of age during the years the magazine was being published. More than any other organ of its day, and more than either Marsh or Olmsted had done, the magazine addressed a broad array of urban environmental issues, including not only solving the physical shortcomings of the modern city but also preserving and enhancing natural beauty within, near, and far away from them. During a crucial decade, *Garden and Forest* recruited a wide array of people to write for its pages. It became, however briefly, a key voice for its time, a voice that articulated a comprehensive vision for the relationship between nature and urban society.

2   TWO MINDS, ONE MAGAZINE

WILLIAM A. STILES had neither the time nor the mood to celebrate Christmas and the new year of 1888. Besides his routine editorial writing for the *New York Tribune*, he had accepted a new job as managing editor of the forthcoming weekly magazine *Garden and Forest*. The idea for this new publication had come from Charles S. Sargent, the founder and director of the Arnold Arboretum at Harvard, but he was hit by a sudden case of typhoid in mid-December 1887. Sargent's unexpected illness disrupted the entire plan. Stiles felt that he was "left hanging in air." The publishing company had to be formed as soon as possible; several blank advertising pages in the magazine had to be sold; thirty thousand names had to be organized for mailing the prospectus; the correspondence from the contributors had to be answered. However, the most overwhelming and urgent work to be done at this moment was to get enough money to publish the first few issues of the magazine.[1]

Sargent himself was one of the major financial backers, and all the other investors were his friends and long-term benefactors of the Arnold Arboretum, including Frederick Ames, Jack Gardner, and Horatio H. Hunnewell. After sending $250 to Stiles, Sargent was preoccupied by his bout with typhoid, leaving all the challenges, especially the financial ones, to Stiles. After working extremely hard for two months on preparing for the day of publication, Stiles had not yet received a single dollar for his service; on the contrary, he had to pay for many things out of his own pocket. He was confident and eager to see the success of the magazine, but both he and it faced strained financial circumstances. He barely had any personal contact with those rich patrons from Boston, and he did not want to approach Sargent or his wife about business matters when Sargent was so ill. Articles and plant specimens were coming in from everywhere, and he had already sent out fifteen thousand announcements about the magazine. Money or no money, it was clear that "we can't stop—or make any show of stopping," because "this has all been done in his [Sargent's] name, & his honor is at stake."[2]

For help in launching the magazine, Stiles went to Frederick Law Olmsted, a frequent correspondent and mentor. From 25 to 30 December, he wrote to Olmsted almost every day, and Olmsted did not disappoint. He was generous in both advice and money. Right after he received Stiles's letter, Olmsted sent encouragement, along with five hundred dollars. And a couple of days later, a check arrived from Boston businessman Frederick Ames, rescuing the magazine from its first financial crisis. Stiles wrote to thank Olmsted, promising optimistically that this was a "safe investment." He was looking forward to publishing a first-class, or even the best, magazine in its field.[3]

In the winter of 1888, after being postponed for almost three months, the first issue of *Garden and Forest: A Journal of Horticulture, Landscape Art, and Forestry* was published in New York City. It cost ten cents, and a yearly subscription cost four dollars. As everyone had expected, the magazine proved to be superior to any others in its category.[4] The content was broad, the editorials were insightful, the essays were well chosen, the layout was tasteful, and the illustrations were superb. For the next ten years, *Garden and Forest* maintained this high quality in all aspects. Stiles was right in his judgment that the magazine was going to be interesting and influential on many subjects related to plants, design, and conservation. He would never be able to deliver on his financial promise, however. Although a great success in many ways, the magazine would fail as a business proposition. In the last issue, published on 29 December 1897, Sargent announced the end of the magazine in a short note on the final page:

> With the present issue, which completes the tenth volume, the publication of GARDEN AND FOREST ends. . . . This experiment, which has cost a large amount of time and money, has shown conclusively that there are not persons enough in the United States interested in the subjects which have been presented in the columns of GARDEN AND FOREST to make a journal of its class and character self-supporting. It is useless to expend more time and money on a publication which cannot be made financially successful, and must, therefore, sooner or later cease to exist.[5]

The magazine, from its shaky beginning to its disappointing end, was not a profitable investment for its investors and patrons.

However, the significance of *Garden and Forest* was not determined by its profitability. Its reputation and influence went beyond the geographic boundaries of North America, reaching Europe, South America, and Asia. Its pioneering discussion of forestry stirred up a nationwide debate over the preservation and management of forests. Its enthusiastic advocacy of urban parks and landscape architecture in general promoted the idea of including nature in designing modern cities. The magazine appeared at a critical moment when environmental concern was becoming a powerful force. Affording a common forum for different professions interested in present and future environmental issues, the magazine recruited contributors from a wide spectrum of reform.

"ONE DAY, A MAN looked up—and saw a tree." So wrote Edward E. Hale about Charles Sprague Sargent. The founder and first director of the Arnold Arboretum at Harvard and the author of the fourteen-volume monumental work *The Silva of North America*, Sargent saw, knew, and celebrated numerous trees during his long life, many more than most people. Although he accumulated some enemies among his fellow humans, Sargent was a real friend to all trees.[6]

Sargent did not show this zealous interest in trees as a child. Born in 1841 to one of the longest resident and most famous families in Boston, he was the second and the only surviving son of a successful banker and railroad man, Ignatius Sargent. In the Boston suburb of Brookline, the senior Sargent purchased a property known as Holm Lea (Norse words meaning "inland island pasture"), the largest private estate close to the metropolis. Like many of his wealthy contemporaries, Ignatius Sargent dedicated his leisure time to horticulture and transformed his domain into well-managed parkland. The younger Sargent spent several of his earliest summers at Holm Lea and then, after 1852, lived there year round with his parents. But he did not leave any record of when his love of plants began. After he grew up, this rather cold and reserved man rarely mentioned his childhood. "I have virtually no information about his early life," his long-term colleague Ernest H. Wilson recalled. "On one occasion, being in a reminiscent mood, he drove me around and pointed out the house on Joy Street, Boston, in which he was born. Passing the Arlington Street side of the Public Garden, he remarked that there he used to put on his skates, and that opposite the Harvard Club he frequently fished for smelts through the ice." These words are probably the only record through which people could connect the boy Charles with some sort of outdoor life.[7]

Sargent also did not show any outstanding talents when he was in school. After he left the Epes Sargent Dixwell School for boys, he entered Harvard College in the fall of 1858. Either because his intelligence matured rather late or because he could not adapt himself to the traditional way of teaching that emphasized memorizing texts and parroting the professors, Sargent ranked third from the bottom in a class of ninety when he graduated in 1862. More surprisingly, he was among the very few who did not take the course of botany taught by his future mentor Asa Gray, the great scientist who billowed the sails of Darwinism in North America. Although published in 1859 and immediately introduced to the United States, Darwin's *Origin of Species* seemed not to have any impact on Sargent as a modest Harvard undergraduate.

The Civil War exploded when Sargent was in his junior year at college. Lacking any interest in politics, he kept silent on the war. Like most of his classmates, however, he joined the Union army and stayed in uniform until 2 August 1865. His military career did not leave any imprint on his later profession. When he was in the army, he mentioned almost nothing in his letters about the vegetation he saw while in the Gulf Coast region. After he was discharged, Sargent followed the tradition of his age: acquiring a gentleman's education by traveling in Europe. Wandering over the old continent for three years, he might have visited some gardens and parks, but, once again, no records or comments survive from such experiences.

Sargent went back to Boston when he was twenty-seven years old, ready to establish himself in society. Although very methodical and practical, he did not find or want a career in business. He took on the responsibility of managing his father's estate and, according to his own account, set out to become a self-taught tree expert. This occupation might have been suggested and encouraged by his second cousin, Henry Sargent, and a distant relative, Horatio H. Hunnewell.

Both Henry Sargent and Hunnewell were in their late fifties at the time. They belonged to the same social caste—wealthy and well educated. Henry Sargent was the first cousin of Ignatius Sargent, and, like other Sargents, he had amassed a great amount of wealth, which allowed him to semi-retire and indulge in his hobby—horticulture and landscape gardening—when he was in early thirties. His country place, known as Wodenethe, was right across the Hudson River from Andrew Jackson Downing's estate, and Henry Sargent became a close friend and admirer of Downing, whom Judith Major calls the father of American landscape gardening.[8] Both the taste and the estate of Henry Sargent conformed to Downing's artistic principles: simple and natural. From his cousin, Charles Sargent learned his early lessons in landscape gardening and found his own taste eagerly matching Downing's ideals.

Hunnewell had accumulated a fortune through banking, real estate, and railroads, and he too invested part of his wealth in an estate in Brookline. Henry Sargent frequently visited that estate and encouraged his relative's fascination with horticulture, especially rhododendrons. In turn, Hunnewell became Charles Sargent's adviser and a lifelong sponsor of the younger man's career. Under the influence of these two mentors, Sargent set about realizing the horticultural potential of his father's estate, Holm Lea. Its grand scale, diversity of species, and naturalistic style gave scope to his imagination. He proved a fast learner in his own garden.

In 1872, an opportunity came that would help Sargent establish a professional reputation and become a national leader in forestry and botany. He was hired for the position of professor of horticulture at the Bussey Institution at Harvard, a position formerly occupied by historian Francis Parkman, who had resigned because of poor health.[9] Sargent had never taught a class before. Right after this appointment, he also became the curator and first director of the newly founded Arnold Arboretum in Jamaica Plain, south of Boston, and, in November 1873, he was appointed director of the Botanical Garden in Cambridge, a position he held until 1879. He stayed at the Arnold Arboretum for more than a half century, until his death in 1927.

For many people, Sargent's appointment was a mystery. At best, he was a knowledgeable amateur gardener and the supervisor of a private estate, with neither long experience nor an impressive formal educational background. But Asa Gray, the greatest botanist in North America at the time, appreciated his diligence and administrative talent and endorsed him for the position. Sargent's family wealth and social position certainly constituted another advantage in securing his appointment.[10]

Full of ambition and enthusiasm for his fledgling career, Sargent planned a second trip to Europe. This time, however, Sargent would visit many gardens and meet many important figures in botany, including Joseph Hooker at the Kew Royal Botanic Gardens in London. Unlike his earlier trip, he would travel with his bride, Mary Allen Robeson, the daughter of a rich merchant family in Rhode Island. Twelve years younger than Sargent and a graceful and gentle woman, she and Sargent wed in the same month that he became the director of the Arnold Arboretum, and everything was perfect for the young couple's travels.

Sargent, although overly serious and a bit arrogant, was a handsome young man. He possessed abundant health and wealth and was thus a desirable husband. Mary Sargent, with her outgoing, mild-mannered character, complemented him in many ways. Later, she became increasingly religious; Sargent, on the contrary, never showed any hints of religious belief.[11]

When the Sargents returned from Europe in early 1874, there was a bright career ahead for the new professor. His goal was ambitious but simple: he intended to build the best arboretum in the world, even better than the much-admired Kew Gardens. He was optimistic about accomplishing this goal, for he believed that the natural environment of New England was much more suitable for growing diverse plant species than was that of England. Plants would thrive in Jamaica Plain as well as they did in their native habitats, if they were cultivated scientifically. Money was always the primary need and the toughest requirement of such a program, but, for Sargent, this task turned out to be easier than for other people. His own property, strong social connections, and great administrative ability paved a broad and smooth financial way for the arboretum. But Sargent had to deal with something else that the director of a botanical garden usually did not have to face. He needed to acquire the training, at least at an elementary level, to be a scientist.

Fortunately, Sargent had near at hand Asa Gray. Gray was an awe-inspiring figure because of his nimble intelligence and amazingly broad knowledge.

Born in 1810 in a humble family, he had joined the Harvard faculty as a botany professor in 1842. Sargent took full advantage of Gray's knowledge and followed his scientific lead. Sargent's career steadily advanced over the years, but as the first issue of *Garden and Forest* neared publication in the winter of 1888, his mentor died, only a month after Sargent was taken ill with typhoid.

The first editorial of the magazine, unsigned but almost certainly written by Sargent, was dedicated to Gray. An obituary might not have been what Sargent originally planned to write for the first issue; he had planned to "write editorials for the earlier numbers, setting the tone" of the magazine. Still, he managed, while celebrating Gray's marvelous achievements in botany and modern science, to explain what a botanically informed magazine could contribute to society.[12]

Sargent believed that Gray would forever be counted among the nineteenth century's greatest scientific minds not only because of his accomplishment in taxonomy but also because he drew "broad philosophical conclusions from the dry facts he collected and elaborated with such untiring industry and zeal." Gray, he wrote, "did not devote himself to abstract science alone; he wrote as successfully for the student as for the professional naturalist." Most important, botany was not the sole concern of Gray's intellectual life. Sargent pointed out that "one of Asa Gray's chief claims to distinction is the prominent and commanding position he took in the great intellectual and scientific struggle of modern times, in which, almost alone and single handed he bore in America the brunt of the disbelief in the Darwinian theory shared by most of the leading naturalists of the time." But Sargent also expressed regret that Gray had left his crowning work, *Synoptical Flora of North America*, unfinished, although there was enough to keep Gray's "memory green . . . as long as the human race is interested in the study of plants." (Sargent took pains to ensure that such a fate was not his. Two years after Gray's death, he published the first volume of his own monumental work, *The Silva of North America*, and, in 1902, he put a period to this lifetime achievement with the completion of the fourteenth volume.) In the last paragraph of the editorial, Sargent concluded that the most valuable legacy of Gray was that his life "teaches how industry and unselfish devotion to learning can attain to the highest distinction and the most enduring fame" in an age of materialism. This was a life that Sargent himself craved and expected *Garden and Forest* to promote.[13]

If Gray was Sargent's tutor in botany, George Perkins Marsh introduced him to a more comprehensive understanding of the natural world, especially the forest. In a letter to Robert Underwood Johnson, editor of *Century* magazine, Sargent frankly admitted that he owed his "interest in forests and forest preservation to [Marsh's *Man and Nature*] almost entirely." Presumably, Sargent had read the book when he was supervisor of Holm Lea. Its influence was deep and complex, and it was the main force pushing him to investigate the nation's forests and advocate their conservation.[14]

In 1879, Secretary of the Interior Carl Schurz, who was sympathetic to forestry issues, wanted to have a report on the condition of the nation's forests included in the nation's tenth census. Gray recommended Sargent to conduct the investigation, and Sargent accepted the assignment. The report was supposed to provide "a list of the trees of North America with their geographical distribution and economic uses." Serving as the "Expert and Special Agent of the Tenth Census of the United States," Sargent enlisted a diverse group of botanists, collectors, and nursery experts. In 1880, for the first time, Sargent went deep into the nation's western territories and forests, studying the existing dangers and problems, such as fire and grazing, and their relationship with other aspects of nature. In 1883, he finished compiling, organizing, and evaluating all the data obtained from his field trips and published his first major work, *Report on the Forests of North America*.[15]

This report was the first systematic and extensive work on the nation's forests to be based on observation and study in fields and laboratories. With effective and orderly presentation of copious data, Sargent tried to convey the same message that Marsh had preached in *Man and Nature*—that the nation's forests had to be protected and managed as soon as possible; otherwise, this great wealth of nature would diminish and, subsequently, American civilization would decline. Twenty-five years later, Sargent claimed that "this report, I think I can say without vanity, marked the first real step taken in this country toward forest preservation, and I believe that it was owing to this report that the early forest reservations were made. In any case, very little was known before the publication of this report about the forests of the country, their composition and productive capacity."[16]

In the essay "The Protection of Forests," published in the *North American Review* in 1882, Sargent expressed the conservation idea in a more direct and simple way. He analyzed the relationship between forests and rivers in both East and West, warning that if the government and public could not be awakened as soon as possible, North America would soon be entirely stripped of its forests. "The future prosperity and development of the country," he stated, "are so largely dependent upon the preservation of the forest."[17]

"The Protection of Forests" immediately attracted attention among opinion makers in the East. The *New York Times*, for example, published a long article on Sargent's essay, proclaiming that "Prof. Sargent's knowledge of the extent, condition, and laws of growth of our forests is probably more full and accurate than that of any other man in the country, his professional studies as a botanist and his special investigation in connection with the preparation of forestry bulletins of the Census Bureau giving him that pre-eminence." Sargent had gained a reputation as the nation's foremost authority on forest issues.[18]

Subsequently, Sargent was invited to join the Northern Transcontinental Survey sponsored by the railroad promoter Henry Villard, who wanted to collect information about the land resources owned by his northwestern railroad interests. Raphael Pumpelly, a geologist and formerly a Harvard professor of mining engineering, was the director of the survey. Sargent accepted the invitation in order to satisfy his own curiosity about the forests growing in the mountains of the Pacific Northwest. At the end of June 1883, when he finally finished the report, he headed for the mountains of Montana. Stiles, then an editorial writer for the *New York Tribune*, went along with him for the sake of adventure.

For Sargent, the most significant outcome of this survey was an essay published in September 1883 in *The Nation* in which for the first time he proposed to establish a national forest reserve on the site of what would later become Glacier National Park. The sublimity of the scenery obviously touched Sargent, but what made him more concerned were the vulnerable headwaters of three rivers: the Missouri, the Columbia, and the Saskatchewan. For this reason, he pointed out that "there seems to be an entirely proper opportunity for the Government to establish a great forest preserve." This forest preserve "would contain perhaps some 8,000 square miles of mountain territory, absolutely unfit for agriculture or grazing, and only valuable as a reservoir of moisture."[19]

The ecological and aesthetic concerns of Sargent and some other members of the Northern Transcontinental Survey failed to meet their railroad backer's profit-oriented intentions, and Villard cut off funds for the survey. It would be interesting to know how Sargent resolved the conflict between his objection to railroads invading the forests and the security of his personal wealth, which had been acquired mainly from investing in railroads. In 1880, Sargent took the place occupied by his father on the board of the Boston and Albany Railroad and later was elected one of the directors. When the senior Sargent passed away in 1884, the son inherited not only Holm Lea but also his father's stock in the railroad company. This wealth shielded Sargent from any financial problems, but in the years when he was engaged in promoting conservation, Sargent stood firmly against the railroad companies and their ambition to exploit the nation's forests.[20]

It was not rare in the late nineteenth century for the affluent class to feel some passion for nature. From Sargent's own family, such nature lovers as Henry Sargent and H. H. Hunnewell had also made money from railroad investments. Some railroad barons, such as E. H. Harriman, a friend of John Muir, the nation's most beloved naturalist, "sought beautiful scenery to adorn their lives and therapy to soothe the cares and nervous prostration brought on by their intense work habits." Sargent was different. If the standard had been based on social status and wealth, he belonged to the same category as Harriman; if the standard was deep commitment to conservation, Sargent deviated from his social class. Underneath his imperious and stout physique, he was essentially a scholar with a sincere love of nature, an idealist in many ways. His steadfast love of and lasting interest in nature could not be fed by a mere vestige of scenery or some labor in a greenhouse. The natural world for him was more fascinating than the human world.[21]

He did enjoy his wealth and the comfort and security it brought. More importantly, this wealth was vital to the publication of *Garden and Forest*, but Sargent did not have the desire to make his wealth grow, which was just as well since he had no time to think about its increase. He did see the local and national economic benefit from constructing railroads, and, like most of his fellow environmental reformers, he embraced modern technology. He did not find it necessary to choose between the development of the economy, such as railroads, and the extinction of forests, if people would only restrict their greed and destructive behavior.

Sargent may not have bothered to think much about the contradiction between his commitment to the conservation movement and his personal wealth derived from the railroad business. What made him more bewildered and frustrated was politics. S. B. Sutton was right that Sargent was extremely conservative in politics and loathed any form of governmental intervention. He neither understood Washington's political games nor liked to be involved in them, but his anxiety about the future of the nation's forests forced him to deal with politicians. At least on the issue of forest conservation, he wanted to see a strong hand of protection and control extended by local and federal government.

Driven by this motivation, Sargent agreed to chair a commission appointed by New York State to "investigate and report a system of forest preservation" in the Adirondacks. He undertook the task in 1884 and wrote the major part of the report. In it, he analyzed both the function of the Adirondack forest in preserving the headwaters of the Hudson River and the Erie Canal and the value of its natural beauty. The report also warned about threats to the forest, such as fire. Because of the complicated geocultural landscape of the Adirondacks, in which the state-owned land abutted private lands, the management of the forests became much more difficult. Thus, the report insisted that the appropriate way of preserving the Adirondacks would be that, "under different circumstances[,] the state might acquire the whole Adirondack forest by purchase." But considering the difficulty of fulfilling that goal, the commissioners suggested that the state could demonstrate its ability by managing the forest on a small scale at first.[22]

Sargent was disappointed to see the passage of an alternative bill that established the Adirondack Forest Commission, consisting of politicians who knew nothing about forests. In the years that followed, the inefficiency of the commission supported Sargent's belief that forests had to be managed by experts shielded from the interference of politicians.

In the 1880s, while much of Sargent's attention was devoted to forest issues, he was also becoming influential in the field of urban environmental planning. In 1882, he allied himself with Frederick Law Olmsted, and, after nine long years of negotiation, they successfully made the Arnold Arboretum a part of Olmsted's "Emerald Necklace." This string of parks and parkways, starting from Boston Common and ending in Franklin Park, was one of Olmsted's most successful designs for incorporating nature into the urban landscape. It was also Sargent's vision. The Arnold Arboretum promised to open its gates to the public as a part of the city's park system, while the institution remained affiliated with Harvard.[23]

Sargent could not be more satisfied with the result of this agreement. First, the most serious challenge facing the arboretum—fundraising—was substantially mitigated by municipal support. Second, Sargent never intended to build an urban green space merely for a limited group of scientists to do their research. Instead, his idea of an arboretum was to instill the public with knowledge of botany, to stimulate their interest in science, and to increase their love of nature. As a personal payoff, he got the assistance of Olmsted in designing the landscape of the Arnold Arboretum, which emerged as a masterpiece of naturalistic design, not a mere flowerbed or plant exhibit.[24]

Cooperation between Sargent and Olmsted began in 1873, when Olmsted first got involved with expanding the Boston park system. They continued to collaborate on several other projects, including tree planting along Commonwealth Avenue and preserving redwood forests in California. On Sargent's side, he admired the simple and natural style expressed in Olmsted's works. On Olmsted's side, he respected Sargent's professional knowledge of horticulture and botany that helped fill the gap in his own education. When, in 1881, Olmsted settled his family in Brookline permanently, his friendship with Sargent grew even stronger. Thus, Sargent became to some extent one of the earliest urban environmental reformers, as well as one of the first advocates of forest conservation.

SARGENT'S PARTNER in *Garden and Forest* was the New York newspaper professional William A. Stiles. But it was Olmsted again who recruited Stiles for the job of magazine editor. Stiles was born on a farm near Deckertown, in northern New Jersey, in 1837. He was the only son of Edward A. Stiles, who founded Mount Retirement Seminary, one of the best educational institutes in that part of New Jersey. William received an education in his father's school before he went to college. Quite different from Sargent, who was always well behaved, Stiles was so mischievous that his father expelled him from the classroom at least once every term. He was a good scholar, though, showing special talent in such fields as Latin, music, and mathematics.[25]

Looking like a shabby hick, Stiles went to Yale in 1857. At first, his classmates thought he was very "'green' and awkward," but he changed their impression quickly. He soon gained a reputation for his wit. One day he was called on to solve a problem in geometry, and he gave a satisfactory answer. Then the professor asked him, "But why does A equal B?" and Stiles answered,

"Because two and two make four." The class laughed. The professor realized that "the geometrical fact was in the lad's mind as clear as the sum in addition." His classmates and teachers hailed him as a "natural mathematician." Later on, the *New York Times* recorded some of his views on the connection between mathematics and such fields as art, botany, nature, and landscape architecture: "Mathematics is logic, system, form. Art is form in its high development. Botany is the study of nature's growths, and from examinations of nature's methods one learns the natural arrangement of plants and trees and of the paths through the collection of lawn, bush, and forest, and thus nature and art again commingle and again are proved identical." These words explained why he could find pleasure in such seemingly different things. All of them, including nature itself, belonged to the same orderly and rational world, which Stiles grew up loving and respecting.[26]

Stiles became widely admired in college. "His manner of speech, his caustic humor, and his kindliness of heart," it was said after his death, "added to the simplicity of his tastes, frequently tempted his friends to compare him with Abraham Lincoln." He graduated from Yale in 1859 with honors and became a teacher in his father's school, while studying law at the same time. But his poor health, especially his severely impaired vision, forced him to give up teaching. In 1864, he left on a sea voyage to San Francisco, via the Isthmus of Panama, hoping to get some benefit for his health. He did recover from his eye ailment while in California. After briefly teaching literature and music in Oakland, he accepted a position in the engineer corps that was building the Central Pacific Railroad across the Sierra Nevada. His health collapsed from the exhausting work. When he managed to get back East, he was close to death and completely blind. His sisters nursed him back to health, and Stiles spent the rest of his life living with one sister's family, never marrying.[27]

During his year-long illness, Stiles discovered another world, full of vitality and freedom, so much different from that of his bedridden life. He could not see, but he could hear; he could not move, but he could think; he could not touch, but he could sense the world outside his window. That outdoor world offered plants, trees, flowers, birds, insects, wind, and water. When he got better, he spent hours and hours roaming his father's farm, observing plants and studying the Latin names, characters, and habits of various species. "This love of plants grew to a passion, and he became an expert in botany," a writer pointed out. His interest in plants expanded to include horticulture, scientific agriculture, forestry, and, most importantly, urban parks. Unlike the landscape architects who worked directly with plants and land, Stiles applied his pen to defend their work and promote making the city environment more natural.[28]

Meanwhile, he devoted much energy to Republican Party politics. For a while he served in the Custom House in New York as a "gauger" (tax collector), a political appointment he did not find interesting. Then in 1880 and again 1883, he ran as a Republican for the state senate in New Jersey but was defeated by narrow margins both times. After the second defeat, he accepted an appointment as the secretary of the state senate but stayed only one term.

A more lasting kind of political engagement came through journalistic writing and editing, what one observer called a batch of "vigorous and characteristic political articles for the *Tribune* and other papers." In late 1870, Stiles gave a talk to Yale alumni in New York. The editor and publisher of the *New York Tribune*, Whitelaw Reid, who was present, immediately offered him a job as an editorial writer with the *Tribune*. He held this position until the end of his life. At the beginning, his writing focused on local political issues, especially New Jersey political matters, "where his knowledge of English and his crisp, clear-cut form of expression made him a powerful adherent of whatever policy he was supporting." In 1883, he was also employed as agriculture editor for the *Philadelphia Press*, one of the oldest major newspapers in Philadelphia. From this point on, Stiles's writing focused on creating urban parks and protecting them from any wanton intrusion and destruction.[29]

An artistically designed urban park was, for him, the ideal combination of art and nature. Urban parks provided places where stressed urban residents could relax and contemplate. Stiles, like Olmsted, was an egalitarian who believed that everyone should have access to nature's beauty as enhanced by art.

As a political writer, Stiles's ultimate goal was to extend American democracy. In a letter to Olmsted, he wrote, "I have found that the sharpest attack nowadays is to make common cause with the poor as against encroachment of classes. No one dares to speak slightingly in public of the right of poor children to clean air & grass & trees & birds." These were amenities that Stiles felt morally obligated to preserve in cities. As a loyal adherent of Olmsted's art, Stiles also concurred with Olmsted's social ideals. He intended to use the power of his pen to defend Olmsted's works and their underlying values.[30]

Before he became editor of *Garden and Forest*, Stiles was well aware of Sargent and his views. They had worked together on the Adirondack survey. At that time, Sargent had criticized one of Stiles's editorials because its description of the grassy charms of a mountain's summit was "quite incomplete." Stiles thought that the criticism was correct, but he argued that "it isn't easy to keep on describing scene after scene and object after object in nature." Where he could not agree with Sargent was that he "should have left out the list of big trees," because Stiles believed that "facts are valuable to some extent always."[31]

In letters to Olmsted, Stiles gave more personal views of Sargent. The "professor" had invited Stiles to go to Europe with him and Henry Codman, Sargent's nephew and one of the most promising young landscape architects around. Knowing the demanding character of Sargent, Stiles hesitated to accept the invitation: "With the professor I should be a subaltern under marching order—with a rush here or there as might be best for his purposes of course, but without any free agency of mine." Yet he respected Sargent's knowledge of botany and forestry and anticipated the "highest educational value of the trip." The disadvantage of being overcommanded by Sargent would be "balanced of course by the advantages of his instinct & the superior opportunities for learning." In the end Stiles did not go and was right about his prediction: Codman was soon exhausted by his uncle's "marching order."[32]

In fact, physically and mentally, Stiles and Sargent were quite different and even opposite individuals. The Boston botanist was rotund and strong, while Stiles, whose health had never been robust, was "tall, being 6 feet 3 inches in height, angular, and of spare build." Besides having a difference in physique, the two men differed considerably in wealth. Stiles had to live on his newspaper salary and a modest outside income (his brother-in-law managed his father's farm for him). In explaining to Olmsted why he could not travel in Europe with Sargent, he confessed it was partly due to a lack of money. He was responsible for supporting several young relatives, which cost him "more than several trips to Europe." He regretted that it was "hardship" that kept him from going.[33]

The two men were even more different in temperament. Sargent had the reputation of being bossy and condescending. It took a long time and close acquaintance to touch "a sympathetic kindliness as underlying any superficial reactions." Stiles, however, was easygoing, good humored, and made friends easily. Sargent was usually distant and quiet in personal relations, although Ernest Wilson, his colleague and succeeding director of the Arnold Arboretum, claimed that "toward ladies he [Sargent] had a charming, deferential manner." Stiles, however, was a "celebrated after dinner speaker," and "whenever his tall, gaunt, Lincoln-like figure was seen to rise at the post-prandial board, for speech or story, the treat of the evening was known to be assured."[34]

The difference between these two men also lay in their personal interests. Sargent's world was occupied by plants. From Holm Lea to the Arnold Arboretum, from the parks of Boston to the forests of the West, from North America to the far corners of the earth, plants were his career and his hobby. Stiles, however, had a wider variety of interests. Many remarked on his "versatility." Music was one of his natural gifts, which "came from his mother, a woman of strong intellect and great refinement, from whom, too, came his ready and brilliant wit and keen perceptions." In his memoir of Stiles, Sargent wrote that "music was one of the vital and influential forces of his life." Sargent, in contrast, had such limited talent in music that his family even dared to make fun of him. Stiles was also interested in sports like football, baseball, and horse racing; he had a professional's critical insight regarding those games. Also unlike Sargent, he entertained himself by solving tough mathematical problems.[35]

However, their biggest difference lay in their attitudes toward politics and religion. Contrary to Sargent's indifference to politics, Stiles was fascinated with political games as much as he was with sports. In terms of religion, Stiles was "a constant and profound student of the Bible and truly reverential," a fact that was, however, unknown to many, "even some of his intimate friends." When the church of his hometown lacked a pastor, he took charge of the pulpit for many months. In later years, he sometimes played the organ in front of the congregation, and "at such times his face took on a deep seriousness, as reverential as it was sincere, and with nervous intensity showing in his dilated nostrils and in the strong touch of his fingers, he led in sacred song the congregation of the church where his father and grandfather had been honored deacons."[36]

It is almost impossible to discern this religious conviction from Stiles's published essays. Parks, he argued, should be free of all forms of religious preaching, including that of Christians, for it would disturb the tranquility offered by nature. Like most American intellectuals in his time, Stiles had been profoundly influenced by Ralph Waldo Emerson's transcendentalism, which aimed to search for God and his miracles in the Creation—that is, in nature. Stiles once joked to his friends that since he had written so many essays on urban parks, he could compile them into "a book as big as a family Bible," and this book would express a profound reverence toward nature and its beauty. Finally, it was this love of nature that made these two dramatically different persons, Stiles and Sargent, kindred spirits.[37]

In his memoir of Stiles published in *Garden and Forest*, Sargent reminisced in an uncharacteristically poetic and sentimental tone: "he loved Nature in all her aspects, delighting in the beauty of trees and flowers in the forest and in the garden, and in their harmonious arrangement; he loved the song of birds, quiet sylvan lanes and sparkling waters." Their interest in nature overlapped in many ways. Stiles regarded the defense of urban parks as his primary mission, and Sargent also believed in their importance and actively promoted the park movement, locally and nationally. Sargent was among the pioneers in preserving American forests and wild scenery, a cause that also attracted Stiles's concern. Sargent was the expert of experts in botany, dendrology, and horticulture, and Stiles was an enthusiastic learner in these fields and equipped himself with more knowledge than a mere amateur would have done. His essay "Orchids," published in *Scribner's Magazine* in 1894, was regarded as an outstanding treatment of this family of plants.[38]

Essentially, the two men pursued the same thing—a balance between nature and human beings in an ever-progressing civilization. This common goal ensured a solid foundation for their ten years' cooperation. Their differences, however, made the magazine, the outcome of their cooperation, more diverse, interesting, and inclusive.

APPARENTLY, *SILVA* was Sargent's first choice for the new magazine's name. As *Silva*, the magazine's scope would have been substantially narrower. Initially, Sargent regarded the magazine as an organ associated with the Arnold Arboretum, and, through it, he intended to "extend and popularize the knowledge of trees and their cultivation, and of gardening and garden-botany." In his original plan, the new weekly magazine would be a scientific journal mainly focusing on botany, horticulture, dendrology, and forestry. When Sargent selected Stiles to be the editor, however, the focus and title of the magazine shifted, from the scientific-sounding "silva" to the more popular and vernacular "garden" and "forest." Stiles's close connection with Olmsted guaranteed that there would be a powerful and lasting voice for landscape architects in its pages.

In a letter to Olmsted, Stiles thanked his friend for the suggestions that "the Park or Public works notes ought to be made features," for they would be the best way of "connecting the paper with actual news." He admitted that he and Sargent had some divergence over who should be included among the magazine's contributors and audience. For instance, they disagreed on the names and expertise of contributors listed in the prospectus. Stiles complained that Sargent "crossed off [Bernhard] Fernow's [name] for example—the best equipped man in the country for what we want." Even worse, Sargent did not want Charles A. Dana's name in the first number, for he was afraid that "it would strike the scientific eye unfavorably." As the editor of the *Sun*, Dana was one of the most prominent journalists in the nation but only an amateur in horticulture in Sargent's eyes. For Stiles, having Dana's name associated with the magazine would enhance its influence; even more important was that Dana had for years been sympathetic with those promoting urban parks. Stiles was aiming to "keep too much technical science out" of the magazine and to bring more "society" in, for he believed that the magazine should be relevant to the development of not only science but also society. Only by doing so could they make "a paper distinctly different & better than any yet seen."[39]

After much compromising between the two editors, the first issue of the magazine appeared on 29 February 1888. Fernow's name was absent in the prospectus, but Charles A. Dana's name was listed along with landscape architects suggested by Olmsted. Sargent designated himself the "conductor" who would have "general editorial control" of *Garden and Forest*, while Stiles was to be the managing editor. The editorial office was in the Tribune Building, New York City, which meant that the real editorial work in fact was on Stiles's shoulders. Most of the communication between Stiles and Sargent relied on postal correspondence, with a few telegrams and personal meetings.[40]

The first number also set up the goal for what would be the next 513 issues—to cover a full range of topics from botany to horticulture, from forestry to landscape architecture. As the subtitle, "A Journal of Horticulture, Landscape Art, and Forestry," indicated, the magazine would be devoted to all these subjects, but, more importantly, it was devoted to promoting a more general environmental awareness in the nation, particularly among a distinctly urban audience, while addressing nature's place in a changing society.

The magazine usually comprised nine to twelve pages in the main body, followed by four or five pages of advertisements. In general, *Garden and Forest* included eight sections or "departments": editorial, new and little-known plants, foreign correspondence, culture, forests, correspondence, recent publications, and notes. In some issues, there were also sections devoted to entomology, exhibits, expositions, and meetings of different associations. The editorial section mainly commented on four distinct themes: preservation of the nation's forests, protection of urban parks and advocacy of landscape architecture, description of plant species growing in North America, and general ideas about the relationship between nature and humans. Stiles probably wrote most of the editorials on urban parks, while Sargent wrote those on native species and some articles on forestry. Occasionally, others, such as Mariana Van Rensselaer, provided unsigned editorials.

The noneditorial departments had more narrowly focused subjects. The new and little-known plants department described recently discovered or exotic species, many of which had been sent to the Arnold Arboretum from all over the world, especially from North America and eastern Asia. Some specimens were also sent to the editorial office of *Garden and Forest*, and if Stiles could not identify them, he would consult with either Sargent or other botanists at Harvard.[41] The foreign correspondence section printed letters on plants and botanic gardens from foreign countries, especially the Royal Botanic Gardens at Kew in London. The culture section concentrated on horticulture. The forests section carried articles on forests and forestry theory and practice around the world, especially in Europe. The recent publications section introduced books and articles published on all the fields related to the editorial focus of *Garden and Forest*. The entomology section discussed problems caused by various pests and disseminated information about new pesticides and other insect-control techniques. The section on meetings, exhibits, and expositions reported activities of such groups as forestry, horticulture, and floriculture associations and printed excerpts of papers presented at their meetings. It also recorded exhibits of flowers and plants and in 1893 published a series of essays on the world's fair in Chicago. Some of the magazine's issues reported the wholesale and retail prices of flower and plant markets in various cities.

The correspondence and the notes sections were, in contrast, exceptionally broad. The former received letters on such diverse subjects as amateurs' observations in their backyards, professionals' travels around the world, the relationship between forest and civilization, and the connection of urban parks to society. Sometimes there were editors' responses to questions or comments given by correspondents. The notes section provided information on new species or presented a brief obituary or a note on an urban park or road in an American or foreign city.

In addition to its well-written and edited text, *Garden and Forest* was also striking for its numerous illustrations, which were regarded as superior to those of any other magazine in its field. Each issue carried one to three illustrations, which could be drawings of gardens or parks, portraits of significant figures, designs of landscape architecture, or photos of trees or plants. But a large percentage of them were paintings of plants rendered by Charles Edward Faxon, a staff employee of the Arnold Arboretum and one of the best botanical illustrators in the nation. He prepared 285 illustrations for the magazine and did most of the drawings for Sargent's *The Silva of North America*. Sargent thought that his works united "botanical accuracy with graceful composition" and hailed him as one of "the few great masters of his art."[42]

Each magazine section and illustration was supposed to promote the major mission that Sargent and Stiles bestowed upon the magazine: addressing nature's role and survival in an urban civilization. To fulfill the mission, both Sargent and Stiles thought that *Garden and Forest* should educate not only the general public but also policy makers. Its educational content ranged from elementary information on botany to theoretic discussions of the field, from the basic techniques of gardening to the most updated and complicated methods of horticulture, from the physical benefits of roadside tree planting to the spiritual implication of urban parks, from the introduction of foreign ideas and the practice of forestry to the social imperative of sustaining the nation's forests.

From the outset of publication, *Garden and Forest* asserted its educational intentions: "it will place scientific information clearly and simply before the public, and make available the instruction of all persons interested in garden plants [and] the conclusions reached by the most trustworthy investigation." Furthermore, "it will be a medium of instruction for all persons interested in preserving and developing the beauty of natural scenery." The editors believed that good taste in the appreciation and comprehension of natural beauty, and systematic knowledge in understanding nature's laws, unlike the innate love of nature, needed to be cultivated. "The general public," wrote the editors, "does not know good from bad in gardening, and, therefore, this is the requisite lesson to teach it." "The truer gardener" was not to "cater to public taste, but to educate it."[43]

Meanwhile, the magazine declared that it would also "give special attention to scientific and practical forestry," educating both the public and the government about the significance and urgency of rational management of forests. More than once, the magazine declared its role "in forming public taste and guiding public sentiment in this direction." Repeatedly arguing that "Americans as a nation need instruction in the laws which govern forest growth and forest management," *Garden and Forest* took on this responsibility. To make its editorial voice stronger and more influential, *Garden and Forest* collaborated with other publications, periodicals, newspapers, pamphlets, and books.[44]

For instance, in its opposition to a proposal to host the 1892 world's fair in Central Park (before Chicago was chosen to hold the fair, New York City had offered another possibility), *Garden and Forest* echoed the city's hostile public media. It pointed out that in the past the newspapers of the city had saved Central Park from being ruined by different types of assaults more than once. And this time, the magazine exulted, "when the question of appropriating a portion of the park for the World's Fair was under discussion, the unanimity of the press, outside of the daily papers, was surprising. Journals in the special fields of architecture, art and engineering, and the leading literary, pictorial and religious weeklies, with scarcely an exception, took a firm stand against the invasion." When these publications joined to form an organized power, *Garden and Forest* was in their vanguard.[45]

On forest issues, *Garden and Forest* searched for the same political impact. Being the first magazine in the nation that systematically discussed forestry matters, *Garden and Forest* forged an alliance with *Century*, one of the nation's most popular magazines among intellectuals, while endeavoring to gain more support from other publications. The editors believed that "the public must be enlightened and aroused to active interest in the matter; and the concerted and energetic action of the press of the whole country can alone accomplish this." Its frequent contributor Jonathan Baxter Harrison placed such a high value on the educational function of *Garden and Forest* that he predicted optimistically that, "if such a journal as GARDEN AND FOREST . . . could be read habitually for some years in every school and institution of learning in this state, and by ten or twenty thousand of its leading citizens, we might then have here such conditions of knowledge and thought as would constitute the soil and atmosphere needed to produce a better civilization, and a practical and effective system or method of forest preservation and management might then be evolved." Certainly, the nation seemed in need of more such magazines and journalism. One editorial in *Garden and Forest* indicated that "there is no subject which at present more urgently requires the attention of journalists, educators and statesmen, and of all thoughtful men in this country" than improving the critical relationship between forest and civilization.[46]

In addition to building alliances with other media powers, Stiles and Sargent were also trying to spread their ideas through their personal activities. After Stiles accepted the position as managing editor of *Garden and Forest*, he became associated with several other nongovernmental organizations, such as the American Forestry Association, the New Jersey Forestry Association (of which he was the vice president), the New York Forestry Association, and the Tree Plantation Association of New York City.

The most important step Stiles took in his campaign for promoting nature in cities was his acceptance of a seat on the New York City Park Board in November 1895. For years, *Garden and Forest* had criticized the decisions and actions made by the old park board, which turned out to be ineffective in defending New York City parks from defacement or inappropriate development. Worse than that, the previous park commissioners, who were ignorant of the art of landscape architecture, showed no respect for the designers' professional skills and choices; the commissioners had distorted or ignored the landscape architects' original intentions. The most intolerable aspect of the commissioners' service was that they had no sympathy for or interest in nature, nor did they feel or respect the aspiration for contact with nature among urban residents. Therefore, when Stiles was offered a position on the board by Mayor William L. Strong, he "accepted [the position] without hesitation, as he is an enthusiast on the subject of the possibilities of the parks."[47]

The appointment of Stiles was a victory celebrated by landscape architects and their supporters, no matter which political party they belonged to;

in fact, they had been urging the mayor to make Stiles a park commissioner for years. Traditionally, the park commissioners had held their positions for political or economic reasons. Stiles's colleagues on the commission, S. V. R. Cruger, Smith Ely, and Samuel McMillan, had all grabbed seats out of political or economic self-interest. Both Cruger and McMillan had real-estate investments in the city, and the latter was "one of the wealthiest builders in New York." Ely was a former mayor and the only Democrat on the commission, and his appointment was supposed to balance the power between the two parties. Stiles was the only one among them who had "technical knowledge" about balancing nature and art in urban parks. The *New York Times* declared "there was no political influences [sic] at work to secure the office for Mr. Stiles." Being the managing editor of *Garden and Forest*, Stiles had "a National reputation among experts as the authority on the subject of parks, and his appointment as a Commissioner is considered the best and most fitting that has been made."[48]

The new job on the park board demanded a lot of time and energy from Stiles, so he recruited another person to help with the editorial work at *Garden and Forest*. The new assistant editor was Mary B. Coulston, but her position was never acknowledged in the pages of the magazine. She signed her contributions only with initials—M. B. C.—and only in the index of the tenth volume could one find her full name listed. To be sure, Stiles's name was not listed either, except in the first volume, but Coulston's contribution to the magazine would have been obliterated had it not been for acknowledgment in the *Cyclopedia of American Horticulture* and in her obituary.[49]

In the *Cyclopedia*, edited by Liberty Hyde Bailey in 1902, Coulston, who wrote the biographical entry for Stiles, was described as a former assistant editor of *Garden and Forest* from Ithaca, New York. After her untimely death in 1904, an obituary was published in the *San Diego Union and Daily Bee*, a newspaper published in the city where she had taken up residence after leaving New York. There one finds a few more words about her early life:

> Mrs. Coulston was a native of Pennsylvania—where she lived during
> the early part of her life. Her principle [sic] life work has been with the
> associated charities and more especially with "Garden and Forest," which
> up to a few years ago was the best horticultural paper of the country. She
> was on the staff of the magazine for ten years, having begun as pioneer

writer, and having worked up to the position of associated editor and finally editor-in-chief. . . . In her capacity of editor on this paper she became well and favorably known among horticulturists in this country.[50]

The obituary, the most detailed biography of Coulston available, leaves her role at the magazine obscure.

Presumably Coulston was not associated with *Garden and Forest* in its early years. From the first to the sixth volume, there was only one horticultural correspondence sent by an "M.B.C.," from Philadelphia. In the seventh volume, published in 1894, Coulston's name began to show up in the correspondence section more frequently, and her address indicated that she had moved to New York. Given Stiles's new obligation as a park commissioner, it is likely that Coulston was hired as assistant editor in 1895; in the last few months of the magazine, she might have become the chief editor because of Stiles's deteriorating health.[51]

As for overworked Stiles, his position on the Central Park board gave his pen more influence than ever, but it was an influence that would soon come to an end. Every Wednesday a new issue of the magazine came out; every Thursday he went to his park board meeting. His frail constitution and intensifying illness could not stand the physical stress. It was during one of those board meetings, on 2 August 1897, that he collapsed and never recovered. He died of cancer on 6 October 1897.

With Stiles gone, there was no one on the Central Park board who had a real love of nature or was concerned about the presence of parks in an urban society. Evidence of that change came when a group of people in New York City submitted a proposal to the board to name one of the newly built small parks after him. In their petition, they claimed that "for more than twenty years . . . he had been striving to lead the public mind to understand the legitimate purposes for which our parks were created and to prevent their misuse through unwise legislation or the mistaken views of their temporary custodians." His persistent effort exerted on behalf of Central Park justified ranking him next to Frederick Law Olmsted and Calvert Vaux, the original designers of the park, as being responsible for the "usefulness and beauty" of "this glory" in the city. The petition failed, however; no park would be named after him. Board members protested that he had lived across the Hudson River in Jersey City part of the time and that new parks could be named only after "the distinguished men of this city." Hypocritically, they proceeded to name a park after a person who spent most of his life in Auburn, New York.[52]

In his obituary for Stiles, Sargent wrote, "His pen saved Central Park from the speedway which threatened to ruin its rural character and destroy its true value . . . and he made it impossible to use Central Park for the Columbian Exposition." In Sargent's view, Stiles had influenced the public and the policy makers as "an educator in all that relates to parks, reaching the public ear through the press, which had unbounded confidence in his judgment and integrity of purpose[;] his service to the people has not been merely local; his example has stimulated and his words have instructed, and now in every American community there are [those] who understand the significance of city parks and the difficulties which those who labor to make them most useful have to encounter."[53]

Two months after Stiles's death, Sargent ceased publication of *Garden and Forest*, partly due to the editor's death and partly due to financial difficulty. For a long time the magazine had been a success, not least for Sargent the scientist. Using *Garden and Forest* as his outlet, Sargent had year after year reported on research at the Arnold Arboretum, exchanged views with his peers, and popularized the knowledge of botany and horticulture. It was in *Garden and Forest* that he published his botanical discoveries during a field trip to Japan in 1893, articles that subsequently became the book *Forest Flora of Japan*. It was the beginning of comparative research—a project that is still active today—into the vegetation of eastern Asia and North America undertaken by the Arnold Arboretum. Also in *Garden and Forest*, Sargent published several other important essay series, such as "Notes on North American Trees."

Near the end of 1897, Sargent complained to his friend John Muir that "the year ends badly for me because it will see the demise of *Garden and Forest*. For ten years I have worked like a dog to get this paper established because a paper of the kind seems needed in this country, but it is no go." He had put too much money into the magazine and could not "sink more."[54]

The magazine was probably doomed to expire with or without financial problems. Not only was Stiles dead but Olmsted was old and sick, and Sargent was discouraged. How could he alone maintain the momentum of *Garden and Forest*? If *Garden and Forest* had survived, it probably would have become a forerunner of the still active *Journal of the Arnold Arboretum*, a magazine Sargent started in 1919 and one that was more purely scientific than *Garden and Forest* had been. But that would come twenty years later; in 1897, Sargent felt it was time to turn away from the publishing world.

Garden and Forest's record of achievement, however, was not inconsequential. The nation's most popular newspapers and magazines frequently quoted from its pages, and public opinion was undoubtedly influenced through its articles during the decade of its publication. In its day it had been a unifying voice speaking to all those across the nation, particularly in the axis of urbanity that stretched from Boston to New York, who were earnestly seeking environmental reform.

3 SHAPING NEW PROFESSIONS

〜〜〜〜〜〜〜〜〜〜〜

THE LATE NINETEENTH CENTURY was a formative period for many fledgling professions dealing with the human environment—forestry, gardening, urban design, and even conservation. The advocates of those new
professions were seeking self-definitions and identities. They wanted to set
standards and justify these new areas of expertise that were challenging the
domain of vernacular knowledge. Before that time, ordinary citizens without any special training, mostly farmers, had long decided how to create and
manage the landscape. They utilized the forests, laid out their villages and
towns without formal knowledge, and decided what was useful and what was
beautiful. Now those decisions were beginning to fall into the hands of men
and women who claimed more rigorous training and expertise.

In the late nineteenth century, urban professionals began to promote
themselves by editing periodicals and establishing organizations, and it was
this trend that in large part motivated the publication of *Garden and Forest*. One
of the major missions of the magazine was to make a case for the new environmental professions and to encourage new theories and concepts in more
traditional professions, such as botany and horticulture. This promotion of
professions was a key part of the editorial effort of *Garden and Forest* to reform

urban society and its relation to nature. In one editorial, the magazine criticized the public's lack of respect for "technical knowledge" and argued that "changes in the conditions of life here during the last twenty-five years have rendered [that knowledge] far more necessary than it was before. The need of special training in the management of public parks increases steadily, just as the requirement for technical knowledge in the other pursuits of civilized life is made more imperative by the increasing variety, complexity and costliness of modern ways of living."[1]

Both editors and contributors thought that professionalization was part of progress, an irreversible trend coming in the wake of urban industrial life. To adjust to that "variety, complexity and costliness" of modern society, scientific or other systematic knowledge was essential. The new professionals' work would ideally not be limited to private patrons and employment. They believed professionalism should be at the service of the whole society. This promotion of expertise came from a faith in the expanding potency of modern science, which would, these new professionals and their supporters thought, enable people to understand the laws of nature in a more profound way. Through better knowledge they could better incorporate nature into civilization and make it serve the needs of humankind.

If the ultimate goal was to sustain civilization, however, the magazine staff were not altogether sure what that meant. Its writers debated what names to call their professions and what ideas they should pursue. They posed such questions as whose expertise should prevail and whether the various environmental professions would agree on goals and methods or if they would be in competition.

During its ten years of publication, *Garden and Forest* attracted more than 630 contributors, nearly a third of whom wrote more than three pieces for the magazine.[2] Geographically and socially, these people spanned a wide range. Mainly, they came from New England and New York, but the magazine also maintained a regular group of contributors from the Midwest and the West Coast and from foreign nations such as Germany, France, England, and Japan.[3] Among the contributors were many scientists, including leading domestic and foreign botanists, entomologists, and horticulturists; joining them were other experts with professional training, such as florists, nursery experts, landscape architects, and foresters, along with knowledgeable "amateurs," such as art critics, journalists, ministers, and devoted nature or plant lovers. The majority of these contributors were male, but there were about thirty female authors who wrote for the magazine, and several of them were among the most regular and influential figures in *Garden and Forest*.

The magazine did not seek a rigid uniformity among its contributors. In terms of their vision of nature, some were more passionate about gardens, while others were more attracted to forests; some were fascinated with cultivating individual plants, while others were engaged in designing a more comprehensive landscape. Many contributors enjoyed domesticated scenery, while others preferred the rugged wilderness. A large group extolled the beauty of nature above other values, while others ranked its usefulness over everything else. Their social concerns were not completely the same either. Some had political ambitions, while others pursued academic achievements. Some of them put more emphasis on government responsibility and regulation, while others put their hope in the improvement of public intelligence and morality. With regard to their attitudes toward science and art, some of them relied solely on science, while others leaned toward art. Many of the contributors not only wrote on multiple environmental topics for the magazine but also worked on a variety of nonenvironmental issues in their careers. With this diverse but collective assistance, *Garden and Forest* was determined to promote the new environmental professions as guides in shaping a new society. It was not only natural resources that needed expert regulation; so too did urban spaces, such as streets, playgrounds, parks, and the nature growing within cities—trees, flowers, and other plants. Different forms of resources demanded different experts.

It would not be feasible to examine the career and thought of each of the six hundred–plus contributors, but based on the essays they wrote for *Garden and Forest*, they fall into several categories. By examining a few representative figures, this chapter reveals the collective mind of the magazine and makes it possible to discern the differences and even the conflicts that were roiling the world of late-nineteenth-century American environmental thinkers.

BOTANY WAS THE scientific foundation of *Garden and Forest* and of the fields and new professions it promoted. In its pages, the magazine included some of the most prominent names in American botany: William J. Beal, Charles E. Bessey, John M. Coulter, William G. Farlow, Merritt L. Fernald, George L. Goodale, Edward L. Greene, Charles Mohr, Louis Hermann Pammel, Cyrus G.

Pringle, Mary Treat, William Trelease, and Sereno Watson, and such important figures from foreign nations as John Macoun from Canada, Max Leichtlin from Germany, and William Botting Hemley, George Nicholson, and William P. Watson from the Kew Royal Botanic Gardens in England.

It was a time when some traditional subfields, taxonomy for example, still held a significant niche in botany. Collectors sponsored by government or private agencies were exploring new regions and identifying new species, and such work was faithfully reported by *Garden and Forest*.[4] The magazine also encouraged the transition from traditional to modern botany, from field to laboratory. Historian Andrew Denny Rodgers argues that American botany experienced in the last three decades of the nineteenth century a transition that freed "most botanists from a sole interest in taxonomy. . . . The work of the new subjects of morphology, physiology, mycology, 'vegetable diseases,' anatomy, and the like, was taking effect."[5] Essentially, botanists began studying the environmental aspects of plants, their ecology and habitats, along with their individual structure and variation.

While botany was becoming more diversified, it was subject to the "impact of a gathering momentum seeking to develop an American scientific horticulture and agriculture." Thus, some leading botanists increasingly emphasized the utilitarian value of plant knowledge. These botanists believed that, by studying the growth dynamics of plants, they could discover "what nature could be made to perform," rather than merely focusing on "what nature had done." Following this belief, many preeminent botanists showed a zealous interest in agriculture, horticulture, and forestry, and some of them even switched their main research interest to those more applied fields.[6]

All of these trends traced their origins back to Charles Darwin's theory of evolution. In an address given at the Botanists' Dinner in 1913, William G. Farlow, one of Asa Gray's former students, vividly recalled the changes happening in the field of botany and the crucial effect of Darwinism in pushing forward these changes. "It has been my fortune to see the old order of things overturned by 'The Origin of Species,'" he declared, "which, by freeing science from the fetters of a semitheological bias, opened the way to free scientific studies of the distribution of plants and animals and the great question of heredity and evolution." Through Darwin and his American disciple Asa Gray, Farlow and others were inspired to change the course of their science, and that change was a fundamental theme in *Garden and Forest*.[7]

After Darwin, the major influence on the minds of America's professional botanists was Gray, who emphasized the social value of the study of plants. Growing up in a humble family, he strived to make science accessible to anyone who wanted to learn. According to Rodgers, Gray believed that "since science was combined with the open field and forest, as well as the farm field and garden, science service was offered to all worthy comers, and no monopoly would ever be possible nor was it desirable." Many of his disciples followed not only his academic example but also his endeavor to break down the exclusiveness of science, bringing its insights to common people, especially to farmers, florists, and gardeners.[8]

Although coming from various social backgrounds and working in different regions, almost all of the American botanists who published in *Garden and Forest* were somehow linked to Gray.[9] Among them were four Harvard botany professors with diverse specialties—William Farlow, an expert in cryptogamic botany and pathology, George Goodale in physiology, Sereno Watson in taxonomy, and the magazine's publisher, Sargent, who represented horticulture. They had their disputes. Sargent, with his low academic status as arboretum manager, had not gotten along well with his colleagues in his early years at Harvard. According to his biographer, however, when Sargent felt confident as a trained scientist, he managed to respect them and recruited them for his magazine.[10]

Farlow was put in charge of the editorial section for cryptogamic botany and plant disease. Before his death in 1892, Watson wrote frequently for the "New and Little Known Plants" section. Goodale published a series in the second volume of the magazine (1889) titled "Principles of Physiological Botany as Applied to Horticulture and Forest." In introducing this series, *Garden and Forest* confessed that it was inspired by an 1888 meeting of New York florists where it was admitted that "even from a practical point of view some knowledge of botany is necessary to plant growers who aim to get the most out of their business." At the end of his series, Goodale stated that "the history of science has shown over and over again that the results of pure, scientific research are, sooner or later, likely to be turned to the highest practical account." This was, in fact, a general goal of *Garden and Forest*, which promoted the idea that science should apply a more down-to-earth approach.[11]

Besides these Harvard professors, botanists from the West and the Midwest also wrote for the magazine. The relatively unknown vegetation in those regions stimulated botanists to focus more on native flora—its structure, history, and relationship with the environment. While botany itself was becoming more and more fragmented into such specialties as physiology and morphology, it also saw the emergence of a new integrated point of view, "the science of the development of communities," which was especially strong in the Midwest. Eventually this new botany took the name "ecology." The name was coined by the German scientist Ernst H. Haeckel in 1866, but it was not widely adopted by botanists and other scientists until the 1890s, about the time that *Garden and Forest* ceased publication.[12]

Among prominent midwestern contributors was Charles E. Bessey. Born in 1845 in Wayne County, Ohio, Bessey attended the Agricultural College of Michigan, then went on to study botany with Gray, after which he became professor of botany at the University of Nebraska and also served as dean of the agricultural college there. Bessey was interested in forestry and undertook a tree-planting experiment in Thomas and Cherry counties in Nebraska. Among his greatest achievements was making the University of Nebraska a national center for ecological research. Some of Bessey's writings revealed an interest in the natural succession of vegetation in the landscape. In a *Garden and Forest* essay titled "Are the Trees Receding from the Nebraska Plains?" Bessey indicated that on the plains of Nebraska one could observe "the slow changes due to natural causes, and having nothing whatever to do with men's activities."[13]

Another of the magazine's midwestern contributors was William J. Beal. He too had studied at Harvard, working with Louis Agassiz for a while and then with Gray, from whom he learned the physiology and morphology of plants, along with Darwin's theory of evolution. From 1871 until 1910, Beal taught at the Michigan Agricultural College. In a *Garden and Forest* essay titled "Methods of Botanic Study," Beal argued, "in the new botany, for which we are speaking a good word, we set pupils to studying plants before books. . . . Free use is made of our botanic-garden, the crops in the vegetable-garden, fields and experiment station, and the thickets along the river." For the magazine he reported regularly on forestry issues in Michigan, especially the management of a college forest preserve that he thought would show some "practical instruction of forestry" and furnish suggestions "as to the best method of managing our woodlands."[14]

Louis H. Pammel was another botanist writing for *Garden and Forest*, and he too showed enthusiasm for forestry issues. After receiving a degree in agriculture from the University of Wisconsin, he studied with Farlow at Harvard and then accepted a position at Iowa State College as professor of botany. He had a strong interest in the native vegetation of Iowa and became one of the most active advocates of the conservation movement in that state. Another important contributor was William Trelease, the first to hold the Engelmann Professorship in the Shaw School of Botany at Washington University in Saint Louis. Becoming the first director of the Missouri Botanical Garden, he also saw in the applied field of horticulture the means not only to make a garden or even a city bloom in all seasons but also to demonstrate humankind's role in the evolution of the natural world.

These botanists all made *Garden and Forest* a magazine of science, to some extent, opening the minds of its readers to the importance of the scientific study of plants to modern America. A different but related profession was the study of horticulture, which the magazine also promoted.

During the decade when *Garden and Forest* was published, horticulture grew rapidly in many dimensions. The strongest impetus came from expanding markets among urban residents. With the assistance of newly invented chemical and mechanical techniques, horticulturists accelerated the commercialization of nature. New species of domesticated fruits, vegetables, and ornamental flowers were produced and marketed every year. The magazine noted, "As our vast territory has been brought under cultivation, all plants, and especially those grown for fruit, have responded with wonderful facility to the demands which new climates and new human wants have placed upon them." Horticulture, like agriculture, intended to make nature act according to human will and demand. However, while agriculture aimed to meet humans' basic need for subsistence, horticulture aimed to satiate other desires, such as those for beauty and ornament. Horticulture as a practical business could not blossom until a large number of people were no longer toiling on the land, striving for basic existence.[15]

Garden and Forest regularly reported the activities and meetings of horticulturists or florists, updated the wholesale and retail price of flowers, plants, fruits, and vegetables in New York and Boston, and published hundreds of articles and notes on new methods, technologies, pesticides, and fertilizers, in addition to introducing several hundred species for home cultivation. At least five hundred contributors could call themselves horticulturists. As a leisure activity, horticulture was popular among the upper classes, but as a profession it was an elusive field to define. What was horticulture after all? Should horticulturists be equipped with advanced scientific knowledge, or should horticulture become itself a science, involving its own theories? Was horticulture a hobby or a profession?

Horticulture's major subject is the cultivation of plants, including trees, fruits, vegetables, and flowers. It had been traditionally regarded as manual work for low-paid gardeners who had relied more on experience and vernacular knowledge than on science. But in the late nineteenth century, significant changes occurred in horticulture that pointed to a more scientific basis. As early as 1875, Francis Parkman, the eminent Harvard historian and president of the Massachusetts Horticultural Society, described the profession in these words: "It is an art based on a science, or on several sciences. When pursued in its highest sense and to its best results, it demands the exercise of a great variety of faculties, and gives scope to a high degree of mental activity. . . . The mind of the true cultivator is always on the alert to detect the working of principles and carry them to their practical application. To read the secrets of nature and aid her in her beneficent functions is his grateful and ennobling task."[16]

As Sargent's predecessor in the Bussey Institution and a self-taught expert on flowers, Parkman had a close relationship to the magazine. His name showed up in the list of contributors published on the first page, but probably due to health reasons he wrote only one short piece, on forests in New Hampshire's White Mountains, which was published in the first issue of the first volume.[17] His description of horticulture's mission expressed a dominant view among American horticulturists and botanists: explore its scientific potential, make it practical, and through it pursue a more comprehensive understanding of nature.

It was the task of horticulture to broaden the boundaries of botany, which had been confined entirely to wild plants and their environment, by focusing on cultivated plants. In an editorial published in 1892, *Garden and Forest's* editors wrote that a bias toward the wild was "natural in earlier days, when there was little attempt to apply science to cultivation, but since the theory of evolution has come to be accepted, a new purpose has been given to the study of all natural objects, and cultivated plants especially have gained a fascinating interest because they furnish such conspicuous examples of variation and heredity. The great mass of material which the multiplied species of cultivated plants afford can be made to illustrate the accumulative effect of modified environment and selection under the influence of human care as wild plants cannot possibly do." The magazine endorsed the call for a "broader botany," in the words of Liberty Hyde Bailey, who was the most crucial advocate of applying science to horticulture.[18]

Bailey was born in Van Buren County, Michigan, in 1858. His father operated a big apple orchard, where Bailey spent much of his childhood gaining wide knowledge about nature and horticulture. After graduating from Michigan Agricultural College, he went to Harvard and became Asa Gray's assistant. In 1885, Bailey returned to his undergraduate college as its first professor of horticulture and landscape gardening, but, three years later, he was invited to assume the Chair of Practical and Experimental Horticulture at Cornell University. It was there that Bailey launched not only his influential reform of horticulture but also his legendary career as an extremely prolific writer and environmental philosopher.[19]

During his years at Cornell, Bailey was a regular contributor to *Garden and Forest*, publishing about eighty articles. Many of them discussed specific topics of horticulture, but others were on the general development of the field. He reported on the 1893 world's fair in Chicago; more than twenty of his articles were on the fair's horticultural exhibits. Compared to his life list of more than seven hundred papers and sixty books, the number of articles Bailey published in *Garden and Forest* was not large, but these articles were vital to the magazine's vision of itself.

The fundamental idea Bailey tried to convey in the magazine was that horticulture must become part of modern education and should train people to observe and contemplate the natural world by working directly with plants. His experimental horticultural course, designed at Cornell, was reported in detail in *Garden and Forest* as part of its project of introducing scientific knowledge to its readers. As more programs of horticulture were established in the nation's schools and universities, the magazine devoted more pages to this subject.

Bailey's personal interest and contribution were too broad to define him merely as a horticulturist. At the turn of the twentieth century, he served as the leader of the American country-life movement and the nature-study movement, both efforts by urban people to reform society. The former paid close attention to elevating farmers' material and spiritual lives by introducing them to scientific thinking while inspiring them to discover the beauty of nature and to explore their kinship with nature. The nature-study movement aimed to bring nature into the schools through Arbor Day celebrations, gardening in the school yards, visits to botanic gardens, summer camping, and the study of botany and birds. Its purpose was to restore an intimate relationship with nature among children living in cities.[20]

Historian Allan Carlson argues that Bailey was also the voice of a new agrarianism emerging at the turn of the twentieth century. Agrarianism promoted a social order that was politically decentralized, "socially conservative and economically radical." The central question Bailey asked was how to preserve rural values based on the family unit while bringing advanced technology and science to farmers, who were becoming a minority. It is important to notice that Bailey was concerned with not only farmers' destiny in an urban society but also nature's position in that same society. He was searching for a balanced relationship between nature and people, whether urban or rural. Despite his decentralization bias, he argued that Americans should use the power of government to preserve natural resources and scenery, such as forest reservations and national parks. His conservative social values made him cherish rural family life, but they did not lead him to oppose urban and industrial growth. In *The Holy Earth*, the work containing his essential philosophy, Bailey did not call for a return to the traditional rural order but tried to construct a new relationship between humans and nature and, to some extent, a new religion that recognized the earth as its source of the sacred.[21]

Thus, Bailey preached to his readers, "We shall find our rootage in the soil." By soil, he meant gardens more than fields. Horticulture, defined as the physical and mental experience of working in the soil, offered a substitute for agriculture in an urban age. For some people, it offered a way to make a living; for many others, it offered the means to touch directly the soil and learn about the economy of nature. Even though Bailey advocated kinship between humans and other creatures, he still believed that humans had to exercise dominion but that "dominion does not carry personal ownership." Dominion infused with ethics taught responsibility toward the earth.[22]

Other contributors agreed on the need to promote horticulture in the new era. Henry Sargent Codman, for example, called the attention of Americans to a horticultural school at France's Versailles that was regarded the best in Europe. In discussing Codman's essay, *Garden and Forest* editors pointed out that "the theory of the school is, that instruction in horticulture, if it is to be of any value, must be both practical and scientific." In another editorial, "Horticulture and Health," published in 1896, the editors summarized the magazine's view: "It is very plain that the ampler knowledge we have of Nature's laws, and the fuller command we have of scientific truth, the better we are able to cope with the problems of practical horticulture, which means the transforming of crude and comparatively worthless material into substitutes of value for food or for administrating to our love of the beautiful. A knowledge of botany, chemistry, entomology and geology can all be utilized in floriculture, in vegetable-gardening and in fruit-growing, and any one of these occupations will stimulate the ambitious practitioner to study and cultivate his habits of observation." Science and horticulture should, in this view, be combined so that humans could gain more knowledge about nature and make the earth more bountiful for human needs.[23]

Although they reached consensus on promoting the scientific aspect of horticulture, horticulturists disagreed over several questions in the field. In the eighth volume of *Garden and Forest*, Bailey, E. S. Goff, and Luther Burbank all debated the purpose of their science. Goff, a professor at the University of Wisconsin and a regular contributor to the magazine with about thirty essays, led off with an essay on plant breeding. He called for breeding new plant varieties in agriculture experiment stations. Bailey countered that scientists should put more emphasis on improving present varieties instead of inventing new ones. "Man," he asserted, "does not have it in his power to summarily produce a new variety with any degree of certainty." He argued that "the true method of improving the vegetable kingdom is that pursued by nature—the slow unfolding of one form into another, the carrying forward of the whole body of cultivated forms of any species." Then Goff responded that his experiments had demonstrated the possibility of achieving whatever the breeder wanted. Luther Burbank, one of the most prominent horticulturists in the nation and the developer of the Idaho potato, joined the debate. As a man who had bred more than eight hundred varieties of plants, Burbank had more confidence in the success and stability of human interventions. He argued that "there are fixed laws in the breeding of plants as in other natural forces, and the more we learn of these laws the more certainly we can control results." Admitting the slowness of natural evolution, Burbank believed that humans could accelerate nature's selection process in order to achieve a more immediate result.[24]

The crucial question in this discussion was how fast and how far human power could change the evolution of plants. Compared to Goff and Burbank, Liberty Hyde Bailey was more cautious in claiming human ability to control natural processes, yet he was not unwilling to try to apply this power. Horticulture, after all, intended not only to explore the mystery of nature but also to alter and improve nature for the sake of human beings. On this point, the magazine's horticulturalists were in agreement.

Advocating the scientific foundations of horticulture did not contradict the magazine's effort to promote horticulture as a hobby among urban residents. On the contrary, Garden and Forest argued that acquiring botanic knowledge and active gardening were complementary paths to the same goal: a more harmonious, if dominating, relationship with nature. There were many amateur flower growers writing for Garden and Forest, including the editor Stiles, who was an enthusiastic grower of orchids. Many contributors thought that horticulture was a good way to overcome the stress imposed on people by urban life.[25] However, amateurs were more self-focused in their gardening activities, while professional horticulturists concentrated on producing plant seeds and stock plants in mass quantities to satisfy urban residents' growing demand for such items.

Garden and Forest was strongly committed to the use of ornamental plants. The first issue of the magazine featured "Floriculture in the United States," an essay by Peter Henderson. One of the most famous ornamental horticulturists in the nation, Henderson owned a big market-gardening business operating in New Jersey and New York—a business that claimed in its magazine advertisements to supply "everything for the garden." Henderson pointed out that, at the beginning of the nineteenth century, there had been no more than one hundred professional florists in the entire nation; by 1888, the number exceeded ten thousand. "The present rate of growth in the business," he wrote, "is about 25% per annum, which proves that it is keeping well abreast of our most flourishing industries." A native of Scotland, Henderson thought that "old world conservatism is slow to adopt improvements." American florists, in contrast, were much more efficient, inventive, and inclined to apply new techniques and knowledge. In the end, he confidently concluded that since the love of flowers was innate in everyone, he could "safely look forward in the expectation of an ever increasing interest and demand, steady improvement in methods of cultivation, and to new and attractive developments in form, color and fragrance." Henderson's prediction was not overly optimistic. As urbanization gained momentum, the consumption of green growing plants became a marker for a more civilized life.[26]

For *Garden and Forest*, the profit potential was not the only justification for horticulture. The magazine promoted the notion that the primary mission of horticulture should be to enrich people's lives with a greater diversity, quality, and quantity of plants and to teach citizens to admire and cooperate with nature. One of the most significant contributors on this broader social function was Edward O. Orpet, who published the first essay of his career in *Garden and Forest* in 1889. After that, around 240 articles and notes appeared in *Garden and Forest* under his name, discussing such topics as new species of flowers, fruits, and vegetables and best methods of potting, grafting, and sowing. Next to William Watson of Kew Gardens, who was one of the major foreign correspondents of *Garden and Forest*, Orpet contributed the largest number of articles to the magazine.[27]

Coming to the United States in 1887 when he was twenty-four years old, Orpet had been a nursery expert for almost ten years. His father was a gardener in Cirencester, England, so he grew up surrounded by plants. Like many horticulturists in his day, he had little academic training, but, unlike many nursery workers of his time, he did not give up the cultivation of his intellectual side while he was doing manual work. Reading *Gardener's Chronicle*, the leading horticultural magazine in England, helped him connect with the scientific development of his profession. Coming to the United States presented him with new opportunities, and one of the most important was a chance to fill the gaps in his knowledge of botany and horticulture. For three years after arriving, he lived in New Jersey in the home of a prominent self-educated botanist, George Thurber, from whom he learned much about flora native to the country.[28] In 1888, Orpet became the superintendent of a private garden in Lancaster, Massachusetts, a position he held until 1910. Later on, he moved to Forest Lake, Illinois, then Chico, California, and finally to Santa Barbara, California, where he served as superintendent of parks. A four-acre park he established as a horticultural showplace was named after him.[29]

Orpet exemplified the successful practical horticulturist of his age: trained in the conventional practical way but eager to absorb new scientific knowledge and adopt new techniques. His biographer called him a "plant mission-ary"; his mission was to disseminate plants and knowledge of them. In many editorials, the magazine emphasized the horticulturists' and florists' respon-sibilities as "educators" in shaping the public's choice and taste for flowers and plants. It argued that the recognition of this responsibility represented "horticultural progress" in the United States.[30]

Besides their efforts in "forming public taste in horticultural matters," the magazine editors suggested, horticulturists should also try to protect various natural features, especially in the urban landscape. For example, street trees, with their sanitary and aesthetic values, were one of the more common but vital natural features in cities. In its pages, *Garden and Forest* described the mer-ciless abuse that urban street trees had to suffer and deplored the disastrous consequences that followed ignorant species selection and plantings. The ed-itors and contributors noticed that there was a growing enthusiasm for tree planting in cities and towns. The establishment of Arbor Day symbolized this enthusiasm, but the lack of professional advice might lead people to make poor planting decisions. This was why *Garden and Forest* found suspect the offer made by the city of Boston to give shade trees to citizens who promised to plant them on the street in front of their properties. The proposal sounded attractive; however, warned the editors, "if the offer is accepted by many peo-ple, the appearance of the city will be seriously injured, and the taste of the inhabitants for trees and tree planting will be checked rather than developed." Street trees in cities were different from trees planted in people's backyards, for they required special care to survive the "hardship of a city life"—threats of dust, smoke, and other pollutants. Also, "uniformity is essential in a street plantation," but this could be gained only by wise selection and a unified way of planting. Thus, it was one thing to arouse the public interest in planting street trees, and it was another thing to plant trees in a smart way.[31]

Early in the magazine's existence, the editors pointed out that there were two common mistakes in urban forestry: "the work is done too cheaply, and the trees are badly selected with reference to future effect." To solve these two problems, *Garden and Forest* argued that "handsome trees will never be found in our cities until the work is placed in the hands of responsible and competent officers from the very beginning whose duty it is not only to select the trees and plant them, but to supervise all pruning." These officers should be "experts who know trees, who know how to plant them and how to care for them afterward."[32]

IN THE PROSPECTUS printed in the first issue, the editors claimed that the magazine was devoted to "Horticulture, in all its branches, Garden Botany, Dendrology and Landscape Gardening." In practice, however, the magazine focused on a somewhat different order of expertise: horticulture, followed by landscape art and forestry. Even that order changed over time as the magazine gave more and more space to the professions of landscape architecture and forestry and their role in improving the urban environment and its hinterland. Neither profession was clearly defined, however, nor was their proper place in environmental management altogether settled.[33]

In a letter written to Frederick Law Olmsted, Stiles worried that articles about landscape architecture would not make "a paper that will sell," but "really it is the only feature of the paper that can make it different from or better than any other garden paper." Before *Garden and Forest*, there had been no magazine systematically defining and demarcating landscape architecture as a profession. For years, Olmsted had been striving to gain recognition for his profession, but he had often been a lonely voice. The emergence of *Garden and Forest* created a forum for more vigorous and concentrated discussion of this novel profession. At the time, no more than a dozen people in the nation practiced landscape architecture as a profession, and most of them were contributors to *Garden and Forest*, including Olmsted, his two sons—John C. Olmsted and Frederick L. Olmsted Jr.—as well as Horace W. S. Cleveland, Charles Eliot, Henry S. Codman, Beatrix Jones, Samuel B. Parsons, Frank A. Waugh, Ossian C. Simonds, Warren H. Manning, Harold A. Caparn, and Wilhelm Miller. Then there were enthusiastic supporters of the new profession, including Stiles, Sylvester Baxter, Mary Caroline Robbins, and Mariana Van Rensselaer.[34]

Quite different from their contemporaries in horticulture, many of whom were not native born and usually had humble or even rough childhoods, most of these new landscape architects came from upper-middle-class or wealthy families in New England or New York. This was the case with Olmsted's two sons. Similarly, their friend Charles Eliot was the son of Charles W. Eliot, the president of Harvard, while Henry Codman was Sargent's nephew.[35] Jones was born into a rich New York family; her aunt was Edith Wharton, a famous novelist. Parsons was born in New Bedford, Massachusetts, where he lived until his family's business, one of the nation's biggest and most famous nurseries, was moved to Flushing, Long Island. Robbins was from an elite family in Maine. Van Rensselaer belonged to a wealthy New York City family. There were exceptions to this elite background; Simonds, Waugh, and Miller came from the Midwest and Caparn from England, and all were from more humble backgrounds.

In general, most of these professionals had received the best general education their generation could dream of, thus creating another big difference distinguishing them from the older horticulturists, many of whom were self-educated and self-trained in gardening practices. Many of the landscape architects were graduates of either Harvard or Yale. Codman received his degree from MIT, Waugh and Miller had gone to Cornell, and Caparn studied at the University of London. The three women in the group received private educations by tutors and grew up surrounded by artists and intellectuals. Most of them had traveled in Europe frequently as part of their education. Eliot studied there for one and a half years. Codman had enrolled in the horticultural school at Versailles, near Paris. Jones regularly traveled abroad with her mother or aunt. John C. Olmsted studied architecture in London for a year. Part of Waugh's graduate study was accomplished in Europe. Van Rensselaer, from age seventeen to twenty-two, lived in Dresden, Germany, with her family, and went back to Europe frequently. Robbins went to Europe with her father and studied art in Italy for a year. Baxter studied intensively in Leipzig and Berlin for three years.

Elite social status, highbrow education, or both did not determine their choice of profession, but such rich academic training and knowledge broadened their horizons and enabled them to keep abreast of the most advanced scientific, social, and artistic developments. Meanwhile, their family wealth often provided financial security, for landscape architecture as a career in the nineteenth century usually cost a fortune to study and brought little profit in the early years.

It is also worth noting that many of the new landscape architects were brought up in northeastern cities; thus, their vision of society and nature was primarily urban. They were in favor of the advance of civilization. They admired order and efficiency promoted by expertise. In addition, the transcendental tradition of New England had had an impact on them, making their aesthetic ideals essentially romantic. More important, their social connections brought most of them into the elder Olmsted's authoritative net, converting them to that prophet's artistic and social concepts. Peter Walker and Melanie Simo argue that Olmsted, by "temperament, background, [and] inclination," should stand in the same camp with other American romantic artists, but "what distanced him from them . . . was his drive to build his profession on such solid, pragmatic foundations that America's most aggressive, powerful men of influence would have to recognize the stature and power of landscape architects." To fulfill this goal, the first thing the new professionals needed to do was to separate landscape architecture from horticulture.[36]

They did not intend to sever the connection entirely. Many prominent landscape architects in the nineteenth and early twentieth centuries, such as Andrew Jackson Downing, Manning, Miller, and Waugh, were initially horticulturists.[37] Miller's and Waugh's writings for *Garden and Forest* focused on horticultural issues instead of landscape architecture. Olmsted was not good at horticulture, a failing that he regarded as a serious defect of his career, so he insisted that his son, Frederick Law Olmsted Jr., spend time learning the field. However, the landscape architects did want to challenge the subordination of their field to horticulture and make people recognize that their discipline was essentially a fine art consisting not only of practical skills and scientific knowledge but also of artistic instinct and training. The subject of horticulture was a single plant, but landscape architecture dealt with everything in view, including soil, rocks, water, and plants in order to compose a harmonious living environment.

Throughout its history, *Garden and Forest* pushed its readers to accept the necessity of employing this new profession's leadership in redesigning the nation's environment. Repeatedly, the editors and the contributors argued that the art of landscape architecture must aim at preserving all forms of natural beauty and that "it is this broad and catholic art which alone is satisfying everywhere, and which is just as useful in the preservation of the Yosemite Valley or the scenery of Niagara as it is in planning a pastoral park or the grounds about a country house."[38]

Urban parks most famously represented Olmsted's and his disciples' professional and social ideals. As a complicated and comprehensive public work, an urban park required the hiring of a diverse group of experts, but the crucial need in their making was landscape architects. The magazine pointed out that the development of a park was a long and slow process. Therefore, "a public park," wrote the editors, "in order to be well administered, should have a management of the most permanent character possible." Germany, they thought, had the best public parks, due to the stability of that country's municipal governments. The editors pointed out that the result of this stability was a "harmonious administration of public works by competent and experienced men that assures the most economical and satisfactory results."[39]

Such political maturity was not exactly common in the United States, however. The editors thus had to proffer another way to ensure the permanency of park administration. Their suggestion was to establish boards of trustees composed of experts in landscape architecture who functioned independently but still operated as "public institutions sustained by public support." They observed that this sort of board was already used to manage museums and libraries, so public parks should be administrated in the same way. Public parks "form an institution by themselves, sanitary, educational and esthetic in nature, and it is equally important that they should be kept free from the complications and uncertainties of local politics."[40]

For example, on the controversial proposal to build a speedway or racetrack complex in New York City, *Garden and Forest* reiterated the need for landscape architects in design. The plan for this project surfaced after the public rejected a proposal to build a horse racing complex in Central Park.[41] The horse racing supporters then suggested another site along the west bank of the Harlem River above Manhattan. The new proposal was approved, but soon the magazine found out the decision had been made by the old New York park commission, which had used an engineer to plot the proposed racetrack complex instead of consulting Olmsted's old partner, Calvert Vaux, the landscape specialist.[42] The magazine argued that a landscape architect should be consulted, because only such a professional knew how to "make any effort for harmonizing his work with the landscape." In contrast, a civil engineer, who may have had the skill to connect two points, was ignorant of nature and natural beauty. The engineer took his professional pride from making his work "obtrusively distinct from nature, since in his view, and this is in a manner a true view, it has a beauty of its own which should be displayed. It is his business to make a convenient road and build it as economically as possible." But in failing to bring Vaux into the decision, the editors lamented, the city's "money is misspent; its opportunities are squandered; its natural beauty is obliterated, and with it vanishes an attractiveness and charm which money cannot restore." The fight lasted a year and finally achieved success; a new mayor appointed a new board that turned the supervision of the speedway construction over to Vaux.[43]

In the editors' opinion, the authority of landscape architects should not be confined to urban parks and speedways. According to *Garden and Forest*, it must be applied to reform the entire landscape—from protecting and enhancing landscapes far away from cities, like state and national parks, to creating a far-flung system of parks, like the one in Boston. The *Garden and Forest* editors wrote, "An individual park ought to be an organized work of art. A system of parks requires still more study if it is wisely adapted to the varied wants of all classes and all ages, with facilities for every form of outdoor recreation." The magazine editors believed that such a grand project could succeed only when it was under the control of experts.[44]

To make this case more emphatically in its pages, *Garden and Forest* recruited Mariana Van Rensselaer, and her articles on landscape gardening subsequently inspired a lasting and influential appreciation of this fledgling profession. Born in New York in 1851, she married a wealthy man named Schuyler Van Rensselaer. After his death in 1884, she undertook a new career as an art critic. Her first articles paid special attention to architecture and led her to write a biography of H. H. Richardson, a renowned figure in the field. This project brought her into close contact with Olmsted, who had been Richardson's longtime friend. Never feeling confident in his own writing and becoming more and more occupied by increasing work contracts in the late 1880s, Olmsted was eager to enlist more talented and enthusiastic individuals to inform the public about the growth of his profession. Thus, Van Rensselaer's availability was timely for both her and Olmsted. The art critic was ready to shift her focus, and the landscape architect was in need of just such an author, one who could master the language of the field and bring to it her knowledge of art and history.[45]

When *Garden and Forest* was getting launched, Olmsted included Van Rensselaer in a short list given to Stiles of people who should be asked to write about his profession. Before the first issue came out, Stiles replied that "Eliot has sent me some valuable material—quotations from early landscape writers—German & English—with a catalogue of reference. There's stuff in the young man. Mrs. Van Rensselaer is also very helpful. We are going to be able, I begin to feel[,] to make a paper distinctly different & better than any yet seen."[46]

Van Rensselaer's greatest contribution to the magazine consisted of her well-organized and beautifully written seven-part series, "Landscape Gardening: A Definition." In these essays, she attempted to persuade her readers that landscape architecture was a fine art, ranking with the more commonly recognized arts of design, painting, sculpture, and architecture. It was that art "whose purpose it is to create beautiful compositions upon the surface of the ground." As a compositional art, it should be assisted by specific knowledge and technique, harmonizing the artistic imagination with the natural scenery. For landscape architects, general beauty was at a higher plane than individual beauty. The beauty shown by nature was always scattered and disorganized, but unity, wholeness, and compositional harmony were the ultimate goals of the profession. According to Van Rensselaer, landscape architects possessed "an appreciation of organized beauty—of the beauty of contrasting yet harmonious lines and colors and masses of light and shade, of intelligent design, of details subordinated to a coherent general effect. Yet it is only such an appreciation as this which means a real taste for nature's beauty and which can make the surroundings of our homes really beautiful."[47]

Satisfied with Van Rensselaer's general discussion, and especially with her effort to generate public awareness of the profession, Olmsted wrote to her, "I really think that *Garden and Forest* . . . will hereafter, be thought to have marked the dawn of a new day. And it gives me some satisfaction to think that though I seem to myself to have been all my life swimming against the tide I shall not sink before having seen it turn."[48] Over the next few years, Van Rensselaer's enthusiasm for this new art did not fade. She published a total of seventy-one articles in *Garden and Forest*, including a twenty-one-part series of essays collectively entitled "Art of Gardening: A Historical Sketch."[49] In introducing the series, the editors declared that it was the first substantive work on the history of landscape gardening written in English. Van Rensselaer reached all the way back to ancient Egypt to begin tracing the historical roots of the field, and she described its practice as a fine art all over the world.

Van Rensselaer was not the only female voice heard in *Garden and Forest* on the issue of landscape architecture. In 1891, Mary Caroline Robbins's name appeared in a series of essays, "How We Renewed an Old Place." Published in twenty parts, the series was later compiled into a book under the title *Rescue of an Old Place*, published in 1892. At the beginning of the series, she thanked the magazine for many "practical suggestions which have a help in bringing harmony and beauty out of neglect and desolation, and at the same time to show its readers the pleasure and interest of endeavoring to create, under its inspiration, a garden and forest of one's own." She described how she and her husband revitalized an abandoned estate in Hingham, Massachusetts, fifteen miles south of Boston, through gardening and renovations. Robbins offered a few horticultural and landscape gardening tips, but her series was primarily a work infused with an Emersonian passion for nature and humanity. It is easy to find phrases like these in her texts: "Hope and faith are qualities that find splendid exercise in tree-planting, and no pursuit can be more unselfish. . . . It is by this spirit that we become one with Nature, sharing humbly in her patience, in her vast unending plans, in her bountiful provision for the future."[50]

Robbins was born in 1841 to an elite family in Calais, Maine, and was brought up on the cultural nutrition of New England transcendentalism. When she was twenty, she went to Europe with her father, who was then the US ambassador to the Netherlands. Later, she studied watercolor painting with R. Swain Gifford in New York and then art in Italy. Before she took up gardening, she translated several literary and biographical works from French to English. After her series of essays was published in *Garden and Forest*, she became one of the most enthusiastic advocates for urban parks and landscape architecture and published approximately sixty articles in *Garden and Forest*.[51] Besides the essays on the renovation of her estate, she wrote about the establishment of New England and, later, American parks, including the park systems in Minneapolis and Saint Paul undertaken by Horace Cleveland.

Robbins's articles lacked the systematic structure and understanding of art that characterized Van Rensselaer's. Also, whereas Van Rensselaer's discussion of landscape architecture focused on the profession, transcending the boundaries of nations, Robbins tended to write out of a feeling for local heritage. Van Rensselaer's articles in *Garden and Forest* were mainly about art and nature, but Robbins's works were more about society and gardening. If Robbins did not evince a clear sense about what landscape architecture was as art or profession, she was nevertheless keen on its social and educational value. From December 1896 to February 1897, she published three articles in the *Atlantic Monthly*: "The Art of Public Improvement," "Park Making as a National Art," and "Village Improvement Societies." The central theme of them was the need for a park system that would connect cities and villages, wild mountains and forests, and that would represent the democratic spirit of the United States.

The two women also differed in their gender attitudes. Although pursuing a radically different career from most women in her era, Van Rensselaer was not a typical women's-rights activist. She became a member of the Women's Association for Improving the Public Schools and from 1898 to 1906 served as president of the association (which by then had been renamed the Public Education Association). She insisted that professionals, not politicians, be put in charge of managing the schools. Still, her vision of women's social position and occupation was rather conservative. She argued that "education for women was important to fit them to be the best wife, mother, and housekeeper." Women "may help the world along in a way that is parallel, not identical, with his [man's]." The division between men and women should not be blurred, and the work of them was distinct—"not inferior but different."[52]

Biographer Cynthia Kinnard indicates that Van Rensselaer approved of the idea that some women, those who did not have "female" work to do, should become members of an "intellectual leisure class." However, their work sphere should be confined to home, libraries, or college labs, so that they would not be masculinized by money-oriented work. It was her fear of losing femininity that motivated Van Rensselaer to become a member of the anti–woman suffrage campaign at the end of the nineteenth century. She worried that woman suffrage would lead women to work in government jobs, which she believed were unfit for them. Woman was "the world's educator," while man was the "executive." Instead of claiming new duties, she believed, women should learn how to perform their natural roles to better effect.[53]

Except for the byline on her *Garden and Forest* articles, Van Rensselaer conveyed almost no hint of her sex or her views of gender. She used the pronouns "she" to refer to nature and "he" for humankind, which was common usage in the nineteenth century. In general, her gender views told her that she should sit in her garden, writing on the art of gardening while enjoying her tea, instead of surveying the field, hoeing the earth, and calculating the expense of a project.

Robbins, on the contrary, expressed strongly feminist views and made zealous efforts to find a spot for women in landscape architecture. This activism did not always sit well with *Garden and Forest* staff. In an editorial published in 1892, they failed to hide their gender bias. The essay criticized Americans' excessive attention to indoor decoration and their inability to see the grand outdoor picture. Since American men were "too much occupied to give much attention to their grounds," it was women or hired help who were usually put in charge of such work, for which they were less well qualified. Women were always talented in making a flower garden, the essay noted, but "they are seldom great on an estate where prettiness, variety, daintiness, delicacy are required." The reason was that "landscape-gardening on a large scale is, after all, a masculine art, and requires a certain manly vigor of treatment, an unhesitating despotism, that the gentler sex deprecate as cruel and unnecessary." The editors did not intend to discourage women's activity, arguing that "there is no reason why a woman of taste should not master the science of outdoor beauty, and conform her arrangements to its rules rather than to her own caprice." The editorial continued with the statement that "we would urge upon women to address themselves to the acquirement of solid knowledge on this subject, as the best foundation for taste in the arrangement of their grounds. It is a healthful, beautiful and useful pursuit. . . . All this would be of value to feminine development, both physical and mental."[54]

Robbins responded immediately to this editorial; her letter, "Some Questions about Taste," was published two weeks later. She asked, "Are we women to be confined to the petty and the pretty forever, or may we not aspire to the loftier walks of landscape-gardening, even as some of us venture to try issue with senior wranglers in the higher mathematics?" Her answer to this question was a resounding no, but a thorough education in the profession was required of women as well as men. "The editor of this paper," Robbins wrote, "is just the person to give us a few elementary lessons in the profession we are so eager to practice, and apparently in his eyes so little qualified to adorn." Three weeks later, the editor admitted that he had received some complaint about "the rather ungallant statement that hitherto women had not shown themselves great in creating broad landscape-effects." He proceeded to lay down some fundamental principles in landscape architecture for anyone who intended to practice it. He made no apology for his gender-biased definition of the profession, although he allowed that, by learning and obeying the laws of science, women would find their lack of "an unhesitating despotism" eliminated and "studious women might master [the profession] thoroughly."[55]

This gender controversy did not go further, and Sargent soon found an opportunity to promote more gender equality in the pages of *Garden and Forest*. In 1893, he met through his wife a shy, rich, pretty, and talented girl of twenty years, Beatrix Jones, whom he helped launch as "the dame of landscape architecture." Jones's first published work appeared in *Garden and Forest* in that same year, and she contributed three articles to the magazine. Her career proved at least one thing—that women could be geniuses in landscape design.[56]

On the male side of the gender spectrum the outstanding young recruit was Charles Eliot. Almost three decades junior to Olmsted, he was a loyal pupil of the great master but was even more ambitious and determined to advance the development of the profession of landscape architecture. Unlike Olmsted, Eliot did not take any detours on the way to his beloved career. When he was a teenager, his love of nature and talent in designing were already noticeable. Graduated from Harvard in 1882, he enrolled in the Bussey Institution's Department of Agriculture and Horticulture, since there was no program in landscape architecture then available. He took courses in horticulture, agriculture, topological surveying, and related botanical and entomological fields. In 1883, his studies were interrupted when he accepted an internship with Olmsted, who had taken the expansion of the Boston Metropolitan Park System in hand. So Eliot became familiar with that significant project and with Olmsted's ideas of design through close observation.

After traveling in Europe, Eliot, instead of joining Olmsted and his son in their firm, opened his own office but maintained a close relationship with his teacher, who recruited him to use his pen to promote the profession. In a letter to Eliot in 1886, Olmsted urged his protégé, "You ought to make it a point of your scheme to write for the public, a little at a time, if you please, but methodically, systematically. It is a part of your professional duty to do so." Olmsted had been concerned with the shortage of skillful writers on landscape architecture. He told Eliot that the latter should make himself better than other people writing on this subject, and he tried to persuade him by saying that, "if you consider who and what they are who now write for the public on—or rather around—the subject, you will not think it flattery, if I say that you can easily give the public what [the] public most needs much better than any other man now writing."[57]

In *Garden and Forest*, Eliot published twenty articles, and they covered a broad range of topics, including landscape preservation, the history of landscape architecture in the United States, horticulture, urban parks, and regional planning. Eliot's intention of winning public recognition for his profession was articulated again and again. In 1889, in an essay responding to an editorial, "When to Employ the Landscape Architecture," he listed a long series of questions on how to work the land surface to reach a state of harmony with nature. The key was simply this: "only special study and long observation will fit a man to solve successfully these problems of landscape gardening."[58]

Although Eliot did not write very much for the magazine, some of his most important literary works appeared in *Garden and Forest*, and, conversely, the magazine inspired this talented young landscape architect in many ways. Like Van Rensselaer, he was fascinated with the history of landscape design. While Van Rensselaer surveyed the world's landscape history, Eliot published a six-part series collectively entitled "Some Old American Country Seats," which was one of the earliest efforts at studying American landscape history and showed Eliot's interest in both natural and cultural landscapes.

With this interest in mind and his belief in cultivating a "public spirit," Eliot, along with the Appalachian Mountain Club (in which he played a major role for many years), initiated a new environmental organization called the Trustees of Reservations, the first association of its kind in the world. The purpose of this association was to preserve in the state of Massachusetts, either through private donation or purchase, certain open spaces with unique natural or historical traits and open them for public use.[59]

In February 1890, an editorial in *Garden and Forest* entitled "The Waverly Oaks" had focused on a group of ancient oak trees in Belmont, a suburb of Boston. In it, the editors had suggested that "the age which these trees have attained and the vicissitudes they have survived entitle them to respect, and the people of Massachusetts might wisely secure their preservation through the purchase and dedication to public use of the land on which they stand." Soon, Eliot published a correspondence under the same title and indicated that it was this editorial that had prompted him to send "an imperfect plan of a scheme by which not the scene at Waverly only, but others of the finest bits of natural scenery near Boston, might perhaps be saved to delight many future generations." He urged that all lovers of nature in Boston "should now rally to preserve for themselves and all the people as many as possible of these scenes of natural beauty which, by great good fortune, still exist near their doors." To save the woods near Boston, Eliot called for "an incorporated association, composed of citizens of all Boston towns, and empowered by the State to hold small and well-distributed parcels of land free of taxes . . . for the use and enjoyment of the public." The direct consequence of this call was the Trustees of Reservations, officially established in 1891.[60]

Eliot soon realized, however, that stronger powers than local individuals had to be convinced to preserve much larger pieces of scenic land that were in danger of being encroached on or destroyed by urban sprawl. Thus, the idea of a metropolitan-wide park system began surfacing among Boston's city planners. In May 1892, the Board of Metropolitan Park Commissioners was organized and Eliot was appointed its landscape architect. In his letter to the chair, Charles Francis Adams, Eliot outlined his blueprint for the new park system:

> As I conceive it the scientific "park system" for a district such as ours would include—(1) Space upon the Ocean front. (2) As much as possible of the shores and islands of the Bay. (3) The courses of the larger Tidal estuaries (above their commercial usefulness) because of the value of these courses as pleasant routes to the heart of the City and to the Sea. (4) Two or three large areas of wild forest on the outer rim of the inhabited area. (5) Numerous small squares in the midst of dense populations. Local and private action can do as much under the 5th head but the four other call loudly for action by the whole metropolitan community.[61]

For *Garden and Forest*, the plan of a metropolitan park system was like a new gospel—a revelation that would lead people to defend all manifestations of natural beauty within and near the nation's cities. The magazine kept close watch over this Boston innovation and recorded its progress.

However, it was not Eliot who wrote on Boston's parks for *Garden and Forest*; rather, it was a Boston journalist named Sylvester Baxter, who published sixteen essays in all. Baxter was born on Cape Cod in 1851, the son of a sea captain. In 1868, Baxter visited New York City's Central Park, where he was fascinated by the masterpiece composed by Olmsted. In the same year, Baxter went to Boston, hoping to study architecture at the newly established Massachusetts Institute of Technology, but he failed to do so for financial reasons. After dabbling in various fields for three years, he decided to undertake journalism and worked on the staff of the *Boston Daily Advertiser* from 1871 to 1875. His report on the reconstruction of the burned parts of the city after the

Great Fire of Boston in 1872 led him to become interested in city planning.[62]

In 1875, Baxter was sent to Europe as the newspaper's foreign correspondent, and he studied at the universities of Leipzig and Berlin, where he found a model for American city planning. Three decades later, in his essay "The German Way of Making Better Cities," Baxter wrote, "In no other country has the art of city planning been carried to so high a degree as in Germany today. This is due to several important factors. Among them are the extraordinary industrial progress in the past quarter century, the highly organized character of German institutions, the thoroughness with which the Germans attack their problems, and the strongly idealistic quality of the national temperament. The unification of Germany in 1871 made possible the development of large plans and vast enterprises, political, economic, and industrial." These words revealed the essential social vision of Baxter, his favorable attitude toward centralized and organized institutions, and his admiration for industrial and scientific advancement.[63]

After Baxter returned to the United States, his journalism career became even more colorful than it had been before his international assignment. From 1879 to 1905, he served on the staff of the *Boston Herald* and also edited and published *Outing Magazine*. He showed inexhaustible energy and lively curiosity in digging up new subjects. A list of his publications covers a stunning array of subjects, from landscape architecture to city planning, from anthropology to archaeology, from German cities to Japanese poetry, from utopian socialism to Indian life, from bicycles to trains and trolleys. In *Garden and Forest*, he even wrote on the orange fruit worm and a delicious tuber called *Apios tuberosa*. In the 1880s, he traveled the American Southwest, not as a hasty and casual tourist but as an insightful and considerate observer, investigating and writing about the untamed landscape, the Zuni lifestyle, and the archaeological and anthropological discoveries of his friend Frank H. Cushing and the Hemenway Expedition.[64]

In 1888, right after the publication of Edward Bellamy's pathbreaking *Looking Backward*, Baxter became one of that author's most famous and loyal adherents. That year, he joined with other Bellamy followers and formed the Boston Bellamy Club, and, three months later, they organized the Boston Nationalist Club. In 1915, he wrote an introduction to the memorial edition of *Looking Backward*. Although he favored government control as much as Bellamy had and admired science even more strongly than his hero did, he did not want to promote a characterless, standardized urban landscape. He did not believe that the expansion of the metropolis he called for should squeeze nature out of human sight and contact.

In an essay published in *Garden and Forest* in 1889, Baxter called for the preservation of the public forest of Lynn, Massachusetts, and it was later incorporated into the Boston Metropolitan Park System. He indicated that what made such a piece of wilderness particularly precious and important was that it was located with "the densely populated and bustling city close at hand." He believed that such a place should be held by government for public use and enjoyment and that park designers should try to exclude artificial things from the wild scene except for what was necessary for public access, such as roads and walks. At the end of the essay, Baxter concluded, "Its value to the neighboring New England metropolis can hardly be overestimated. Lynn is already, geographically, a portion of Boston, and will be knit closer together with the central city as years go on."[65]

For Eliot and Baxter, a beautiful design was not the only goal a landscape architect should pursue. In "The Necessity of Planning," published in *Garden and Forest* in 1896, Eliot pointed out that both architects and landscape architects were often "deceived with ornament" and prone to regard beauty as the sole aim of their professions. He argued that "in all the arts which serve the use, convenience or comfort of man, from gardening and building down to designing the humblest utensil which it is desired to make beautiful, utility and fitness for intended purpose must be first considered." Fitness was the "law," and beauty was only secondary. Any plan must be "a skillful combination of convenience with effectiveness of arrangement." A landscape architect should be strenuous "in demanding studied planning and adaptation to environment and purpose in the laying out of whatever work may need to be done to make the wildest place of private or public resort accessible and enjoyable." Planning with fitness in mind was as necessary for a forested park as for the construction of "formal gardens, rectilinear avenues and courts of honor."[66]

Eliot's idea of meeting a wide array of human needs in designing the landscape was not radically different from the combination of utility and beauty advocated by Downing and Olmsted, but Eliot's stress on large-scale, comprehensive planning enriched the content of the new profession. In writing to Mary C. Robbins, Eliot criticized her "unfortunate identification of 'landscape architecture' with 'landscape gardening'" and argued that "'landscape

architecture' includes and covers landscape engineering, landscape gardening and landscape forestry," which "means the designing of all things and
arrangements necessary or desirable for the use and convenience of human
beings occupying the surface of the earth." In a follow-up letter to Robbins,
he stated, "Landscape gardening means such nice arranging of lawns, trees,
shrubberies, water and so on as Mr. Sargent may practice on his private place,
or elsewhere, but . . . it is not a broad enough term to indicate the scope of
the profession which Mr. Olmsted and some of the rest of us have been trying
to establish."[67] The material of landscape architects included not only natural
entities but also artificial objects. The final product of a landscape architect
should be the harmonizing of the two spheres. Only when they were composed in harmony could the landscape realize its highest utilitarian *and* aesthetic values, and only then could the social mission of a landscape architect
be accomplished.[68]

WHILE LANDSCAPE ARCHITECTS were seeking a professional role in reforming
the nation's environment for the sake of beauty, health, and convenience, a
new profession devoted to the practical protection and use of the nation's
forests was also taking shape. In the process of forming this profession of forestry, *Garden and Forest* again played a crucial role. As the magazine claimed, it
was "the only journal published in the United States which discusses compre-
hensively questions relating to our forests as they affect the welfare of the individual and of the nation." The man who would become the most prominent
forester in the country, Gifford Pinchot, lauded the magazine's publisher: "I
think his [Sargent's] greatest service to Forestry—but one—was made through
Garden and Forest, which distributed more information about American forests
and forest trees than all other periodicals combined."[69]

Strictly speaking, there were only two well-trained professional foresters
in the United States in the 1890s—Bernhard E. Fernow and Carl A. Schenck—
and both were born in Germany. "Forestry" and "forester" were not new
terms in English, but most Americans in the late nineteenth century had neither heard of them nor considered forestry as a profession. When Fernow's
wife, Olivia R. Fernow, had announced her engagement to him in 1879, her
friends had asked, "What is a forester? A Robin Hood who takes from the rich
to give to the poor?" Fernow soon found out that the Robin Hood image was
not exclusive to the unenlightened or uneducated. Even people with advanced

learning were unfamiliar with the term, and many of them confused forestry
with tree planting or arboriculture. Most of the early forest preservation advocates in the United States were botanists, horticulturists, geologists, or other
scientists who took an interest in the outdoors. During the last decade of the
nineteenth century, however, forestry began appearing in the headlines of
leading newspapers and magazines. *Garden and Forest* was the most prominent
of these and the most influential organ of information.[70]

Based on this view, Jonathan B. Harrison hailed the aim and function of
Garden and Forest in an address to the annual meeting of the Pennsylvania Forestry Association:

> A long course of education of the people regarding the facts of the subject
> will be necessary before adequate legislation can be devised or efficiently
> applied. What we chiefly need now is an era of teaching and instruction
> regarding the subject—teaching that shall be intelligent and intelligible,
> comprehensive, coherent, systematic, iterant and authoritative, because
> based upon competent knowledge. The greatest step in advance ever taken
> in this country in connection with forestry subjects has been made this year,
> in the establishment, in New York, of a journal devoted to the discussion of
> forestry in all its aspects, and to the dissemination of knowledge in relation
> to this subject.[71]

The magazine he referred to was *Garden and Forest*.

The magazine's voice on matters of forestry and forest professionalization
will be the subject of a later chapter. Here it suffices to say that for ten years
the existence of the magazine allowed forest professionals such as Fernow
and Pinchot and amateurs such as J. B. Harrison to express and exchange their
views on a common platform. More importantly, the magazine managed to
achieve a balance among various disciplines and opinions, maintaining comprehensiveness in its effort to establish new professions and give new defini-
tions to the traditional ones. In both aspects, *Garden and Forest* was successful.

In 1899, eleven practitioners founded the American Society of Landscape
Architects, and most of its early members had been contributors to *Garden
and Forest*. In 1900, Pinchot initiated the Society of American Foresters, a national professional and educational organization. In the twentieth century,
these new professions would keep growing and changing, but their enduring
principles had some of their origins in *Garden and Forest*.

What the magazine failed to anticipate, however, was that professionalization could undermine the comprehensive thinking the magazine tried to promote. Melanie Simo points out that "it is a familiar story, the progressive breaking down of complex wholes into manageable (or profitable, or analyzable) parts. In time, special tools and new words allowed people to discuss increasingly finer distinctions among increasingly fewer people." If the search for professional esteem did not necessarily lead to contempt for other professions and amateurs, at least to some extent it created obstacles for more cooperation and dialogue among them. This fragmented consciousness was the logical consequence of increasing professionalization, as the new professions became more tightly focused. Just as the encyclopedic knowledge of the eighteenth-century naturalists was cast into the shadows by modern specialized scientific disciplines, so also the environmental professions displaced older, more integrative bodies of knowledge. The balance between beauty and utility, city and countryside, garden and forest, and nature and culture that *Garden and Forest* sought to fulfill would become more difficult to achieve in the wake of professionalization.[72]

The fundamental force that pushed professionalization forward was the accumulation of knowledge and, in the broadest sense, the progress of science and other bodies of systematic knowledge. A "profession" is a kind of work that requires specialized education—not just general knowledge open to anyone with the ability to read and write, or anyone who has gone to college, but formal training—or a more formally instructed "knowing how." In forestry, one had to go to school to learn not simply how to cut down a tree but how to determine at what age to harvest a tree and how to replant a forest most successfully. This was not the simple folk knowledge of a farmer who owned a woodlot and exploited it. Gifford Pinchot had to go to France to attend formal classes to learn forest biology, mensuration, and economics; it was acquiring that specialized knowledge that earned him the label the "first American forester." Similarly, Charles Eliot studied his art and science of landscape architecture through working with the great pioneer in the field, Olmsted. In that case there was no school yet, but Eliot could learn his profession by observing the leader in the field.

Garden and Forest insightfully and correctly predicted the coming age of professionalization. It sensed the quiet transformations happening in the world of science and also grasped the more visible and dramatic changes in society. In an increasingly urbanized and industrialized era, the age-old human-and-nature relationships became too complicated to be solved merely by government legislation and public enthusiasm. Neither, it seemed, could simply fall back on folk knowledge and personal experience to solve them. The magazine and its hundreds of contributors all sensed that the old knowledge system was often imperfect and sometimes vicious or wasteful or unjust. It seemed increasingly outmoded. Even though professionalism and its foundations in modern science could be imperfect too and might present some potential conflicts and dangers, overall the trend seemed to be toward progress in human understanding of nature and society. The times called for new professionals to use their training and knowledge to deal with increasingly intricate social and natural problems in order to make life not only more efficient but also more healthy, more beautiful, more deeply satisfying to the intellect and emotions, and more sufficient for material needs.

GARDEN AND
FOREST GALLERY

〜〜〜〜〜〜〜〜〜〜

T HE VISUAL ICONOGRAPHY of *Garden and Forest* magazine was an important
part of its environmental message: to naturalize the city and harmonize
its people and their lives within the broader context of green plants, forests
and other habitats, and the general forces of nature. The illustrations in this
gallery are representative of the magazine's pages and exemplify its ideals.
The gallery includes photographs, line drawings and etchings, and designs for
parks and private estates. Together, the images reflect the era's sense of what it
should mean to be urban—to conserve nature, to design with nature, and yet
to civilize the landscape for human satisfaction. In the magazine editors' idea
of civilization, natural beauty and human needs—even the most utilitarian
needs—find a common unity.

GARDEN AND FOREST.

PUBLISHED WEEKLY BY

THE GARDEN AND FOREST PUBLISHING CO.

OFFICE: TRIBUNE BUILDING, NEW YORK.

Conducted by . . . . Professor C. S. SARGENT.

ENTERED AS SECOND-CLASS MATTER AT THE POST OFFICE AT NEW YORK, N. Y.

NEW YORK, WEDNESDAY, JANUARY 30, 1889.

TABLE OF CONTENTS.

The Nation's Forests.

THE first step in the effort to provide for the conservation of the forests on the national domain should be the withdrawal from sale of all forest-lands belonging to the nation. It will not be necessary to preserve and maintain all these forests permanently, but the extent of forest-territory which will be required by a practical plan of forest-preservation and management for our Western mountain regions cannot be at once precisely determined. A thorough examination of these regions, and of the agricultural country depending upon them for its water supply, will be necessary, in order to show what forests must be retained, and what tracts of timber can be put upon the market without injury to the important interests involved. Until such an examination has been made, none of the forest-lands now belonging to the United States should be sold.

The second step should be to commit to the United States army the care and guardianship of the forests belonging to the nation. There is in time of peace no other work of national defense or protection so important as this which the army can perform, and it is plain that under existing conditions the forests on the national domain will not be—indeed cannot be—adequately guarded and protected by any other means. The measures which have been tried, including those now in operation, or nominally in operation, have proved almost entirely ineffective. The forests on the public lands are pillaged by settlers, and by the employees of railroad and mining companies, without scruple or limit. Other instruments will have to be employed if the forests are to be preserved. Their complete and final destruction, with that of the soil which sustains them, is, under the present system, or want of system, only a question of time, and of a very short time. The officers of the United States army are educated by the nation for its service, and they constitute a body of men not equaled by any other in our country in their equipment for guarding and protecting the great forest-regions belonging to the nation. They possess every kind of fitness for this work in greater degree than any other class of men, and if authorized by law to undertake this service they would have the power and the means necessary for its performance, while everybody else is at present inevitably powerless and incapable. As there is likely to be very little work for the army hereafter in the care of the Indians, it will be available for this service of guarding the national forests. The work can be done well by the army, and it would cost nothing, or very little, while any other plan would necessarily be both ineffective and costly. This guardianship and defense of the nation's forests by the army of the nation should be continued and maintained until a sufficient number of adequately trained and equipped foresters has been provided by the national government for the administration of a complete and permanent system and policy for the management of the forests on the public domain.

This brings us to consider the third step. This should be the appointment, by the President, of a Commission to make a thorough examination of the condition of the forests belonging to the nation, and of their relation to the agricultural interests of the regions through which the streams flow from which have their sources in these forests, and to report, with the facts observed, a comprehensive plan for the preservation and management of the public forests, including a system for the training, by the government, of a sufficient number of foresters for the national forest service.

The Commission should determine what portions of the existing forests on the public domain should be permanently preserved, and in what manner the remainder should be disposed of. The national forests can be so managed that they will be perpetually reproduced, and will yield forever an abundant supply of timber for the inhabitants of the adjacent country, and a revenue which will more than sustain the cost of the forest service. A National School of Forestry should be established at a suitable place in one of the great mountain forests on the public lands, and its equipment should be as thorough and adequate for its purpose as is that of the National Military Academy at West Point.

THE "Elizabethan home" has long been a synonym in American ears for all that is most beautiful in domestic architecture, and, at the same time, most comfortable and home-like. But exact observation and clear judgment have less to do with this feeling than traditional sentiment and the reports of tourists enchanted by the picturesque accessories of English country dwellings. The following description—quoted from the pages of the *American Architect and Building News,* where a recent address by the English architect, Mr. J. A. Gotch, is discussed—gives a more exact idea of Elizabethan architecture than those that are commonly presented to us.

"In planning these homes nearly everything was sacrificed to show. People who lived contentedly with their dogs in rooms carpeted with rushes, which were changed once a week, could hardly be expected to be very squeamish in regard to niceties of arrangement, and it is common to find the bedrooms opening from each other after the fashion of a New York tenement-house, without any corridor for reaching them separately, while in some very magnificent mansions the suites of rooms allotted to visitors could only be reached from the reception-rooms by crossing the court, which, it is needless to say, had no provision for sheltering from the rain or snow the festal clothes of the persons who walked through it. So inconveniently planned, according to our notions, are the Elizabethan mansions in this respect, that they can hardly be used at all by a modern family. One or two of them have been remodeled by the rather heroic treatment of building a corridor around the court-yard, like a cloister, so as to reach the farther bedrooms without going through all the others, but this darkens half the windows, besides spoiling the court. In other cases a portion of the house has been rebuilt, at a great expense, according to our ideas, but most of the Elizabethan palaces, splendid as they once were, have been allowed to go to ruin, simply from the impossibility of utilizing them for a modern family without very costly alterations. Even the reception-rooms, magnificent as they are, accord ill with the

---

The standard front page of the magazine was plain and simple in its presentation. Inside, however, the magazine pages were filled with artistic work that evoked the beauty of plants, the possibilities of creative landscape design, and the threats facing the environment, especially the forests.

Garden and Forest, 30 January 1889, 49. Anschutz Library, University of Kansas.

Entrance to the Arnold Arboretum.

This pen-and-ink drawing depicts the entrance to the Arnold Arboretum, established by Harvard University in 1872 under the directorship of Charles Sprague Sargent. The landscape architect Frederick Law Olmsted designed its roads and grounds. In 1882, the Arnold Arboretum was deeded to the city of Boston, Massachusetts, and became part of Olmsted's park system for the city, the famous "Emerald Necklace."

Garden and Forest, 7 March 1888, 17. Anschutz Library, University of Kansas.

Rhododendron arborescens, or smooth azalea, one of the many flowering plants *Garden and Forest* promoted as an appropriate ornament for the urban environment. Its natural range extended from New York State down the Appalachian mountain chain. Charles Edward Faxon, a staff employee of the Arnold Arboretum and one of the best botanical draftsmen in the nation at the time, drew this figure and prepared a total of 285 illustrations for the magazine. *Garden and Forest*, 17 October 1888, 401. Anschutz Library, University of Kansas.

The adornment of home interiors with flowering and nonflowering plants was another aspect of the magazine's focus. Indoor gardening was supposed to encourage a sensitivity to the green world that the editors hoped would then extend to the whole urban environment and result in the conservation of beauty across the American landscape. This photograph is of a Chinese narcissus growing in water.

Garden and Forest, 21 March 1888, 44. Anschutz Library, University of Kansas.

William Augustus Stiles (1837–1897), editor of *Garden and Forest* and editorial writer for the *New York Tribune*. Stiles, a longtime friend of Frederick Law Olmsted, was one of the leading defenders of New York's Central Park.

Garden and Forest, 13 October 1897, 401. Anschutz Library, University of Kansas.

The Meadows in New York's Central Park illustrate both the pastoral aspects
of Frederick Law Olmsted's park designs and one facet of the magazine's
vision for America's cities.

Garden and Forest, 9 May 1888, 125. Anschutz Library, University of Kansas.

This *Garden and Forest* illustration of a temple in Japan speaks eloquently of
the magazine's far-ranging interest in the history and aesthetic principles of
landscape design.

Garden and Forest, 18 April 1888, 89. Anschutz Library, University of Kansas.

Garden and Forest featured this photograph of an unidentified site of forest devastation in Michigan as part of its campaign against overcutting, watershed destruction, and aesthetic damage in the nation's timberlands.

Garden and Forest, 19 November 1890, 563. Anschutz Library, University of Kansas.

America's most famous native tree species, the redwood or sequoia (*Sequoia gigantea*), celebrated by the naturalist John Muir, was under assault by timber cutters. The magazine sought to bring the elegance of this tree and the threats to its existence to the attention of readers and to promote forest conservation.

Garden and Forest, 26 November 1890, 575. Anschutz Library, University of Kansas.

A magazine for tree lovers in the countryside as well as the city, *Garden and Forest* celebrated the grandeur of America's native species. This photograph taken in Chester County, Pennsylvania, is of a solitary tupelo (*Nyssa sylvatica*) growing along a rural road.

Garden and Forest, 11 July 1894, 275. Anschutz Library, University of Kansas.

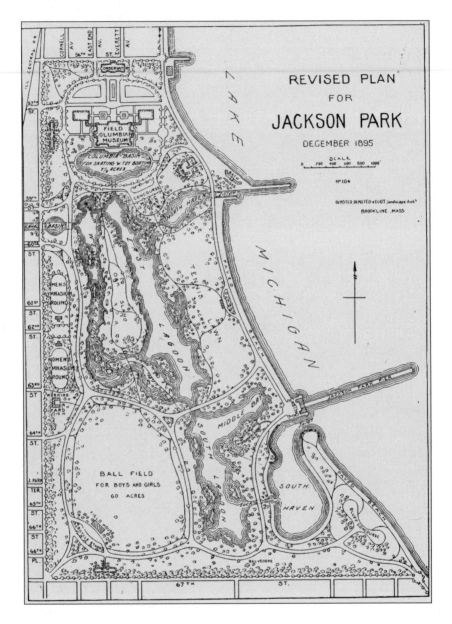

This drawing of the proposed Jackson Park, Chicago, Illinois, was from the firm of Olmsted and Olmsted, 1895. The park was to be the permanent legacy of the World's Columbian Exposition of 1893, the world's fair whose grounds Frederick Law Olmsted had also designed.

Garden and Forest, 20 May 1896, 205. Anschutz Library, University of Kansas.

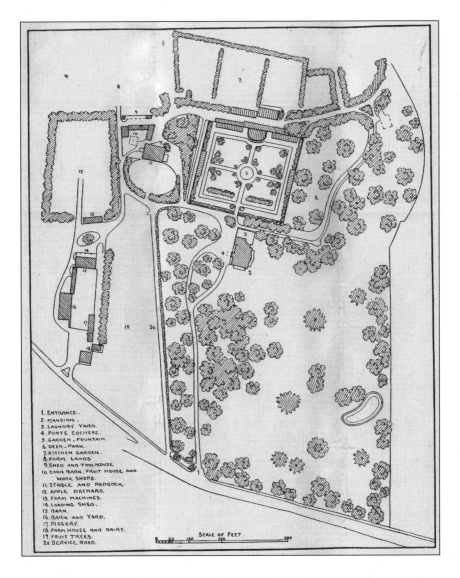

1. ENTRANCE.
2. MANSION.
3. LAUNDRY YARD.
4. PORTE COCHERE.
5. GARDEN - FOUNTAIN.
6. DEER - PARK.
7. KITCHEN GARDEN.
8. FARM LANDS.
9. SHED AND TOOLHOUSE.
10. CORN BARN, FRUIT HOUSE AND
    WORK SHOPS.
11. STABLE AND PADDOCK.
12. APPLE ORCHARD.
13. FARM MACHINES.
14. LOADING SHED.
15. BARN.
16. BARN AND YARD.
17. PIGGERY.
18. FARM HOUSE AND DAIRY.
19. FRUIT TREES.
20. SERVICE ROAD.

SCALE OF FEET

The new profession of landscape architecture, which was a central part of the
magazine's "natural city" ideal, relied heavily on wealthy landowners who
wanted to create beautiful grounds for their dwellings. This architectural
plan, published in the magazine to serve as a model, was for the Belmont
estate near Boston, Massachusetts.

Garden and Forest, 10 July 1889, 327. Anschutz Library, University of Kansas.

4

NATURE AND CIVILIZATION

꧁ᘒᘒᘒᘒᘒᘒᘒᘒᘒᘒ꧂

L ATE-NINETEENTH-CENTURY Tunis, a small French colony on the edge of the
vast desert in northern Africa, might have seemed remote and exotic to
most people living on the other side of the Atlantic Ocean. Although Tuni-
sians could trace their history back to the tenth century BC, for most Americans, who as a whole were marching in the vanguard of an industrial and
urban era, this semiarid part of the world was only semicivilized. Still, a sixty-
eight-page report on the cultivation of olive trees written by the director
of agriculture in Tunis, Paul Bourde, captured the attention of the editor of
Garden and Forest. An 1893 editorial, "The Desolation of Central Tunis: Was It
Caused by the Destruction of Forests?" recapitulated the story of that colony's
rise and fall, from raw desert to civilization and back to desert.[1]

After describing the natural environment of Tunis, the essay briefly introduced the history of Tunis. It cited Bourde's view that there never had been
"high, continuous forests" in that desert country. Its only "forests" had been
cultivated fruit trees. "The country," wrote the editors, "is exceptionally favorable for one kind of culture and is not at all suited to another. Before the
Roman invasion this cultivation was unknown and the country a desert. The
Romans introduced it toward the end of the first century, and became rich;

the Arabs destroyed it in the eleventh century, and the country has become a desert again." Although the Arabs had tried to procure pasturage in this arid land, "the substitution of a nomad and pastoral population for a stationary and fruit-growing population was only effected at the cost of immense disasters." The Arabs had destroyed culture and ecology, a dual assault that led, and always leads, to the decline or collapse of a civilization.[2]

For a modern reader, this essay strikingly anticipates the perspective of environmental history. From the prosperity that followed the conquest by Romans to the decline that resulted after Arabs occupied the land, the essay stressed that a people's way of understanding and using the natural environment can have a powerful impact on the waxing and waning of civilization. While the level of civilization in Tunis might never have been comparable to that of the late-nineteenth-century United States, author J. B. Harrison pointed out that "the laws and forces of nature will not make exceptions in our favor, though we are a great country."[3]

A recurrent theme of *Garden and Forest* was to achieve a more modest, respectful, and careful domination of nature in this new age—to find out how nature could better serve civilization. During ten years of publishing the magazine, Sargent and Stiles tried to integrate a variety of voices into a discussion of how that might be done. Mainly anthropocentric in their stance while soberly recognizing the power of nature over the fate of human history, the editors and all their contributors promoted a more harmonious and prosperous society in which nature played an indispensable, if still subservient, role.

The connection linking gardens, representing a tamed nature, and forests, a wilder one, was not "nature" but "civilization." It was civilization that needed both gardens and forest, and it was for the sake of civilization that both should flourish. In her series of essays on landscape gardening, Mariana Van Rensselaer wrote, "Every step in civilization is a step away from that wild estate which alone is really nature; and the further away we get from it, the more imagination is needed to bring the elements of existence which nature still supplies into harmony with those which man has developed." Both gardens and forests required the human imagination, and the contributors tried to incorporate, through their advocacy of trained intelligence, the different forms of nature into the fabric of civilization, so that the latter could be more advanced, refined, and secure.[4]

Although part of the new urban age, the magazine's contributors were privileged to have more frequent physical and mental communication with nature than most urbanites, for they had to work with it directly. This contact not only gave them fuller knowledge and understanding but also led them, so they believed, to a more realistic assessment. They were aware of the still powerful agency of nature in shaping human society while also seeing the destructive power that humans could exercise on the environment. This was a relationship that needed careful thought, not sentimentality or hostile feelings.

Garden and Forest was consistent in valuing civilization over nature. For contributors and editors, civilization meant, of course, Euro-American civilization. They did not deny that there were other civilizations existing outside the Western world. Compared to most people in that era, the magazine editors and contributors showed a surprising acquaintance with and sympathy toward non-Western cultures. Many of those contributors interested in landscape architecture and art wrote essays on Oriental and Persian gardens and on Chinese and Japanese landscape art and floriculture. In general, however, their interest in more ancient civilizations was superficial and passing, merely a search for novelty and exotica. The botanists and horticulturists writing for the magazine were more intrigued by the natural species of those remote places than by their cultures and societies. For the foresters, the only sound model came from the Europeans. They discussed the forestry of India, but that system was mainly the work of European foresters. None of the magazine's contributors advocated adopting non-Western cultural ideas or elements into the human-nature relationship. Their approaches and philosophies were unmistakably Western.

Living at the crucial turning point of American history when the nation was becoming the most powerful empire in the world, the writers and editors had good reason to embrace their own civilization. Under the surface of their optimistic celebration, however, they were deeply anxious about the direction that their civilization might take. In one editorial, "Attacks on Civilization," the editor warned, "It is a matter of importance for the American people to learn as soon as possible that under the conditions of our national life, nothing in our civilization will keep very long. It must be perpetually reproduced, must in some way always be the fresh expression of the life and thought of the time, or it will decay and vanish."[5]

Facing the seemingly endless expansion of the empire, the editors tried to remind people of the inseparable bond between cities and their rural roots, between civilization and the soil on which the former was built. In "The Soil and National Development," the editor wrote these words: "Our people cannot all live in cities. If men will not themselves cultivate the soil, they must still eat what is brought out of it, and the subsistence and civilization of the entire population must depend at last upon the fertility of the land. We cannot advance much farther in civilization, or national development, until the nomadic methods of agriculture by which the soil is now mercilessly exhausted and ruined, shall give place to a practical and enlightened policy which will preserve permanently unimpaired the fertility of cultivated lands." In this forward-marching, industrial-urban age, the magazine reminded readers of basic but easily forgotten foundations of all civilizations. The hope was that Americans would see that their success was dependent on the earth. Solutions to problems occurring in urban civilization could be found not only within cities but also in the wider natural world.[6]

Worried about unplanned urban sprawl, a degrading industrialization, the closing of the frontier, the abuse of land, an impending "timber famine," and an accelerating trend toward materialism and social inequality in the distribution of wealth, the magazine editors and contributors expressed an urgent need to find a way for American civilization to survive and continue to progress. The way ahead seemed clear and obvious: enlightened conservation and better environmental design. "The new interest in forestry and related subjects in this country," wrote the editors, "is a natural development. It is time for it. It is an important next step in our national progress. The production among our people generally of a vital and intelligent appreciation of the true place of forestry and landscape-art among the forces which improve mankind would constitute a real advance in civilization." They were confident that they could find remedies within their own culture and believed in its promise of self-perfection.[7]

In its relatively short run, *Garden and Forest* raised questions of lasting significance: How should civilization regard nature? What should it mean, "to love nature"? Could science assist in promoting the appreciation of nature, or was its role mainly to subdue it and make the natural world function in a more efficient and modern way? How could the country reinforce its democracy through rectifying the relationship between nature and society?

THE MANY TANGLED MEANINGS of nature did not bother intellectuals living at the end of the nineteenth century as much as they would bother those of more recent decades.[8] There was no doubt though that nature was as ambiguous a term then as it is today. In a review of the popular nature writer John Burroughs's new book *Riverby*, the reviewer pointed out that Burroughs lacked the "high moral purpose which drove Thoreau into wilderness"; in compensation, his book showed a healthy degree of relativism. The author cited Burroughs's own words: "We cannot all find the same things in Nature. She is all things to all men. . . . In her are all manner of tastes—science, art, poetry, utility, and good in all. The botanist has one pleasure, the ornithologist another, the explorer another, the walker and sportsman another; what all may have is the refreshment and exhilaration which come from a loving and intelligent scrutiny of her manifold works." Burroughs might have been describing the contributors to *Garden and Forest*. What was nature to them? Many of them were busy re-creating a "natural" landscape in and around cities or "improving" wild nature to make it more useful or accessible. Were their products natural or artificial? To what extent were their achievements still a form of nature?[9]

Instead of seeing nature merely as a single object, humble like an aster or sublime like Yosemite Valley, they defined nature more as a universal force, one not created by humans, one that was spontaneous and self-regenerating, one that had long been in a contest with human beings and had always been the ultimate winner. An early editorial observed,

> Studying little by little the influence of the forest, we come to understand the intimate relation between man and nature—that relation which is a struggle of rival forces, in which the silent, mighty mother inevitably wins the battle. If at the first glance man seems her ruthless adversary, the tormentor of the earth, the wrecker of woods, the destroyer of beauty, the boastful pigmy [*sic*] who would assault a colossus, we soon come to learn that in wronging her he but evokes a doom as sure and terrible as his assault has been reckless and violent.[10]

Similarly, in an essay on the preservation of a Massachusetts forest, Sylvester Baxter stated that, compared to permanency and endurance in nature, human power was only a "passing incident, transient and erasable. . . . The abiding impression is that of Nature herself, and humanity appears to be but one of her forces, temporarily modifying the earth's surface, like the beavers, the ants or the earth-worms. And how the trees serve to veil the structures of man!" Once human beings were absent, it would not take many years for nature to wipe out all their traces and "relapse into utter wilderness."[11]

By recognizing nature as a powerful cosmic force, these contributors had to solve a problem—not whether such works as landscape gardens were nature or not but how to balance and harmonize these opposing forces in a modern society. They never denied the power of the artist or professional in creating a park or a garden; on the contrary, they aimed to make the public recognize and respect this power. However, this recognition did not lead them to deny the existence of nature even in gardens designed by humans. In an essay on the relationship between formal and natural landscape architecture, the editor pointed out that "it is important thus to realize that no garden or park or landscape picture can be treated in a 'natural way'—that the work whose result comes nearest to Nature's cannot be more than naturalistic work; for this realization will, in the first place, teach us to apply a right standard when we judge works of naturalistic kinds." The essayist continued: "no garden can be altogether artificial, and none can be altogether natural." But no matter in which style or which form, "nature must be allowed her freedom to some extent, even where all the trees are clipped and all the grass is shorn and all the flowers are set in pattern-beds. Within the prescribed shapes and lines she must grow her flowers and foliage as she will, and she must supply light and shadow and the atmospheric envelope. And, on the other hand, artificial, formal elements must enter into every landscape which man's foot is to tread and man's eye is to enjoy as a work of art."[12]

Nature, as a creative cosmic force, exists everywhere, but wherever there are humans, nature's force mixes with human force. The distinction between the wild and the tamed would thus depend not on what the scene looks like but on which force was superior to the other in a given place. In the wilderness, although humans might have some small impact on the landscape, the predominant force is natural and human culture would be subordinated to nature. In a city park, however, human force would be more fully in charge, controlling and directing the nonhuman.

A fascination with the beauty of wilderness did not necessarily require a rejection of the more humanized landscape. The line between the natural and non-natural had always been ambiguous and fragile, for in many cases landscapes "do not show us what nature wants to do or can do—only what man and nature have chanced to do together." The magazine urged people not to overlook the human landscape surrounding them; although more artificial, it could supply order and convenience, as well as intentionally designed beauty, which was more suitable for daily human life.[13]

Furthermore, the magazine pointed out that although there were conflicts and struggles between nature and human beings, there also existed harmony and cooperation. In its editorial "The Beautiful in the Surrounding of Life," the magazine recommended John Ruskin's way of thinking. In the *Poetry of Architecture*, that English philosopher of art had written that on the primitive level in the evolving relationship between nature and humans, the latter relied on wilderness and rarely thought of changing it. Later, because of the need for food, they were forced to adopt agriculture. Then, villages, towns, cities, gardens, and palaces all came into being. In this long process, "mother Nature stands ready to adopt it as her own, and to make of it [a] landscape rich in meaning and pathos such as no primitive wilderness can show." At the end of the essay, Ruskin hailed the charm of farms in Sweden, villas on the shores of Lake Como, the English deer park, the Italian village, and the American colonial towns of Hadley and Deerfield. After all, the editor concluded, "the beauty of these memorable humanized landscapes is nothing extraneous; it is not something added to the landscape after the main lines have been laid down; it springs directly from the fact that these fields, trees, ways and buildings have been arranged first with reference to the needs, uses and enjoyments of real life in their respective lands and climates, and it is their perfect conformity to these principles which constitutes the essence of the beauty we admire."[14]

The editors of and contributors to the magazine were not philosophers and did not really intend to pursue the nature they were dealing with through the labyrinth of philosophy or theology. They cared more about social and practical issues rather than metaphysical ones. On the whole, they did not bring to their writings any strong religious stance toward nature but tended to follow a more scientific and pragmatic view. In their works, which might be as large as managing forests and big urban parks or as small as hybridizing a species of orchid, they claimed to follow the rules of nature rather than of God.

Deeply influenced by the development of modern science, most of the contributors to the magazine, rather than emphasizing that nature was the direct and special creation of God, relied on Darwin's theory of evolution. "The survival of the fittest" was one of the doctrines they frequently used and quoted. In one of the editorials on the uses of flowers, the editors wrote, "Monsieur Joigneaux claims that the love of [flowers] is one of the important differences between man and the brute, but, unfortunately, modern science reveals that, after all, the primary cause of the color and fragrance in flowers was to make them attractive to birds and insects; and as the Poppy-bee and Australian bower-bird manifest quite as keen an appreciation as we do of their decorative value, the Frenchman's theory has no more substantial basis than the vainglorious assumption that the universe was made for man, and that he is superior at all points to other created things." Darwin taught them, contrary to traditional Christianity, that the world had an independent evolutionary history apart from humankind and that, from nature's point of view, humans are not superior to other forms of life.[15]

Furthermore, in nature the writers and editors sometimes felt a kinship connecting them with all those other lives, which indicated at least some taint of romantic and pagan animism. In comparing lovers of natural scenery and nature, the editors said of the true lover of nature, "When alone in the dense forest or in some sunny glade a mysterious sense of kinship with the silent forces working all about him, or a dim consciousness of a haunting presence, comes to him unbidden and ravishes his soul with suggestions of a more awful beauty some day to be revealed, and after such hours of communion with nature he can return to the noisy world refreshed in spirit and strengthened for the inevitable conflicts of life." For those who, like Stiles or Robbins, still maintained a faith in God and Creation, nature, as suggested in the previous chapters, rather than the Bible, was the more vivid and tangible manifestation of the design of God.[16]

Still, some faint influence of conventional Christian thinking was traceable in the pages of the magazine, such as a stress on the ideal of stewardship and reverential contemplation of the Creation, both part of the Christian legacy. In an issue published in 1891, *Garden and Forest* cited words from Ruskin again: "God has lent us the earth for our life; it is a great entail. It belongs as much to those who are to come after us, and whose names are already written in the book of creation, as to us; and we have no right, by anything that we do or neglect, to involve them in unnecessary penalties, or deprive them of benefits which it was in our power to bequeath." Throughout the magazine's history, it advocated an ethic of stewardship—or, more narrowly put, the principle that Americans and their governments should manage the earth and take care of it.[17]

There was, however, a subtle difference between traditional Christian stewardship and the perspective of *Garden and Forest*. These contributors in general thought that humans, instead of being the temporary managers of earth, were the actual owners of the land, and rather than waiting for the second coming of Christ, when they would give the earth back to him at the end of time, they were concerned about maintaining earth's fertility and richness for future generations. In the editorial "The Defacement of Natural Scenery," the editors wrote, "Few persons ever think of natural beauty as a possession worth considering by 'practical' men, much less as a public possession which it is a patriotic duty to preserve and transmit to posterity." Two years later, another editorial repeated that "natural beauty is to a certain extent an inheritance of all the people, that it has a real value like pure air and fresh water." It asked readers to realize that their descendants would appreciate that natural beauty more and more over time if it could be preserved, "for this feeling has grown in depth and strength with the growth of the race, and it will probably continue to grow."[18]

By considering natural beauty as a common secular need, the magazine editors and writers further distanced the publication from expressions of traditional Christianity. Natural beauty served a real and legitimate need, and citizens had a responsibility to preserve it for the public good. Maintaining and improving the condition of the earth, for many of the contributors, did not mean turning every inch of the land into a farm or making a profit from it. Beauty was always a central goal in their schemes of "improvement." The dream of remaking their continent so that it would "blossom like a garden" did waft through their desires and imaginations. However, they thought it was also important to preserve a wilder beauty, especially in this urban age, because "wild landscape—the scenery of the natural world—possesses infinite interest and charm for those of us who live caged in towns and cramped in houses, and we greatly enjoy both traveling in search of it and reading the praise of it." The garden and the wilderness were not contradictory because both displayed the beauty of nature.[19]

In an editorial about Yellowstone National Park, the editors wrote, "The preservation of the national park is a matter in which a large number of people throughout the country feel a deep interest and patriotic pride." Moral refreshment and elevation would come from communing with nature in the national park. According to the editor, "Contact with natural beauty is one of the potent agencies for establishing sound minds in sound bodies; and since this is the source and condition of all well-directed ambition and effort, a reckless destruction of this beauty is a blow not only at one of the highest and most satisfying pleasures of the people, but at the public health and the public wealth." When comparing formal landscape gardening with the natural style, the author argued that the formal one was appealing because of its beauty alone, but a natural landscape could reach the "nobler part of man's nature." It suggested something beyond pure beauty composed of perfect color and form, and "its essential charm is in the inner meaning to which it gives expression so as to move the feelings and touch the heart." This deeper meaning could come only from unaltered nature.[20]

Another editorial, "Nature and American Literature," prompted by William Curtis's newly published *Literary and Social Essays*, emphasized the deeply humanizing aspect of nature. In reviewing Curtis's book, *Garden and Forest* acknowledged that it had been less interested in purely literary themes than in practical issues, but in this book the editors discovered how important "a deep and genuine love of nature" had been to New England's classic writers: "In Thoreau this enthusiasm for nature was combined with a stern moral purity; in Hawthorne, with a rich, though somber, imagination, and in Emerson, with a noble and serene philosophy, but in the moral fiber of all the three was the granite strength of the New England hills, and to their inspired imaginations the tranquil scenery about Concord was a symbol of the repose and balance and harmony of the universe." In placing all these pioneering literary artists in their natural habitats, the editor tried to convey how important nature was to the civilized arts and how useful its influence had been in inspiring great writers.[21]

The world of those writers, however, was receding, and no one could hold on to it. Americans were not mere passengers on a train heading toward an uncertain future; they were the locomotive's engineers. They might long for a lost world where nature had been only partially tamed by a gentle and wise human hand and guided by a strong moral tradition, but they should not fight to hold on to the past. A modern landscape, according to the magazine, should integrate the virtues and beauty of the New England past with the progress and convenience made possible in the modern age.

To fulfill this goal, the magazine editors believed that it was necessary to locate a compromise position between a traditional attitude toward nature (expressed by early nature writers) and a resolute faith in modern science and industrial progress. In its Christmas 1889 issue, the magazine reviewed a little book by Bradford Torrey entitled *A Rambler's Lease*, which deplored the burdens of modern life and urged a regimen of two "rambles" every day to allow people to experience the beauty of nature and to escape those burdens. Torrey further suggested that to refine this aesthetic mood, the rambler should study at least one natural science but "make sure that [this] acquaintance with outdoor life is sympathetic and not merely curious or scientific." The reviewer added, "Only by a combination or alternation of the two moods—the two attitudes—can the truest enjoyment be extracted from the natural world."[22]

Garden and Forest's favorite recommendation for popular scientific education was botany. This field would reveal the intricate workings of nature's economy and at the same time would display the humble but authentic beauty of nature. In an editorial, "Botany for Young People," published in 1890, the editors argued that the study of botany could aid youth in discovering the colorful world of nature. They rejected the prevalent notion that, in science, "the more one learns about plants the less will one appreciate their beauty. The scientific attitude is held up as the reverse of enjoyment; scientific knowledge is proclaimed to be deadly to artistic or poetic feeling." Not so, said the editors; by pulling a flower apart to learn its interior structure, a person could come to understand the wonder of reproduction. Only when the truth of the interior was revealed could the beauty of the exterior be more wisely and fully appreciated: "The exterior suggests the interior, and a knowledge of the interior explains the lovely individuality of the envelope." By studying botany, people would become acquainted with the hidden truths of nature.[23]

Rather than waiting for beauty to expose itself, men, women, and children would learn to look for beauty with purpose, until such seeking would become a spontaneous habit. They would detect beauty in the most "unpromising places." The person trained in botany would not miss the most subtle and hidden aspects of nature. "He will," said the writer, "delight in the exquisite beauty of the infinitesimal blossoms of the Door-weed on which passive, uninstructed observers will never have perceived a blossom at all; and will be enchanted by the flowers of the Pigweed even, despised of the multitude, but honored by him as a treasury of interest. Nor, surely, will his new appreciation of such humble charms lessen his feeling for the splendor of the Iris he finds in the swamp or the Meadow Lily that flaunts by the way-side."[24]

Later, the editor received a letter from a person identified merely as "W. G. R.," who recalled Yale president Timothy Dwight's comments on the subject. Dwight had said that "science everywhere brings us into a close relationship with nature. . . . There is cheerful hope for the youth whose mind and heart are stirred with love for all the truth and beauty hidden in the natural world." To attain this close relationship with nature, the editor urged students of botany to break through the walls of a laboratory and the pages of a book and step into the field, experiencing nature in the most direct and lively way. In another piece, the editor repeated that the essential point in studying botany was to approach objects directly, not to read about them in books. "This contemplation of nature," he wrote, "on what may be called its imaginative or poetic side differs widely from the mere study of natural science, but it implies some knowledge, and a growing knowledge, of Nature, and science is only knowledge systematized." The essay went on to say that some critics were afraid that too much absorption of knowledge would lead to overemphasizing nature to the detriment of human interest, but the author argued that this knowledge was "normal and wholesome," while "the indifference to Nature and the insensibility to her kindly influences, is morbid."[25]

For all its progressive-mindedness, the magazine still held to a more traditional view of nature as a benevolent and harmonious system. This did not mean that the writers and editors were ignorant of the brutal side of nature described in phrases like "nature red in tooth and claw," but they believed the world was actually less competitive and cruel than that. The most visible creatures living in this world were the beautiful birds, furnishing human life with colorful feathers and lovely songs. Humans might have to fight against the so-called "pests"—such as various insects attacking crops and English sparrows displacing native American birds—but this war was not a jungle of violence and bloodshed but more like the positive, creative struggle between civilization and savagery. And when compared to the cold-hearted industrial world, nature represented a world full of tender feeling and many lessons in virtue. Recoiling against the modern alienation from nature, the magazine's contributors wanted science to help people touch the soil, the trees, and the flowers, to discover nature's basic goodness and order. When scientific knowledge was coupled with the aesthetic instinct, a true love of nature would flourish.

Garden and Forest's editors and contributors tried to give a new definition to the love of nature—one appropriate for the urban gardener. An editorial published in 1888, "The Future of American Gardening," claimed, "The basis of good gardening is the love of nature. To nature the gardener who would be something more than a mere cultivator of plants must turn for inspiration. From the study of nature alone can be learned composition, harmony and fitness in arrangement, and without these the gardener can never hope for success in the creation of a landscape." In fact, according to the magazine, this love of nature expressed through gardening should be the foundation of the human relationship with nature, working with botany to produce a purposeful, lifetime search for truth, order, and beauty.[26]

The highest love of nature, argued the magazine, was a profound emotion mixed with memory and imagination, and it appeared only when civilization had developed to a high degree. It began as an instinct even among the "savages" and was the "birthright of every healthy child." Over time, however, achieving the fullest love of nature required a high level of education so that one could appreciate a beauty that was spectacular, awesome, and unfamiliar. The magazine was sure that this advanced love required cultivation and learning. It went beyond the superficial and obvious: "The true test of a love of nature is that one who gives interested attention to all natural effects and forms . . . finds beauty where the average eye sees none." Thus, the highest love penetrated the surface and touched the essence of nature.[27]

The true lover of nature, William Blake had written, could "see a world in a grain of sand and heaven in a wild flower." For the editor of *Garden and Forest*, this aphorism suggested that appreciating nature was not a matter of seeking only the most dramatic expressions of scenery, the showiest and grandest panoramas, but was more a matter of finding subtle meaning in the ordinary and near at hand. The flowers strewn by the night rain, the light and shadow of foliage under the sun, the golden grass waving in the blowing wind, the bare but elegant trunk of a tree standing in snow—all these common but truly mysterious things suggested the vitality of a holistic natural world and inspired a deep poetic sentiment that came only with high civilization and learning.[28]

But loving the most everyday, familiar elements of nature did not mean

that a person should be indifferent to dramatic scenery. For the highest kind
of lover,

> great things impress him, but small ones enchant him, and he gathers
> pleasure from the road-side grass as well as from the giant Oak or the sky-
> line of a rugged mountain range. There is a beauty of the Lily and a beauty
> of the Pine, a beauty of the mountain and a beauty of the plain, a beauty of
> wide outlooks and a beauty of enclosed and sequestered corners. One kind
> of necessity excludes another kind; but that does not matter to him, for all
> arrest his eye, interest his mind, and make appeal to his imagination and his
> heart.[29]

This inclusive love of nature extended even to the city's streets. The tamed
face of nature inside cities, the face that urban people were encountering and
experiencing every day, should not be regarded as less significant than the
remote and wilder part of nature. Neglecting either part would be a mistake,
for it would lead to the collapse of the entire picture. Because the nature
surrounding humans every day might seem too commonplace or trivial, the
editor and his favorite landscape architects wanted to awaken their readers, to
help them discover Blake's "heaven in a wild flower." They had accepted that
the majority of people in this urban world would henceforth have to live their
daily lives with whatever nature they could find along the street, and they
were determined to help them find and cherish it.

The love of nature's beauty was combined with a respect for nature's po-
tency. As suggested at the beginning of this chapter, these contributors defined
nature as a great planetary and cosmic force, one that was shaping human activities and competing with human power. Throughout the volumes of *Garden
and Forest*, numerous editorials and essays exalted this force. In "Forest and
Civilization," J. B. Harrison wrote, "Man has no power to create a new world.
He has not yet learned how to take care of the one which he inherits, but his
ability to wreck and exhaust it is very great. The accumulation of the soil of
the planet, out of which must come everything that supports human life, civilization and happiness, has been the slow, patient process of vast and unimag-
inable periods of time, and it has been chiefly the work of vegetation." The
magazine content pointed out that, whether in the creation of a landscape
garden or the management of a productive forest, humans always needed to
work with nature rather than against it. The laws of nature must be heeded.

For a landscape architect, nature suggested the ideal type of beauty; for a botanist, nature implied a complex structure and economy; for a horticulturist, nature was the greatest hybridizer; and for the forester, nature's process of growth and succession should guide the practice of that new profession.[30]

For landscape architects and those promoting particular theories about the natural world, as Mariana Van Rensselaer did, nature in many ways was their master, supplying the materials they worked with, showing the models they should imitate, stirring their imagination, and helping them and their fellow citizens achieve spiritual goals. Nature, after all, was the original source not only of *their* art but also of all art and notions of beauty. As Charles Eliot stated, "Love of beauty and of art must surely die if it be cut at its roots by destroying or vulgarizing the beauty of nature." The magazine editors complained that, in the United States, nature had undergone "needless cruelty." However, once Americans thoroughly "learn the great lesson that the highest art is found in following suggestions of nature, an endless variety of climate and of season awaits our effort, and with an untold wealth of native plants America should have the most effective and diversified gardens in the world."[31]

Take this reasoning seriously, and the civilized artist had to admit that nature imposed limits on his or her work. No artist could ignore those limits: "The artist in landscape must consent, at any given place, to do what Nature then and there prescribes, or, at least, permits. To try to wipe out her work is futile; to try to conceal its character and supply a new one can result merely in an abortion which is admirable neither to the genuine lover of Nature nor the genuine lover of Art." In her series on the principles of landscape gardening, Van Rensselaer wrote that nature had done many things that a landscape architect could not do—"from the building of mountains and the spreading of seas to the perfecting of those 'particulars' which turn the keenest chisel and blunt the subtilest [sic] brush—to the curling of a fern-frond and the veining of a rose." When asked to give advice on designing a specific place, the contributors always answered that they could only suggest this fundamental rule: acquire knowledge of the place, its landscape, its types of soil, climate, and vegetation, and even its history and legends, as fully as possible before the work starts. Only when artists know how to wisely use the resources of nature and work within the scheme of nature can they truly integrate their art with this unbounded and relentless force.[32]

In a spirit of reverence for the natural world, the contributors to *Garden and*

Forest vehemently criticized human blindness and arrogance toward nature. Their discussion of the relationship between irrigation and native vegetation of the arid West exemplified their critical views of arrogance toward nature. Like most of their contemporaries, Stiles, J. B. Harrison, and other major contributors to the magazine believed that the West needed to be improved and utilized. They also dreamed that "some time the day may come when it will be said: There is no desert! The encouragement of irrigation will hasten that day for our country." However, they also challenged several prevalent views about the West and its development. First, they confronted the popular itch to abandon the desolate farms in the East and head for the promising West to look for "inexhaustible" new land. They pointed out that "our people have acquired a habit of boasting of the country's ability to feed the world and of our exhaustless wealth in general. But natural resources are not infinite." If this trend persisted, the editors warned, one day, even with the help of irrigation, the land in the West would stop being productive and profitable.[33]

In addition, contrary to many boosters and settlers, they doubted that there had been any increase in rainfall on the Great Plains since the coming of the plow. The magazine cited the geographer Henry Gannett's refutation of this fantasy. The editor pointed out, "Here are conditions which no action of man can influence." The natural West was doomed to be arid, and only artificial irrigation could turn some parts of that region's deserts and semideserts into a garden.[34]

Another and even more controversial issue was whether constructed storage reservoirs could ever replace nature's reservoir: the forest. The answer again was no. Even though *Garden and Forest* echoed the common faith in the transforming power of irrigation, the editors and contributors maintained their awe of nature. In the summer of 1889, news about the disaster that followed the collapse of a dam and the destructive torrent of a flood in the Conemaugh Valley near Johnstown, Pennsylvania, came to the magazine. The editors were astonished by the disaster, but what made them more uneasy was that the federal government seemed determined to follow the advice of the US Geological Survey, led by Maj. John Wesley Powell, to build similarly dangerous dams and reservoirs in the mountains of the arid West.

According to their reading of Powell, a reading that Powell disputed, his approach to the West advocated that all forests should be cut away at the headwaters of the western rivers so that the water would flow into artificial reservoirs instead of soaking into the ground.[35] The magazine editors, however, questioned the safety of such constructions to contain the wild and destructive floodwaters, and they further challenged the power of modern technologies to prevail against the cosmic force of nature. The editors' warning and advice are valid even in our own day:

> It is also to be observed that the splendor of the achievements of inventive and mechanical genius during our own time, seems to justify the most daring and audacious expectations for the future, and it is not wonderful that men should imagine that nature imposes no limitations which may not be removed or overcome. Some influential engineers in this country think so highly of their profession and its work that they even propose to disregard and reject the natural provision for guarding the sources and flow of rivers, and to substitute for the mountain forests, which are the natural storage reservoirs, a system of artificial storage reservoirs constructed with walls, dams, and embankments. If this method is ever tried it will result in frequent and ruinous catastrophes.[36]

J. B. Harrison responded to the Johnstown tragedy with a similar warning. "There is no reason," he wrote, "to suppose that engineering ability will ever enable us to dispense with the natural function of mountain forests in storing water and regulating its flow." In 1890, another shocking disaster happened. A highly acclaimed masterpiece of modern engineering, Walnut Grove Dam in Arizona, burst under the pressure of rising floodwaters. Lives and property were lost. The editor asked why fellow Americans had this drive to build artificial works that were obviously less safe and less effective than forests, the storage mechanism furnished by nature itself that could blunt the more destructive elements of nature.[37]

In the technologically confident Victorian era, the magazine's editorial voice could be aberrant and discordant. Compared to its contemporaries, *Garden and Forest* stood for a more cautious response to the power of nature. This did not mean that the editors and contributors rejected the prevalent belief in the advancement of modern science and the convenience, profits, and comfort brought by it. As devout as their belief was, however, they struggled not to be blind and scientifically superstitious.

In addition to questioning some of the most ambitious reclamation schemes, the magazine initiated one of the earliest debates over the use of pesticides. As indicated earlier, the editors and contributors in general believed that the war between humans and pests was a war between civilization and savagery. In her series of essays "How We Renewed an Old Place," Mary Robbins wrote, "He [the caterpillar] becomes a menace not only to existence, but to Christian character, by developing the savage instincts of our nature; and, therefore, on every ground, both physical and moral, he is an enemy of the public peace who should be taken in hand by the authorities and be doomed to extermination." Others were less warlike and religious in their crusade against pests, but they were equally determined to exterminate these redundant natural beings in the civilized world. Their method was one of the most celebrated inventions of modern science—chemical pesticides.[38]

Yet, interestingly, a month before Robbins's declaration of war against pests was published, T. H. Hoskins sent in a short passage, "The Abuse of Insecticides," expressing a quite different view on the use of pesticides and even the so-called pests. A horticulturist from Vermont, Hoskins wrote more than eighty articles for the magazine. His general tone was consistent with that of the magazine, but on this particular issue his stand diverged from that of most other contributors. In "The Abuse of Insecticides," even though he also admitted that one of the "great things" to see was the application of insecticides all over the country, Hoskins could not stop worrying that the growing use of arsenic as a garden and orchard poison was likely to cause an unanticipated harmful consequence in human and animal health. "The symptoms of this form of poisoning," he warned, "are so very obscure that even the most skillful diagnosticians may fail to recognize them." Thus, instead of using this potentially dangerous poison in his own orchards, he tried to take full advantage of the benefits that insects could bring. He suggested, for instance, that "the codlin[g] moth is rather a benefit than an injury in well-managed orchards," because it could thin the fruit trees and save human labor. Other insects, such as the curculio, which was a type of weevil, could be held in check by non-poisonous, mechanical methods.[39]

The provocative message sent by Hoskins immediately stirred up a debate among horticulturists writing for the magazine. The first person responding to it was a notable biologist from Rutgers University, Byron D. Halsted. Also a frequent contributor to the magazine, he wrote almost seventy articles focusing on plant diseases. Ardently embracing the coming age of pesticides, Halsted disagreed with Hoskins's caution. He believed that, even though the application of large quantities of poisons could lead to some danger, "the standard fungicides, when properly applied, are practically harmless. Their effectiveness is now generally admitted." It took almost a year for Hoskins to answer this opponent. In a longer article, he started with these words: "Perhaps I am too conservative for this progressive age, but I cannot help thinking that we are doing more spraying in our orchards now than we shall do ten years hence." After reaffirming the benefits of the codling moth, Hoskins pointed out that the major problems in the New England orchards were not those insects but humans deciding to plant inappropriate species of fruit trees. "Spotting and Cracking of our varieties of apple and pear are simply indications of a weak constitution or an imperfect adaption to our soil or climate," he wrote. He indicated that farmers in New England were too intent on planting western European fruit trees despite the dramatic difference in climate between the two regions. He strongly recommended instead the planting of varieties from areas that were more similar to the region, like eastern Asia. He predicted that "when we get stronger races of tree-fruits we shall not wait long for quality, while we shall have constitutions vastly in advance of the old stock, and consequently greater resistance to both insects and disease."[40]

Apparently, as he admitted, Hoskins was too confident that orchardists would adopt his idea of the biotic control of insects. Great production and consequent great profit that followed the application of pesticides stimulated much broader use of these lethal chemical agents. After all, this was a war of civilization against savagery, of modern science against backward local knowledge, of the market economy against subsistence farming. On this issue, Liberty H. Bailey was much more "progressive" than his Vermont colleague. Several weeks after Hoskins's articles were published, Bailey attempted to refute his argument. "My own opinion," Bailey wrote, "is decidedly opposed to that of Dr. Hoskins. I am convinced that ten years hence three times more spraying will be done than now." Moreover, "we shall, no doubt, greatly cheapen and simplify the methods of spraying, but the practice, as a whole, is, in my opinion, one of the distinct advancements of modern times in agricultural and horticultural practice." What could poor Hoskins say after the leading horticulturist of the country blew the triumphant horn of pesticides? A month later, Hoskins sent in another letter to the magazine, claiming "without doubt, the spraying will go on. I would be among the last to favor its prohibition. Its immediate benefits are manifestly important." He did not completely give up, however. Instead, he suggested, "It is a most interesting question, whether, in availing ourselves of poisons, we are not at the same time prolonging the evils, or, perhaps, making them persistent." Unfortunately, he did not press this warning any further and went back to arguing that the best remedy for insect problems was to find the fittest tree species for any particular natural environment.[41]

Soon the editors and contributors of the magazine started pushing forward state programs to eliminate plant diseases and insects through various means, especially the wide use of pesticides. In the rising age of modern science, technology, and professionalism, it was too early for Hoskins to make his voice accepted by even his most knowledgeable colleagues, not to mention profit-oriented farmers. It required a much longer time for scientists to discern the danger hidden in those supposedly beneficial inventions and an even longer time for the public to be willing to recognize and admit the vulnerability shared by humankind and the biosphere around them. The year 1892 was not the time for people to understand words that would be written by Rachel Carson seventy years later: "The 'control of nature' is a phrase conceived in arrogance, born of the Neanderthal age of biology and philosophy, when it was supposed that nature exists for the convenience of man. The concepts and practices of applied entomology for the most part date from that Stone Age of science. It is our alarming misfortune that so primitive a science has armed itself with the most modern and terrible weapons, and that turning them against the insects it has also turned them against the earth."[42]

Those early American scientists and environmental reformers were not stupid or arrogant. They tried, at least, to take this issue into account and open a window for different perspectives. They could not transcend the limits of their era, however. Their general view of nature was not biocentric; it did not put the welfare of nature and nonhuman living things on a par with that of humans, as suggested by Carson. In fact, advancing human interests consistently was central to their concern. They did love nature, because its beauty could please their eyes and calm their weary spirits. They did respect nature, because its force could either encourage or halt the progress of their civilization. In the end, however, the welfare of humans seemed to require a campaign to exterminate all pests.

An editorial on tree planting firmly articulated this stand. "The tree is not an end in itself," declared the editors. "It does not exist for its own sake. It is valuable solely for its effect upon human health and human psychology, for its relations to the welfare of the men, women and children who see it." But why was it important to preserve forests? Apparently, it was because forests were useful to human beings, whether as a place for people to restore health, find beauty, and enjoy peace and freedom or as the source of fuel, furniture, irrigation water, and railroad ties. A just appreciation of nature was based on both its aesthetic and its economic values. Thus, their goal was to manage nature, as much as possible, and make it serve all those human needs in a better way.[43]

According to *Garden and Forest* editors, "the notion that a true lover of nature is one who lets nature alone, is the feeblest of fallacies." They went on to say that humans had been interfering with nature from the beginning of civilization. Inevitably, "he [man] comes in conflict with her [nature's] tremendous forces; he cannot relax his vigor for a day or he will be overgrown." Preserving the beauty of wilderness was necessary and should be done as soon as possible. Still, not all of nature's untamed beauty should be preserved; it would be better to preserve that wildness far away from the dwelling places of human beings. The editor pointed out that "there are very many beautiful spots on earth, but very few of them are beautiful in a way that fits them, untouched by art, for association with the homes of men. A primeval forest would be a priceless possession on some distant part of an estate; but to permit it to come up close to a splendid dwelling would be an offense against appropriateness and harmony, and therefore against beauty." In her "Landscape Gardening: A Definition," Van Rensselaer wrote that "a real taste" for natural beauty required "an appreciation of organized beauty." Although often she showed great interest in wild natural beauty, longing for "a sense of breadth, vastness, freedom and the spontaneous action of elemental forces" bestowed by the less directed forces of nature, she never doubted that "beauty under human control would be the most appropriate and harmonious form for the inhabited world."[44]

In the essay "The Forest: The Need of Forest Policy in Pennsylvania," William Buckhout added that "it will not be wise to leave the work of restoration wholly in the hands of nature" because the species that nature selected to recover the land might not be the one humans needed. Also, forests without human managers were vulnerable to various sorts of attacks from humans or nature, like grazing, cutting, or a lightning-set fire. In another essay, Buckhout maintained that nature's process of self-restoration was ineffective. Forest expert Bernhard Fernow was even more blunt. Because "nature has taken no account of time or space" in producing timber, it was necessary to instill economy into "the use of our inheritance." It was imperative "to make the soil do full duty in producing only that which is useful to man." In forestry, "protection standing alone is irrational and incomplete." On this issue, the editors of and contributors to the magazine maintained a fairly unified voice. In an editorial on the timber supply, the editors wrote that "it is a wasteful policy to allow them [forests] to struggle on without assistance, even in a region where trees will spring up of themselves whenever they have an opportunity, for skilled forest management means an increased production of improved material."[45]

Whether in economic or aesthetic terms, the contributors saw many defects in nature that weakened its appeal and value to people. Just as the forester could improve on timber production, it was the artist's job to gather nature's scattered points of beauty and transform them into a "composed" picture. Mutation and decay were blemishes on the face of nature; art and science could work together to eliminate these unpleasant spots and lead to permanence.[46]

Thinning a woodland was a good example of how art and science could cooperate to improve on nature. An overgrown woodland needed the human touch, but that touch needed to be guided by judgment and taste. Good judgment came from thoroughly knowing the patterns of tree growth, while taste derived from training in art. Because nature would not always be compatible with human interests, the belief went, nature must be altered. Although the law of the "survival of the fittest" was universal, the fittest was not necessarily the most beautiful.

"Do not spare the axe" was one of the most consistent bits of advice the magazine offered. Cutting and thinning were necessary not only for forest management but also for gardens and parks. It was an effective tool for helping people reach the goal they expected. "Man can intervene," wrote the editors, "and by judicious and systematic thinning help the strong to destroy the weak more quickly and with less expenditure of vital force. Thick planting is but following the rule of nature, and thinning is only helping nature do what she does herself too slowly, and therefore too expensively. . . . Of the implements required to produce a fine tree the axe is certainly the first and most important."[47]

What then was a fine tree and what was a poor one? The standard was set by the human mind. In an 1893 editorial, the magazine stated that "nature is bountiful in prospects, bountiful in material for making them. Supreme as she is, man is her ruler, and, without him, her highest charm lacks significance, since his is the eye to see, and, therefore, it is his right to subject her to his fancy, and he seldom has more delightful employment than in producing harmony between her munificence and his own artistic needs." These words gave a legitimate excuse for humans to put wild beauty under control and in better order. For the contributors to *Garden and Forest*, art and science were needed everywhere, and the only question was to what degree they should be employed to transform nature.[48]

In its last year of publication, the magazine still promoted its insistence on the necessity of human control of nature. "It is this broad and catholic art," the editors wrote in "Art and Nature in Landscape-gardening," "which alone is satisfying everywhere, and which is just as useful in the preservation of the Yosemite Valley or the scenery of Niagara as it is in planning a pastoral park or the grounds about a country house." In those preserved natural scenes, "proper planning and maintenance" should be applied to protect them from natural and human invasions and destruction. Yet mere preservation was still not the primary goal. The preserved original beauty should be made to fit human eyes in a more comfortable way, and "skillful and reverent treatment" would add "new charm to every feature." The editorial continued: "It will not be enough to let the trees alone in the Tulare Forest [of California]. It must be adapted to human convenience. Roads must be prepared and other arrangements made so that it can be seen, and seen by great numbers of visitors at all seasons, and to the best advantage always." Although signs of human intervention might be erased or hidden, the editor did not want to deny that the ultimate purpose in shaping the environment was for the "use and enjoyment of the people of the United States." Even preservation of nature was a kind shaping of the land for human purposes and required a strong confidence in civilization. Only when that civilization was advanced and strong enough to contend with the force of nature, when cities, towns, and villages were prosperous and improved enough to be secure from the threat of wilderness, could the magazine and its contributors feel more relaxed about allowing some wild, deviant beauty into their organized, civilized life.[49]

Van Rensselaer cited Aristotle's statement that "nature has the will but not the power to reach perfection," but then she switched the statement around, saying it was equally true that "nature has the power but not the will." In other words, it was up to man to "bend her will to his." While learning from nature, Van Rensselaer said, humans could also "liberate, assist, and direct that power."[50]

This complicated thinking—highly anthropocentric but not indifferent to the form and autonomy of nature—arose from an assurance that nature was now humankind's legitimate responsibility. Since nature and its products were the means to achieve prosperity for humans both present and in the future, they had reason to take care of it, but, at the same time, they believed it was their right and duty to alter nature to make it better or more suitable for its current owners, and even for nature's fulfillment. The editors of *Garden and Forest* actually attempted to spread and reinforce this concept of responsible possession among their readers. If people were more aware that the resources and beauty of nature belonged to them, the magazine editors believed, they would be more gentle and thoughtful in their treatment. They would follow a more enlightened kind of utilitarianism.

The idea that humans must exercise ownership and domination of nature had its roots in the Judeo-Christian tradition. In the book of Genesis, after creating humans in his own image, "God said unto them, Be fruitful, and multiply, and replenish the earth, and subdue it: and have dominion over the fish of the sea, and over the fowl of the air, and over every living thing that moveth upon the earth." Despite the usual caveat that humans are only temporary managers designated by God, the notion sanctifies the concept of nature as a possession. That possession should beget utility, no matter in which form, for the sake of human beings or their God.[51]

The concept of possession was further developed by the Christian world. In 1630, for example, aboard the ship *Arbella* as it sailed toward Massachusetts Bay, John Winthrop delivered his famous sermon, "A Model of Christian Charity." In it, he announced the arrival of Puritans in the New World and predicted a bright future for them. At the end of the sermon, Winthrop admonished that, if they kept loving God, following his laws, and carrying out their covenant with him, they "may live and be multiplied, and that the Lord our God may bless us in the land whither we go to possess it. But if our hearts shall turn away, so that we will not obey . . . we shall surely perish out of the good land whither we pass over this vast sea to possess it." For all his strong spiritual focus, Winthrop saw their mission in material terms, to possess and alter the land, a right bestowed on them by God.[52]

Later, John Locke's writings on private property also crossed the ocean, and for early Americans they provided a more secular theory about possessing the land and everything living on it. Locke's theory argues that private property is the product of labor. If a man owns himself and all his behaviors, all the entities improved by his labor necessarily belong only to him. By making labor the foundation of private property, Locke's theory not only intensified the sanctification of private property but also encouraged people to apply their labor to the land and to create a higher civilization out of it.[53]

This idea of possession balanced by stewardship, which was central to *Garden and Forest*'s philosophy, was unmistakably grounded in Western, and even Christian, civilization. As such, it was fundamentally different from the traditional Chinese Daoist vision of nature—a force that is always "generating without possessing" (*sheng er bu you*, in the words of the Daoist philosopher Laozi). In that tradition, nature is not a "creation" but is itself the creator that generates everything in the universe, without possessing anything. Being an independent and free system, nature functions with autonomy and does not exist or fall into ruin because of the changes occurring in human society. The human being is only a part of this "grand transformation" (*da hua*). Suggesting that the alienation of human beings from nature would be disastrous, traditional Chinese philosophy tends to bring humans into harmony with nature, to become "one" with it, rather than putting people in charge of a piece of property or enjoining an ethic of stewardship. From that oneness comes the fulfillment of spirit and freedom. In contrast, the artists and intellectuals of *Garden and Forest*, along with many of their contemporaries, tried to incorporate nature into civilization so that the latter could achieve lasting progress.

At the same time, by regarding nature as a *public* possession, not merely private property, the magazine contributors managed to connect nature with their belief in the Western ideal of democracy. This view followed the mainstream ideology of American society, in which civilization was supposed to be advancing in democratic, not authoritarian, directions. The magazine's authors argued that it was time for the public to realize that they had an obligation to conserve natural resources for all their people and for future generations. Preserving the abundance and productivity of natural resources secured the economic foundation of American democracy, while the shared pleasure derived from natural beauty fertilized the true spirit of popular government and equality.

In his series of articles under the heading "Forests and Civilization," published in 1889, J. B. Harrison analyzed the relationship between forest resource and the sustainability of civilization from different angles. He emphasized the relevance of this resource to public wealth and happiness. In the first article of the series, he quoted a letter from his mentor Charles Eliot Norton, which, in approving Harrison's work, defined the ideal environmental ethic: "all good men, all men who love their country and who desire that the democracy of America should set an example of rational, manly, intelligent and moral national life, must desire your success, as the agent of the American Forestry Congress, in the work which you have undertaken."[54] Mere economic prosperity for all, Harrison was sure, would not achieve the full scope and promise of a democratic civilization. A fuller democracy implied the general elevation of every citizen's morality and a shared right of spiritual and aesthetic enjoyment. This was the ethic that should guide everyone's life.

At its core, the magazine promoted an environmental attitude that was egalitarian and social. In his essay "Private Grounds and Enclosures in Cities and Towns," Sylvester Baxter contrasted European and America ideas about private grounds, concluding that "in Europe the idea is that of seclusion; in the United States it is rather one of inclusion." He added that this difference was partly due to the American idea of democracy—"an intuitive recognition of the fundamental fact of a democratic common wealth: That the individual is a portion of the public, to which he owes the duty of sharing, so far as he may, the enjoyment of the things of beauty that he may be privileged to possess."[55]

Thousands of big and small parks, both urban and wild, came into being during this time period, the 1880s and 1890s, continuing into the first decade of the twentieth century. As the next chapter argues, *Garden and Forest*, from its beginning to its end, defended the idea of full public access to all such places of natural beauty. It was the magazine's faith that only when people had been given free opportunities to achieve a more equal expression of intellectual and aesthetic capability could democracy truly blossom.

In this dramatically changing society, the contributors to *Garden and Forest* intended to redefine nature's role and significance for an urban industrial age. They aspired to an advanced level of civilization as a social goal. That goal required, they thought, a new understanding of nature—not hostility or raw exploitation but a new integration of nature and culture, a more enlightened possession and stewardship. For the first time, they brought nature—not simply its material resources but also its beauty—into the public sphere, breaking down the wall between nature and civilization, overcoming an all too common apathy toward the environment, and introducing ordinary Americans to the experience of beauty previously reserved only to elites.

The accelerating material demands on nature forced these writers and thinkers to become practical and utilitarian toward their surroundings. In addition, the common people's need for nature began to transcend subsistence demands and to approach a more aesthetic and emotional dimension. To satisfy this need, the magazine promoted love for nature and its beauty while at the same time calling for that beauty to be protected. Nature, in short, must be followed as a model for urban life, and yet nature must be mastered.

5　DESIGN WITH NATURE

〜〜〜〜〜〜〜〜〜〜〜

G ARDEN AND FOREST MAGAZINE was deeply engaged in curing the problems that came with the transition from a rural to an urban society.
Those problems seemed to follow the loss of nature and green spaces in
American life. Sitting in his Manhattan editorial office, William Stiles witnessed that loss occurring in one of the most populated spots in the world
and recorded the changes generated by urbanization, but the value of the
magazine went beyond recording loss. Its more inspiring contribution was to
suggest how the future relationship between nature and cities might develop
and bring back what was being lost and more.

Many of the magazine's contributors, as we have seen, were rising professionals living in East Coast cities. They were urbanites who nonetheless
cared about green vistas, and their careers were closely related to both the
city and nature. For many of them, especially landscape architects inspired
by Frederick Law Olmsted, the United States in the late nineteenth century
was not overcivilized but undercivilized, because in the evolution of its urban
phase, nature had been neglected or at least not given enough attention. Civilization, in other words, should mean not only industrial development, material prosperity, scientific progress, advancing democracy, and improvements in

art, literature, and morality but also the conservation of natural resources, the preservation of natural beauty (in cities and in more remote places), and the coexistence of nature and humanity. Cities, representing the essence of modern civilization, should become well-planned, integrated wholes in which humans and nature coexisted side by side.

This criticism of so-called American civilization was not unique in the era the magazine was published; *Garden and Forest* was following in a well-worn path. Its implicit goal of combining the merits of the cultural and the natural suggested a mind-set that had long been apparent in the Western and American intellectual tradition. In the antebellum years, for example, men and women had also dreamed of a landscape that exemplified physical and moral harmony. Then Olmsted appeared on the scene and actually turned this dream into reality. Compared to some of his contemporaries, he emphasized the power of the natural environment to enhance social morality. As Olmsted's intellectual child, *Garden and Forest* carried on this idea and gave it a strong collective voice. For those antebellum critics, the danger of urban decay had been looming on the horizon; for these late-nineteenth-century reformers, the crisis had already arrived and the problems needed to be solved. Like their fellow progressives, the magazine editors and contributors intended to approach those problems in a pragmatic and concrete way.[1]

What made the *Garden and Forest* circle distinct from the other progressive social reformers, such as resettlement workers or antipoverty crusaders, was their view that nature should be considered a necessary element of urban life. Nature had no place in many reformers' social designs, in which human beings were the only concern and the central fact. For the editors and contributors of *Garden and Forest*, without nature, the social environment would be barren and the human soul would be bleak. As one editorial indicated, "Public pleasure-grounds are possessions of rare value when treated with the full knowledge that they are to meet the elementary wants of the human soul by men who have a reverent love for nature, and whose primary aim is to develop the latent possibilities of the scenery on its poetic side and make these kindly influences accessible to all. They are more to be prized, shall we say, than great cathedrals or libraries or museums of science or art." This understanding was shaped by their admiration, however qualified, of the beauty of nature, their respect for the power of nature, and their belief in a universal and intuitive thirst for nature in all citizens, surviving even the uprooting process of urbanization.[2]

The magazine's contributors were aware of the prevalent nostalgia for rusticity, "the growing taste for rural life" in America, but such nostalgia was no solution in their mind. *Garden and Forest* may at times have echoed the popular back-to-nature mood, but it tried to lead this mood in the direction the writers believed more realistic for a new era. The simple life, old-fashioned virtue, direct contact with soil, indeed all those aspects that supposedly characterized a rural age, were haunting their thought, but their concern was not satisfied with sentiment; instead, they wanted to find more practical and forward-looking remedies.[3]

They were not only nature enthusiasts but also aspiring professionals who wanted to start a new trend of actively designing and planning cities. In their view, nature was not a memory one should dig up from the past but a living entity, tangible and useful in the present and the future. In the environmental designs espoused by the *Garden and Forest* circle, a vanishing rural society was not the model they intended to follow. Quite different from traditional agrarians, they insisted that "it is a narrow view which looks upon this rapid growth and increasing importance of urban communities as an unmixed evil. Sanitary science has made life in the town more healthful than it was in the early decades of the century, and more complete organization has multiplied its comforts. If there has been an apparent decline in the social and political importance of some rural communities, the towns have gained what the country has lost." Filled with faith in modernity and education, confident in the emergence of professionalism and expertise, *Garden and Forest* hoped not to restore a lost rural paradise but to realize a distinctly urban civilization, although one in which nature occupied a secure position.[4]

In this vision of the new city, as in the old countryside, nature must be an integral part of life. It must be rescued from chaos and other unpredictable elements and become rationalized and, in some way, humanized to meet the physical and aesthetic desires of urban inhabitants—somehow without ceasing to be nature. Furthermore, the contributors to *Garden and Forest* believed that their ideal of a more thoughtfully integrated landscape did not end at the city limits. While promoting the incorporation of nature into the urban environment, they also tried to extend the scope of this new integration into the city's hinterland. According to *Garden and Forest*, such a wider integration could generate a dual impact—revitalizing urban civilization while at the same time bringing places other than cities into the civilized sphere.

How did *Garden and Forest* try to design this integrated landscape *within* and *beyond* the confines of the city? To answer this question, one must first ask several others: What was the ideal urban environment that the magazine editors and contributors hoped to see constructed? What was the function of urban parks and green spaces? How did the magazine try to shape the public's vision of nature and its relationship with cities? Finally, how did *Garden and Forest* extend its "city natural" vision into nonurban surroundings?

"IMPROVEMENT" WAS A master theme in progressive America, but it was construed in different ways. Like many contemporary reformers, the contributors to *Garden and Forest* believed that it was necessary to address the urban environment across a variety of fronts. Many of the improvements promoted in the magazine were identical to those of other progressive reformers, such as promoting sustainable economic growth, constructing sewer and other sanitary systems, establishing schools, hospitals, and museums, and providing modern public services. In contrast to the common interpretation of "improvement," *Garden and Forest* offered serious criticisms of a purely artificial urban environment that obscured nature with a layer of quarried stone and macadamized streets. "There is a passion for 'improving' vacant land," the editors wrote, "and the only known way to improve it is to cover it up with some construction. The time has not arrived when the people of the city realize that open spaces are quite as essential to health and comfort as solid blocks of buildings or they would never consent to see their property destroyed in this way." In their magazine, the contributors strived to enlighten readers regarding a broader concept of environmental improvement in cities.[5]

"Comprehensiveness" was a commonly announced goal in city planning in this time period. Progressive reformers and planners argued repeatedly that one should not simply address one or two aspects of the city but should aim to shape and improve the whole entity. According to historian Jon Peterson, in the Progressive Era the phrase "comprehensive plan" suggested "a new more expansive meaning, as a vision of generalized control." The city needed an overall plan or direction, meaning more control over all its energies, and this control was to come from having experts in charge.[6]

City planning as a label or full-blown idea did not yet exist in the pages of *Garden and Forest*, but the magazine editors anticipated this new field in many ways, and many of the magazine contributors, especially Olmsted and Charles Eliot, were regarded as forerunners in the field. They shared the vision of a more "generalized control." For *Garden and Forest*, making one or two city parks or planting a few trees was not enough; those few measures alone could not provide a comprehensive rebuilding of the connection between people and nature. What was needed was a more systematic blueprint for all the spaces and all the people in cities. A "generalized control" meant including and ordering everything within cities, including natural habitat and social groups.[7]

The comprehensive environmental vision promoted by the magazine consisted of two aspects. One emphasized the city as an environmental hierarchy with layers and layers of space, ranging from a single family's indoor and outdoor environment to a street or neighborhood and finally to the entire metropolis and its hinterland. The other aspect envisioned the integration of people from all walks of life into a common social order. The first aspect necessitated the professional skills of landscape architects or horticulturists, while the second grew out of those experts' commitment to a more inclusive democracy.

The magazine asserted that "there is no longer any need of argument to prove that ample and convenient open spaces for public resort and recreation are essential not only to the pleasure and comfort, but to the physical health and the mental and moral growth of the people. This is universally admitted." Based on this assertion, *Garden and Forest* devoted its attention to the places where people were most crowded together—where "lives must be passed in the noise and confusion and rectangular ugliness which seem to be the essential conditions of life in thickly crowded cities." Therefore, in pursuing a more comprehensive design, their ambition was to encourage the growing of green things in every corner of the city so that all urban dwellers could have access to nature.[8]

Gardens could come in many shapes and sizes. A working-class family could own a tiny window-box garden, while an entire metropolis could be transformed into a grand garden city. The most elementary and modest gardens were those nurtured by poor families with little or no space. Many of these tiny outposts of nature could hardly be called gardens but consisted merely of several pots of plants arrayed on windowsills or roofs. Too simple to attract much attention, such home efforts nonetheless often provided urban dwellers with their most direct and affordable contact with nature. This type of "green space" did not particularly intrigue the landscape architects writing for *Garden and Forest*, but it captured the attention of another group of contributors who were mainly horticulturists, nursery experts, and florists. Their work was not to organize trees, meadows, and rivers into a big picture, as landscape architects did, but to study and propagate individual plants, making their form, color, and fragrance more variable and pleasant. Among the working class lay many potential customers for their businesses. While profit from plant sales was their main interest, this group of contributors found themselves allied with other contributors in trying to encourage some form of nature in city people's daily lives.[9]

The contributions of horticulturists, nursery experts, and florists were published mainly in the magazine's "cultural department." They were articles for not only professional horticulturists but also amateurs and for not only huge conservatories but also tiny window gardens. The species discussed in those articles included not only expensive and delicate ones like orchids but also many hardy and affordable flowers, such as rhododendron, chrysanthemum, and begonia, for the contributors believed that growing these sorts of flowers would not place any economic burden on a poor family but rather bring inexpensive pleasure and beauty to them. In the words of an editorial extolling the value of water lilies, plants were "for the poor as well as for the rich," especially plants that were "within the reach of any one who can afford a tub of water and a piece of sunny ground large enough to hold it."[10]

From the outset to the end of its publication, *Garden and Forest* maintained a consistently positive attitude toward home plants growing in a little soil. The editors and writers did not deny the charm of cut flowers, agreeing that it was a positive fashion to love and display cut flowers everywhere in the nation. They simply appreciated living plants far more. In the first issue of the magazine, Peter Henderson compared the development of floriculture in America and Europe, decrying Americans' use of more cut flowers for decoration than any other country's populace. It was far less common to find living plants in windows or backyards in American cities than in Europe. Nevertheless, he concluded optimistically that "beneath these flitting fancies is the substantial and unchanging love of flowers that seems to be an original instinct in man, and one that grows in strength with growing refinement." Several weeks later an editorial brought up the same topic and repeated the encouragement for growing living plants at home, both the familiar and unfamiliar varieties. The editor declared, "Not the most splendid bunch of Roses is more lovely than a fine Azalea in full flower." It was not wrong to love cut flowers, yet the "almost exclusive preference for them instead of for flowering plants is a misfortune, especially to persons of modest means, who, by a different expenditure of their money, might buy more lasting pleasures."[11]

The magazine's fondness for growing plants even in pots or on roof gardens originated from a strong passion for nature joined to a search for the public good. E. P. Powell, a frequent contributor on pomology, wrote the essay "Housetop Gardens," which can be regarded as representative of the magazine editors' views on this subject. He stated that in the process of urbanization, Americans had paid more attention to "the glory of increasing the size of cities" than to the "increase of their attendant comforts. . . . Economy and health and pleasure," he added, "can all be combined in roof gardening." The suburbs were not in need of such efforts, but the tenement houses were; roof gardens could turn them into much more desirable places to live. In contrast to buying cut flowers, growing potted plants conveyed some awareness of the vitality of nature. As Powell wrote, "The most practicable immediate use of the roof garden is for the families of professional men and others who long for some contact with growing things, a bit of nature, wild or tame, all to themselves."[12]

While the magazine tried to persuade poor families to buy and grow a few plants, it also wanted to persuade middle- and upper-class families to embellish their yards with plantings on a larger scale. In an 1888 essay, the editors contrasted the seasonal patterns of Europeans and Americans. While wealthy British people came to town during the summer, their American counterparts headed to the countryside for months at a time to escape the heat. Thus, the wealthy American felt no need to be concerned about the living environment in cities during the growing season; this type of gentleman was too busy "drawing down his blinds, boarding up his front-door, and doing his best to give the city the aspect of a plague-stricken, abandoned place." In the essay "Why We Do Not Buy Growing Plants," the editors wondered why the rich did not think about their neighbors who could not escape the heat. This was almost a moral issue in their view, for "if every absent householder spent this little, how great would be the increase of pleasure for the multitudes of weary spirits to whom a week's outing must represent a summer vacation."[13]

As progressives and idealists, members of the magazine's circle of writers believed strongly in the capacity of education to awaken the universal human instinct for nature and raise it to a higher aesthetic and spiritual level. Their educational means were diverse. The magazine itself was meant to be an instrument of education. Besides print media, they also supported formal and systematic nature education in the schools, along with more informal ways of encouraging a love of nature. Gardening was prominent among these ways. By planting a garden, adults and children alike could touch the soil and participate in the marvels of plant growth.

This was not a new hope. Tamara Thornton points out that, in the antebellum period, horticulture first appeared as a hobby among gentlemen before emerging as a popular movement, with flourishing organizations and periodicals. Gardening was supposed to cure the upper class's moral failings, especially the materialism and boorishness created by greed and ambition. At the same time, it was supposed to calm the "spirit of unrest" (in Andrew Jackson Downing's words) and make the nation more stable. After the Civil War, the advocates of horticulture switched their attention to lower social levels, especially the working class and the new immigrants, who were supposedly weakened by vices generated by poverty. Thornton argues that horticulture "was to function as an antidote to the moral failures" of these people. Behind its promotion lay the belief "that horticulture taught republican virtues: hard work, thrift, and the sacrosanct worth of private property." Thus, gardening entered urban schools and was welcomed by progressive educators as an effective form of moral education. A school garden movement burgeoned, while gardening advocates also promoted the educational value of gardening for adults.[14]

Garden and Forest's contributors likewise looked at gardening through a moral lens. Describing a visit to the annual flower show of the Westminster Society in London, J. D. W. French saw much benefit from such exhibitions for all classes of people. The "chief good was that in watching the growth and progress of the flowers under their care the children and their parents were brought into close contact with something pure and innocent and beautiful; something that should speak to the better part of their natures and tell them of Him who has made the earth beautiful and fair."[15]

Beyond promoting this moral, and even religious, uplift from gardening, the contributors of *Garden and Forest* also expressed confidence that this activity would help bridge the social gap created by concentrated wealth and power; it would break down barriers and encourage social equality. Mary C. Robbins regarded gardening as "a common bond between the wise and the ignorant, a pursuit wherein men of different station can interchange roles and mutually impart knowledge." "Beyond any question," she wrote in one essay, "a more general devotion to gardening among Americans would help them to lead lives of greater serenity and sanity. They could afford to read fewer books and newspapers if they only learned these lessons of peace which come from contact with nature. It would be a solace to poor and rich." In other words, it would serve as a means and also an embodiment of democracy.[16]

In that same essay, Robbins asked why gardening was not as popular in the United States as in Europe. Americans, she complained, lacked "a deep root in the soil," which led to a deficiency in local attachment and sense of belonging. In the opinion of the editors of and contributors to *Garden and Forest*, gardening could help strengthen those roots. Gardening would "imbue [a man] with a love for home, to anchor him to that one spot of the earth's surface which he calls his own, and to which he can impart some portion of his own individuality." Robbins urged that Americans needed this "stay and balance." The sense of ownership that came from tending plants and gardens would make people cherish the natural scenery they possessed and realize it was the real wealth they should preserve for themselves and their descendants.[17]

Furthermore, according to the magazine's contributors, gardening, combined with other programs of nature study, would encourage a more scientific understanding of nature and simultaneously instill a profound love of nature. Many contributors to *Garden and Forest*, most prominently Liberty Hyde Bailey, were early voices for the popular nature-study movement. Historian Kevin Armitage argues that, in the Progressive Era, nature-study advocates encouraged children to gain scientific knowledge through rational, objective experimental methods while learning to become morally engaged through intimate contact with nature. They tried to reconcile what had often seemed diametrically opposed values. The same held true for contributors to *Garden and Forest*, who wanted to integrate what the age seemed to be fracturing.[18]

Science, the magazine editors argued, demonstrated that nature had a positive influence on the human body. Introducing natural elements into cities was not merely for sentimental reasons but for "reasons based on the most substantial and practical truth." The fresh air of the meadow or forest would promote people's physical health. "It is asserted over and over again," wrote the editors, "not only by poets and philosophers who give expression to the profoundest truths in our nature, but the curative value of natural scenery is distinctly recognized by the medical profession. All of us have felt the soothing and restful influence of natural beauty, acting in a subtle way through the very highest functions of our being, and tending to establish sound minds in sound bodies."[19]

Schools were not the only place where *Garden and Forest* hoped to awaken the public's sympathy toward nature. The vision of the magazine also extended beyond the windows, roofs, and front yards of individual houses to a much broader landscape. Even more important were public parks and gardens, for they could exercise "a great educational and moral as well as a sanitary influence in city life." For the magazine, the "city natural" ideal was to make nature omnipresent in American cities. In an editorial on the efforts of the Trustees of Reservations to acquire open spaces for public use in Massachusetts, the editors expressed hope that the preservation of natural scenery would "reflect the taste and civilization of the people of the state." They advocated a movement "broad enough from the beginning to include and enlist all who appreciate out-of-door interests and objects of any kind, the preservation of natural scenery, the care of trees, forests and wooded lands, and of fish and game preserves, the purity of the water-supply for cities and towns, the treatment of roadsides, and of mountain and sea-shore commons and public parks and open spaces." This long list suggested the magazine editors' integrative vision. Streets, railroad stations, school grounds, cemeteries, and parks—all of these public domains were targets for design. They urged that "every city should plant its own trees as much as it should pave its own streets." They wanted the railroad stations to show "a truer appreciation of what is most beautiful in gardening." They called for "a much needed reform in the treatment of school-grounds throughout the country," and they hailed the leafy, well-landscaped cemetery as "a simple, peaceful place in which a natural, rather than an artificial, type of beauty has been secured." Chief among all the public places for which the magazine editors expressed concern were urban parks.[20]

If trees, shrubs, and flowers were only supplemental decorations to streets, cemeteries, and other human-created entities, they were the principal objects in urban parks whose sole purpose was to allow the flourishing and blossoming of the nonhuman world. On the surface, urban parks stood as an antithesis to cities. Their curvy, flowing lines softened the usual grid of streets and blocks commonly imposed on the urban landscape. Their fresh air animated the monotonous and strangled atmosphere, and their rural scenery recalled some sentiment and virtue lost in the smoke and dust of an urban age. Urban parks represented the freedom that urbanization stifled, the instinct it blunted, the beauty it encroached on, and the contemplation it destroyed. *Garden and Forest* argued that "the primary purpose of a rural park within reach of a great city is to furnish that rest and refreshment of mind and body which come from the tranquilizing influence of contact with natural scenery."[21]

For almost ten years, the magazine maintained the same tone regarding urban parks, fought against all sorts of invasion of park spaces, and struggled to make Americans understand the true meaning and value of urban parks. Sometimes the editors apologized for repeating their words too many times, but the sad truth behind their apology was that the threat they feared never ceased. If they sometimes failed to stop business interests from invading the urban parks, they were often just as powerless in their attempts to influence other progressive reformers—those who claimed the same social ideals they did—to work toward achieving the public good. Those reformers could be as deaf as business leaders to all their entreaties on behalf of nature. A fierce dispute between city playground boosters, for example, and *Garden and Forest* and other park advocates illustrated this conflict among reformers.[22]

When the playground movement emerged in the 1880s, with the goal of building playgrounds for children and adults in cities, its leaders collaborated with the advocates of the park movement, fighting for the legitimacy and protection of open space in cities. During the accelerating process of urbanization, all reformers lamented the darker side of urban civilization: the growth of slums, poverty, crime, and unhealthy conditions. They all believed that, despite the cultural and economic advantages offered by cities, many urban residents were physically unfit, spiritually desolate, and morally deteriorating. They believed that democracy in the age of urbanization and industrialization could be strengthened and eventually fulfilled by elevating physical circumstances for and morality among all social classes.

The commonality of their social views did not lead all progressive-minded reformers to a unanimous support for nature parks in the city. As the urban population grew, the acquisition of open space in cities became increasingly difficult; once the reformers had succeeded in acquiring land for parks, reformers fought over the proper function of these few pieces of real estate.[23] For *Garden and Forest*, an urban park naturalized an artificial world and preserved an aesthetic element in the grayness of daily life, so that urban inhabitants could gain physical benefit in the healthy, open air and spiritual refreshment through their contemplation of natural beauty. To the playground advocates, in contrast, physical exercise should be the motif of urban parks; thus, the major function of urban parks should be to enclose abundant and safe space for adults and children to release their physical energy vigorously and freely. Also, they recommended team sports most often because they believed the rules and spirit of cooperation could help people better adapt to industrial work discipline and the collective ethos. Tranquility and beauty experienced in nature, argued the playground boosters, were frivolous middle- and upper-middle-class ideals imposed on ordinary factory workers and their children.[24]

In "Playgrounds and Parks," published in 1894, the editors of *Garden and Forest* replied to the criticism playground advocates had presented, and they articulated their understanding of the purpose of an urban park. The editors claimed that they had "pleaded in these columns for more children's playgrounds too often to be accused of not recognizing their value to the community." But they did not think such playgrounds should be built at the expense of scenery parks, for the latter was the only place where one could discover "the purpose of refreshment, of renewal of life and strength for body and soul alike." They pointed out that the truer and broader sense of recreation was expressed when the word was written as "re-creation." Thus, they argued that "the truest value of public pleasure-grounds for large cities is in the rest they give to eyes and mind, to heart and soul, through the soothing charm, the fresh and inspiring influence, the impersonal, unexciting pleasure which nothing but the works of Nature offer to man." To gain this re-creation, natural beauty was the crucial element because it appealed to the very souls of people, both young and old.[25]

Another editorial took the familiar warning "Keep Off the Grass" as its title and reiterated the magazine editors' concern for protecting natural beauty in city parks. To answer the complaint that the "Keep Off the Grass" sign restricted the freedom of people to use those green spaces as they wanted, the editorial noted that the sign was "necessary if the parks are to retain that tender and restful beauty which gives them their supreme value." "The Defacement of City Parks," an editorial published in 1895, rejected any criticism of park defenders. From the editors' lament that "if public opinion has become so demoralized in any city that proper regulations for maintaining the landscape beauty of their parks are denounced as tyrannous, such parks are doomed to desolation," it is not difficult to tell that the gap between the park and the playground advocates had become deep and wide. Once again, the magazine tried to arouse the public's sentiment for natural beauty and some recognition of its indispensability in an urban age. Facing the argument that parks were to use and not simply to look at, the magazine argued that "the beauty of a park is its highest use, and, therefore, to destroy that beauty is not to use but to abuse it."[26]

The essence of the conflict between the park and the playground advocates was not simply what sort of behavior, passive or active, in urban parks would be a better use of the space but what position nature should or could occupy in this age. Park supporters like Olmsted, Eliot, Sargent, and Stiles believed that nature itself had value in improving the city's physical and social environment, while the playground advocates allowed no role for nature in human self-improvement. Even if they were not completely opposed to incorporating nature within cities, they regarded nature as irrelevant to the process of civilization and did not acknowledge any physical or spiritual need for nature among urban people.

This defense of nature-oriented parks set *Garden and Forest* against those who wanted to use the parks for their projects. In an effort to protect Central Park from the construction of a botanical garden and zoo, the editors of the journal wrote, "We frankly say that we would rather never to see it established than see the Central Park—that great monument to American art and priceless pleasure-ground of the poor—curtailed and ruined for its sake or for the sake of any other scientific or political or money-making scheme." They wanted no structures, even zoos, in these spaces, because parks were built to meet people's fundamental need for nature.[27]

In June 1897, in "Natural Beauty in Urban Parks," the *Garden and Forest* editors summarized all their efforts in defending urban parks over the preceding years. Within another four months, Stiles's life would come to an end, and two months later the magazine would cease publication. It is worth quoting this valedictory at length:

> When we consider the almost universal admiration and even affection among civilized men and women for broad natural landscapes, for "scenery as distinct from scenes," and consider its special restoring effect upon those who suffer from the nervous strain of city life, we have the one justifying reason for large urban parks. Small parks and playgrounds, formal squares, plazas and promenades are all valuable for other purposes, but for the highest rest and refreshment nothing will fill the place of stretches of beautiful natural scenery. Artificiality, the needless intrusion of buildings, anything which interferes with seclusion and the actual contact and communion with pure nature, defeats to some extent the highest purpose of such parks. The idea should never be harbored that rural parks can be improved by buildings however noble, by any work of art which is not entirely in harmony with the spirit of the scene, or by so-called decorative gardening, however choice and rare the plants employed.[28]

One question raised by this statement is whether love for broad natural landscape was in fact a universal sentiment. The late nineteenth century was a time of new immigrants coming to US cities from predominantly Catholic European countries. The contemporary critics of Olmsted-inspired parks and some historians later on charged that a so-called universal love for the natural landscape was limited to the Anglo-Saxon or Protestant imagination. The naturalistic style practiced by Olmsted and his followers was often identified as the "English style." Supposedly, this style did not meet the aesthetic vision of other races and ethnicities. However, the critics trap themselves in another form of ethnocentrism—a Western ethnocentric view of human ideals. Even though romanticism's paean to nature did not spread among Western intellectuals until the eighteenth century, a high appreciation of wild natural beauty had been rooted in Eastern cultures for centuries. The ideal of "naturalness" came to the West from such countries as China, Japan, and India, where it had existed for thousands of years; that fact suggests that there is a more universal feeling that transcends other cultural differences between East and West. *Garden and Forest*'s editors and contributors knew about and praised those non-Western ideals of nature and their expression. Mariana Van Rensselaer, for example, introduced Asia's gardens in a series of articles. Although the magazine contributors had a relatively limited understanding of Asian cultures, they discerned a broader love of nature shared by people from other corners of the world.[29]

If the editors rejected artificiality in the parks and sought universal values, did the magazine bring "real nature" into the designed landscape they promoted? The urban parks and gardens they favored were usually restorations and reconstructions of nature, not samples of original nature. As discussed in chapter 4, the magazine and its circle of writers may have been respectful of the laws of nature, but at the same time they believed that nature needed to be assisted by art and science to become more compatible with civilization. They were not so naïve as to argue that they "created" nature; rather, they wanted people to acknowledge the artistic imagination and human effort in those parks. For them, gardens, being highly organized and selected, would satisfy urban people's hunger for nature but at the same time not repel them with any disgusting or terrifying elements.

To a point, the *Garden and Forest* perspective was not so different from that of other urban reformers, such as sanitation planners.[30] While deploring modern humans' detachment from nature, the editors and contributors assuredly did not want "nature" in the form of stampeding pigs and mountains of manure in the streets. Historian Theodore Steinberg points out that, "in the late nineteenth century, reformers bent on sanitation put an end to the city in its down-to-earth form." So too did the contributors to *Garden and Forest*. They wanted to have a selected version of nature, one in which its unseemly aspects were eliminated in order to protect people's physical and mental health. Farm animals and manure had no place, nor did other elements identified with traditional rural life, such as barnyards.[31]

What also had no place in the parks was proselytizing for any religion, for it would distract from the tranquility and tolerance encouraged by the scenery. The editors stated emphatically that they did not want to turn the parks into a platform for any religion, including evangelical preachers. They pointed out that "wandering sectarian preachers are none too gentle, as a rule, when they are characterizing other creeds than their own, and they can easily succeed in making themselves disagreeable. A large proportion of the working people who most need the park are Catholics, and why should they, for example, be forced to hear their faith attacked in their own pleasure-grounds?" Allowing religious preaching in parks, they argued, would be a "manifest injustice." In another editorial, the editors wrote satirically, "Religious enthusiasts are convinced that in some way the salvation of men depends upon their efforts, and that their exclusion from the public parks means practically the ruin of human souls." The editors argued that it was nature, not words from the Bible or other holy scriptures, that would bring about spiritual development. Whether religious preaching could save the evil urban soul or not, its intrusion would, in the editors' view, ruin a park.[32]

The editors' opposition to preaching in urban parks, an activity they believed would turn into "revival meetings" like those so often found in the countryside, was linked to their challenge to another part of rural society: the tradition of frontier individualism. The magazine editors extolled the freedom suggested by vast meadows and unlimited skies but argued that this freedom should not be unchecked or become a license to do whatever one wanted. In an urban public park, restraint was important; visitors should exercise restraint and learn tolerance toward others' behaviors and views, and others should refrain from unauthorized interventions into nature. The sign "Keep Off the Grass" best imparted this simple but widely ignored principle: if people wanted to enjoy the beauty derived from nature, they had to learn how to restrict themselves to particular activities or behaviors.

Historian Donald Worster argues that the "linkage of freedom and restraint may be the most important feature of the wilderness movement," a movement that embodies the "the virtue of restraint." This argument is also applicable to the urban park movement in which the park defenders asked people to accept restraint in exchange for the protection of nature and also for the benefit of other people. But such restraint was dramatically different from the restraints commonly enforced in American rural life or on the frontier. There, people often fought and tried to subjugate nature for private ends. They insisted on the freedom to make up their own rules. Instead of that individualism, the park advocates wanted to instill a respect for the authority of nature as defined and shaped by knowledge and skilled design.[33]

The contributors to *Garden and Forest* did not want to make urban parks a refuge from law and order, for they believed that urban parks, as an indispensable part of urban civilization, should encourage virtue and morality. Over and over, they made this argument: "public parks are quite as essential to the health and comfort and morals of the city as a pure water-supply or a good system of sewage, and . . . a civilized community can no more flourish with-

out them than without hospitals, libraries, museums, colleges and churches."
Urban parks, like the other civil and public agencies, should be incorporated
into the restraining web of urban civilization. They resembled rural scenery
only superficially, for in essence they were urban and modern. Lewis Mumford said of Olmsted: "by making nature urbane he naturalized the city." So
also was the paradoxical ambition of the *Garden and Forest* circle of writers.[34]

To make a city natural meant to design the park as a subtle form of social,
moral, and even political education. That program of design should extend far
beyond the boundaries of the park and out into the suburbs and countryside.
A metropolitan park system, which extended far beyond the boundaries of,
say, Central Park, would help accomplish this goal. When individual parks
inside the city and those in its hinterland were taken together, one could not
miss their integrative function. Isolated rural communities could not have
built such a system, with its wide scope, ambitious plans, coordinated management, and diverse interests. Only when the nation entered an age of increasingly centralized power and wealth and ever-advancing techniques could
such a comprehensive environmental design come into being.

The Boston Metropolitan Park System, which pioneered this enlarged and
integrative planning idea for the country, emerged in 1891. That was when "the
first suggestion was made for a system of parks adequate to meet the needs
of the great cluster of cities and towns that, with the city of Boston, forms
practically one metropolitan community." The next year a preliminary committee, which included *Garden and Forest*'s Charles Eliot and Sylvester Baxter
among its members, was appointed to draft a plan for the system. In 1893,
the Massachusetts legislature passed an act that enabled suburban cities and
towns to cooperate with Boston in securing open spaces. The purpose was
to establish a park system across the whole metropolitan region, crossing the
political boundaries of twelve cities and twenty-five towns. Soon there were
some ten thousand acres protected in the system (today the total has grown
to almost twenty thousand acres, even after subtracting much that was destroyed by highway construction). All of it was protected open space, both for
recreation and water supply. Integrated with the city's existing park system,
the famous "Emerald Necklace" of Boston metropolitan parks covered a diversity of landscapes and extended far beyond the city's boundaries. As noted
earlier, the advocates of this project argued that since the boundaries of the
park system were not confined to one city or neighborhood, the system had

to be managed by a commission composed of experts not beholden to any local interest.[35]

Garden and Forest noted that an 1895 report indicated that the areas to be controlled by the Metropolitan Park Commission consisted of "the Blue Hills reservation, five miles long; the Middlesex Fells reservation, two miles square; Stony Brook reservation, two miles long; Charles River reservation, including the semi-public river-banks, five miles long; the Mystic Valley parkway, two miles long, and the Reservation, three miles long." In contrast to Olmsted's big city parks, which depended on artistic manipulation, original, natural landscapes would be preserved in these far-flung areas. All the parks would be connected with the populous centers by "cheap and rapid means of transportation by electric cars [trolleys]" and by state-funded parkways, which guaranteed access for different classes with different interests and needs.[36]

From the outset, *Garden and Forest* participated in and pushed forward this park project. The magazine regularly reported on its progress, summarized its lessons, and exalted its values. The leading figures behind the project were also important contributors to the magazine who used its pages as the major medium for explaining their work to the public. The editors and contributors also wanted to see Boston become a model for other cities to emulate, thus broadcasting their environmental and social goals.

Being devout progressives, the editors never allowed their belief in advancing the public good to get lost in their work to construct and preserve urban parks. Always they identified parks, wherever located, as symbols of American democracy. Charles Eliot's words expressed this common view in the magazine: "The occasionally so pressing want of that quiet and peculiar refreshment which comes from contemplation of scenery—the want of which the rich satisfy by fleeing from town at certain seasons, but which the poor (who are trespassers in the country) can seldom fill—is only to be met by the country," that is, by bringing the country into the city or bringing city people to the country. Parks, in this way of thinking, met the demand for social and environmental justice, for justice should mean not only reducing working hours, improving the welfare of laborers, providing cleaner water and environment, or spreading public education but also acknowledging everyone's right and capacity to enjoy nature and its beauty. The magazine's praise of Andrew Jackson Downing summarized this notion of environmental justice:

"that rich and poor could breathe the same atmosphere of nature and of art and enjoy the same scenery without any jealousy or any conflict."[37]

Perhaps they were naïve about what parks could achieve, but other reformers could be naïve too. Idealism drove the *Garden and Forest* reformers as it did others of the day, impelling them to construct and protect hundreds of urban parks and other, smaller-scale urban gardens. Everyone in cities could benefit from these places in their daily lives, however much they took them for granted or even ignored their significance. It was a pity, *Garden and Forest* lamented in its pages, that those who were "striving to reduce the hours of labor" failed to discern that they should "have an especial interest in saving the park from any intrusion that even remotely threatens to impair its efficiency, or limit its capacity, of furnishing recreation for themselves and their children." Confident that they would improve their fellow citizens' psychological as well as physical welfare, the magazine editors could not understand why other reformers were so blind to this fundamental need.[38]

WHILE THE CONTRIBUTORS to and editors of the magazine were attempting to incorporate nature into urban people's lives, the "city natural" project was taking on even grander dimensions by moving beyond city limits to incorporate the rural landscape, which had inspired the look of urban parks. Their goal was an integrated landscape, and their plan for it would not be as complete and comprehensive as they wanted unless they expanded their reach all the way into the countryside. While they imported some rural qualities to improve the urban landscape, they also expected urban environmental ideas and professionalism to change rural lives. However, a bland uniformity of country and city, or a suburbanized sameness, was not the outcome they sought. A true civilization, according to the magazine, did not require obliterating local identity, which derived from unique local history and the shaping power of nature.[39]

As cities were growing larger, suburbanization was also occurring. The magazine editors and contributors were certainly not ignorant of the latter change. While seeking to integrate the urban and the natural, they did not encourage readers to escape from urban geographical boundaries. The primary concern was still those people living in cities and the environment around them. Aware of the lurking dangers of conformity and monotony that sprawling suburbanization might bring to the land, they tried to hinder the trend and to preserve the unique local aspects of nonurban landscapes. Thus, in a series of essays entitled "Some Old American Country Seats," Charles Eliot highlighted local natural and cultural beauty; in other essays, he criticized the monotonous new housing construction on the coast of Maine and called for action to save the historic Waverly Oaks near Boston from sprawl. Similarly, J. B. Harrison set out to describe the unique shore towns of Massachusetts. The motive behind their words was to preserve elements of regionally diverse cultural and natural heritage and prevent thoughtless development that ignored that heritage.[40]

It was still too early for the magazine and its contributors to foresee what later would become serious problems created by the mass housing industry, including the loss of biodiversity and cultural variety that the American suburbs so often caused. It would be anachronistic and unfair to argue that the post–World War II suburb was the middle landscape *Garden and Forest* envisioned in its "city natural" project. Whether for big cities or small towns and villages, the magazine editors and contributors tried to explore the uniqueness of natural and cultural landscapes and to save them.[41]

Even though *Garden and Forest* was an urban-oriented magazine, its producers also viewed the changes occurring in the countryside to be matters of concern. Like many other urban reformers, the editors and contributors worried about the future of farmers and rural life. American agriculture went through a radical and traumatic transition during the second half of the nineteenth century, becoming increasingly subordinate to the new urban industrial society. Populism was the most profound and telling reaction to that change, and that political movement expressed the widespread insecurity and anxiety that farmers were experiencing. As a magazine that avoided most political and economic issues, *Garden and Forest* was not ready to judge populism or other rural protest movements, but this did not mean that the editorial stance of the magazine was indifferent toward what was going on in the countryside. From their urban perspective, its writers grasped the interconnectedness of rural and urban economies and the expansion of markets, due most directly to the proliferation of railroads. Convinced of the need for more scientific practices in agriculture and of the inevitability of urbanization, the contributors to *Garden and Forest* did not see the changes in the farm economy as negative on balance, though they had much sympathy for the farmers who had to suffer through the changes.[42]

Admittedly, the increase of wealth and population in cities and their resulting increase in influence came at the expense of rural communities. Feeling uneasy about the decline of those communities, the magazine editors raised these questions: "How can the conservative practices of Agriculture and Horticulture be adjusted to the swiftly changing conditions of this growing country? How is the farmer to command his fair share of the value of the products of the soil? What can be done to make country life more attractive, wholesome and satisfying? Is it possible to restore the tiller of the soil to the position of consequence he once held in the social and political life of the Republic?"[43] Probably no one could give completely adequate answers to those questions. But the magazine producers made very clear that their mission was to integrate the countryside into the civilized landscape, bringing urban amenities to farmers while protecting farmers' connection to the land. The argument they followed in this case was the same as the one they followed in constructing urban landscapes: all human beings are capable of balancing the rational progress of science and economy with the romantic sentiment of nature and beauty. Liberty Bailey put it this way in *The Holy Earth*: "it is possible to hoe potatoes and to hear the birds sing at the same time." A better civilization for both city and country would come from this cultural balance.[44]

In its publication prospectus, *Garden and Forest* announced that it would "cooperate with Village Improvement Societies and every other organized effort to secure the proper ordering and maintenance of parks and squares, cemeteries, railroad stations, school grounds and roadsides." Village improvement societies were local rural groups that had begun to spread in the second half of the nineteenth century. The first of them appeared in Stockbridge, Massachusetts, in 1853, and, by the end of the century, they could be found throughout New England and the Northeast. This movement, initiated by voluntary efforts, was dedicated to improving the quality of life in the countryside and its declining villages and to boosting their public spirit. First advocated by Andrew Jackson Downing, this movement from the beginning was intertwined with the park movement in the cities. The village societies focused on revitalizing rural life by making their local surroundings more organized and attractive, a goal shared by the urban parks movement. In turn, the parks advocates taught their country cousins about the connection between public health and clean, fresh water and air. Because of this influence, the scope of village improvement became more ambitious; advocates emphasized not only making village centers more lovely but also providing a clean water supply and a good system of sewage removal as the first requisites of a high-quality life.[45]

One of the key texts for urban reformers was *The Improvement of Towns and Cities*, written by Charles Mulford Robinson and published in 1901. The previous year, the National League of Improvement Association had been founded. At its first annual convention, the group renamed itself the American League for Civic Improvement, and later it merged into the American Civic Association. However, a decade earlier, the civic improvement movement had already begun to emerge and was noticed by *Garden and Forest*. According to the editorial "The City Improvement Societies," published in 1890, this urban movement actually had much in common with the village improvement efforts and emulated the latter. The major voice of the urban movement, Robinson, who advocated a more balanced landscape between extreme urbanism and backwoods primitivism, was likely influenced by or in tune with *Garden and Forest's* urban designs. The civic movement aspired to bring together the best of both worlds and never wholly rejected the pastoral, or middle-landscape, tradition. Such *Garden and Forest* writers as William Stiles, Mary C. Robbins, and Sylvester Baxter were outspoken advocates of its causes.[46]

Thoughtful observers could not have taken any other position. A growing economic interdependence as well as constant cultural intercommunication made the boundary between rural and urban very permeable. As early as 1888, when the magazine was just beginning, *Garden and Forest* saw the necessity to infuse village improvement with urban principles. After praising the achievements those rural societies had made, the magazine pointed out that "in too many instances the zeal of the few has been only superficial, or what is quite as bad, it has been uninstructed; and just here lies the fundamental reason for the most signal failures." So what these societies needed to do was to look for instructions and assistance from experts in design. In the words of the editors, "If the service of an expert is needed for the preparation of a creditable design for the improvement of private grounds, how much more is special training demanded when an entire town is to be treated with a view to the development of its landscape possibilities!"[47]

The rise of tourism in the late nineteenth century further encouraged planning for a better rural landscape. The "health, convenience, and taste" that *Garden and Forest* urged village improvement societies to seek were not merely to better the lives of rural inhabitants but also to satisfy urban tourists' requirements for comfort and pleasure. A more attractive rural landscape would benefit the rural economy. There was "a tangible business advantage to be gained by country villages when they are made specially attractive to city visitors; and this profit accrues not to the villages alone, but to all the surrounding region, when the farm-houses are open to paying occupation, and a market is provided for the products of the farm."[48]

The effort of *Garden and Forest* to integrate village improvement into a more modern and comprehensive movement was not futile. Even the organizers of village improvement showed signs of wanting to step out of the narrowness of their locality. A note appearing in the last volume of *Garden and Forest* in 1897 indicated that a member of the Laurel Hill association, the first village improvement society in Stockbridge, Massachusetts, desired "a combination between all similar societies in Berkshire County, or, if possible, in a still wider area, to work for rural improvements and for the preservation for public enjoyment of places of great natural beauty or historic interest." Still, although *Garden and Forest* intended to incorporate villages and their rural surroundings into its integrated landscape design, it did not try to impose uniformity on this landscape. In terms of the countryside, local identity and local ecology needed to be respected.[49]

In an editorial on establishing "county parks" in villages, *Garden and Forest* laid out more systematically its approach to rural improvement. First of all, it indicated that "grounds for associated recreation are quite as desirable in the country as in the city," although they were in some ways different. Iowa professor of botany Thomas H. Macbride had identified three justifications for the "county park"—as he termed it—especially important in western states. The first was that the conditions of rural life were even more monotonous than those in cities. Though farmers had intimate contact with nature every day, it came "in painful efforts to wrest a living from the land, to struggle against untoward conditions of climate and to fight for existence with other forms of life continually." Thus, a public park with picturesque scenery solely preserved for recreation would alter farmers' view of nature, encouraging them to appreciate the nature they always fought against. The second justification was that a well-kept county park "would be a perpetual object-lesson in the best means of preserving and enhancing the essential landscape beauty of any given area, and that this would suggest ways of making home-grounds attractive." By realizing the beauty of their homeland, local residents would find their own identity and dignity elevated as well.[50]

The third justification for the county park was the most interesting to *Garden and Forest* (and perhaps most inspiring to modern readers). In the long-settled eastern states, native flora and fauna had diminished severely, but in the West the original landscape could still be found on a large scale. It was urgent to prevent the native animals and plants from being wiped out. The editors cited Macbride's words: "such is the aggressive energy of our people, such their ambition to use profitably every foot of virgin soil, that unless somewhere public reserves be constituted our so-called civilization will soon have obliterated forever our natural wealth and leave us to the investigation of introduced species only or chiefly." It would be misleading to claim that Macbride was thinking in modern scientific terms of healthy and undisturbed ecosystems, but it is fair to argue that he and other Americans lamented the extermination of native flora and fauna and were eager to preserve them as part of an integrated landscape.[51]

The central purpose of this integrated design was to place nature under the regulation of civilization, but regulation could mean protection and preservation in addition to use and exploitation. It not only implied civilizing nature in creating urban parks and gardens but also maintaining nature's economy through safeguarding places where the mission of civilization should not be to humanize the wild but to defend the intactness and autonomy of nature against agricultural development. An orderly nature was desirable in and around the city, but a wilder nature was desirable elsewhere in the country.

The tame and the wild should not exist in completely separated spheres. Purism was not the *Garden and Forest* philosophy. Even in the most tamed garden, wild animals and weeds existed and should be tolerated, while in the wildest areas, traces of human influence could still be discerned. The fundamental difference between the two spheres was that, in the city, the controlling hand must be that of humankind, while outside the city it should be that of nature.

Social activists might complain that the passion for natural beauty that *Garden and Forest* tried to kindle was a middle- and upper-middle-class aesthetic fantasy that those groups tried to impose on the working class. And some wilderness enthusiasts might argue that the version of nature that *Garden and Forest* was constructing in cities was merely illusory or at least overly idealized. However, these enthusiasts could not deny that the work and concerns of these contributors were quite practical; they dealt directly with everyday realities, not abstract metaphors or theories. In the rows of street trees and the urban parks they created for a new American landscape, we can appreciate their well-conceived and pragmatic environmental logic. And the people from different social and education backgrounds who enjoyed this landscape might well agree that here too was a kind of justice.

6   DISTANT FORESTS

◦◦◦◦◦◦◦◦◦◦◦◦◦◦◦◦◦◦◦◦

TODAY, WHEN ONE LOOKS at a map of the United States, one can see extensive patches of green, from the Atlantic Coast to the Pacific, that represent the many national and state parks and national forests. Most of these green areas are located far away from such big cities as New York, Boston, Philadelphia, or Chicago. These green areas are sharply different from major urban areas and express what may seem very different values from those of cities. These seemingly remote and wild areas, however, exist in an interdependent relationship with those big cities. To a great extent, they were established because of the lobbying efforts of the same late-nineteenth-century environmental reformers who were living in cities and designing cityscapes.

Garden and Forest magazine, and particularly its editor and publisher Charles Sprague Sargent, played an important role in creating America's impressive system of forests and parks. Why was this magazine, based in the metropolises of Boston and New York and concerned mainly with urban environmental reform, so concerned about distant forests and wild lands? The answer is that the magazine editors believed that no matter how remotely located the natural hinterlands were, their fate was tied to that of the cities.[1]

In 1888, about the time that *Garden and Forest* was getting off the ground,

Sargent proposed a scheme for the management of forests in the American West. He recommended that the federal government withdraw all the public lands from entry and sale until a thorough survey had been made. He also wanted the US Army to become the guardians of those western forests and to begin preventing forest fires, livestock invasions, and illegal cutting and mining. He then urged Congress to organize a forest commission of experts to investigate the forests of the West; in his Adirondack forest commission report of 1885, he had proposed something similar for that eastern woodland area.

In 1891, President Benjamin Harrison established the first national forest reserves, covering about thirteen million acres, and Sargent and *Garden and Forest* rejoiced. Sargent thought that those reserves and their legislative mandate could substantially change American attitudes toward forests, but he was to be disappointed because no government agency would actively protect the newly established forest reserves. This outcome deepened his distrust of politics and further confirmed his view that only the army, an agency isolated from political pressures, could protect the nation's forests from all sorts of dangers. The successful stewardship of Yellowstone National Park by a small force of troops from the army provided a useful precedent. Meanwhile, Sargent and other conservation advocates, such as Gifford Pinchot and Robert Underwood Johnson, editor of *Century* magazine, intensified pressure on the government to make a thorough investigation of the condition of the western forests.[2]

Finally, their call penetrated the apathy of Washington, and, in 1896, Secretary of the Interior Michael Hoke Smith charged the National Academy of Science (NAS) with organizing a forest commission to survey the forests on the public domain of the West. The president of the academy thought immediately of Sargent and asked him to chair the commission. Other members included academy president Wolcott Gibbs (ex officio); William H. Brewer, a Yale botanist; Gen. Henry Abbott of the Army Corps of Engineers; Alexander Agassiz, a Harvard zoologist; Arnold Hague from the US Geological Survey; and Gifford Pinchot, who listed himself as a "practical forester." Later, Sargent invited John Muir to join them as an unofficial adviser.

Sargent had first become acquainted with Muir in 1893, when the California nature writer called on him at Holm Lea. The first mention of Muir's name in *Garden and Forest* was in 1889, when it appeared in a brief report on a group of outdoor enthusiasts who had climbed Mount Rainier; Muir was introduced as a "well-known student of the Cordilleran glaciers." In the following years, as *Garden and Forest* began paying more attention to national parks, Muir's name and views often appeared in its pages. When Stiles wrote an editorial on national parks, he referred to Muir's essay in *Century* magazine as being authoritative on the subject. Muir's visit to Sargent's home left a good impression on both men, and a friendship developed between the two.[3]

Muir might have been even more different from Sargent than Stiles was, for his enthusiasm for mountains in the wilderness was effusive and limitless. It is hard to evaluate to what extent Muir's passion for nature had penetrated the stubborn Harvard professor's reserved manner, but Muir's appreciation of trees in all their aspects certainly found resonance in Sargent's heart. In an editorial published in 1896, with the same title as Muir's first book, *The Mountains of California*, Sargent did not stint on complimenting Muir's book. He describe it as a "fascinating" work in which "Mr. John Muir tells this history and describes the forests, their trees, and several of the animals which live among them, speaking out of a full knowledge and with the feeling and affection of a devoted lover of nature. . . . No one has had such opportunities for studying the Sierras, or knows them so well; and no one, it may be said, has done so much to preserve their beauty by securing the establishment of the Sierra Forest Reservations." Sargent's pen drew Muir as a lonely figure roaming in California's mountains on a subsistence diet and "without a gun or any companion but his own thoughts." Then, at the beginning of July 1896, the two men met in Chicago and, as members of the new NAS forest commission, set out on a lengthy journey to inspect the western forests.[4]

This journey was the longest, hardest, but probably the most interesting and instructive Sargent ever made in western America. Lasting three months, the tour strengthened the connection between Muir and Sargent, but a conflict between Pinchot and Sargent began to take form. Sargent regarded Pinchot as the most promising forester in the nation, and Pinchot had looked on Sargent as a mentor. But this investigative journey led Pinchot to decide that Sargent's knowledge of forestry was suspect. He even disdained Sargent's judgment, believing that Sargent saw only "individual trees," not a "forest." Sargent, on the other hand, was annoyed by the younger man's cockiness; for almost two decades, Sargent had been praised as the leading authority on forest issues, and it was hard for him to tolerate any challenge, especially from a much younger person. So the suspicion was mutual. In his autobiography

Breaking New Ground, published in 1947, Pinchot was still complaining about Sargent's ignorance of economic forestry and of the report he submitted to the president.[5]

After they returned home, Pinchot urged Sargent to prepare the report as soon as possible so that they could submit it several months before the end of the Cleveland administration. Sargent had hurt his ankle badly, however, and needed time to recover. Then, on the day after Christmas, his Holm Lea mansion caught fire. When Sargent finally could sit down with the other members of the commission to discuss the report, it was already January 1897.

Led by Sargent, the commissioners recommended establishing thirteen more forest reserves, which would add more than twenty million acres to the existing reserves. On 22 February, President Cleveland approved their recommendation and issued an executive order to set the lands aside, but western members of Congress were infuriated, for they thought that the reserves would encumber the development of local economies. Led by Wyoming's Clarence Clark, the Senate passed an amendment that would in effect reopen the reserves to use. *Garden and Forest* raged that "the Senate, deceived by the false statements of the representatives of western mining and lumber companies who became the champions of this amendment, passed it without hearing a single word of protest." Cleveland left office on 4 March, leaving the status of the reserves unsettled.[6]

At first, the new Republican president William McKinley seemed to offer hope to the commission and its expanded reserves. However, Sargent soon found out that McKinley was ready to please Congress by revoking the new reserves. Sargent "explained to him [McKinley] that the President of the United States could not afford to put himself in the position of helping western timber thieves." McKinley ignored the warning and suspended all the newly established reserves, except for two in California, although the suspension was supposed to last only seven months.[7]

For Sargent, his job with the commission was at an end. Although not completely satisfied, he had expected a worse outcome. For Pinchot, the forest issue was not settled; he wanted much more for himself and his profession of civilian foresters than public forests placed in the hands of the US Army. Several days after he signed the report, Pinchot accepted an appointment as a special forest adviser to Cornelius Bliss, the secretary of the interior, who proceeded to set the report aside. Sargent was shocked and felt betrayed by the young man he had supported and advised for almost a decade. In his letter to Pinchot's tutor, the German forester Dietrich Brandis, Sargent accused Pinchot of throwing over "his old friends for immediate political position." He refused Pinchot's gesture of reconciliation and wrote a harsh letter to him: "different persons have different standards which govern their conduct and yours and mine are evidently so unlike that it is useless to discuss the subject of your letter on April 16th."[8]

The 15 December 1897 issue of *Garden and Forest* discussed forestry for the last time before the magazine ceased publication. Sargent wrote a piece protesting Pinchot's stance and his idea of putting the reserves in the hands of civilians: "the experience of the last twenty-five years has shown what the civil agents of the Interior Department can accomplish in protecting the property of the Government, and the utter futility of trying to enforce the laws of Congress and the regulations of the Department without the aid of soldiers, who have shown over and over again their ability to protect successfully and economically forests in the national parks from fire and pillage after the civil officers of the Interior Department had proved themselves entirely incapable of effective action." In a letter to Muir, who supported Sargent's position and was likewise suspicious of Pinchot's personal ambitions to gain power, Sargent asked, "What are we going to do about forestry matters?" He did not want to "sit idly and allow Bliss and his crowd to exterminate them [forests]," but he had no idea how to form a defense. Stiles's death made him lose his "best hold on the New York Papers," and the cessation of *Garden and Forest* as a magazine left him with no way to "have any satisfactory way of reaching the public."[9]

OVER THE NEXT few years, and indeed throughout the twentieth century, the conservation movement fragmented into warring camps. On one side were those who emphasized the preservation of natural beauty (the disciples of Muir), and on the other were those who advocated the "wise use" of natural resources (the disciples of Pinchot). This split was not apparent in the pages of *Garden and Forest* before its demise. On the contrary, the magazine stood for a unified outlook that promoted both the practice of scientific forestry and the protection of natural beauty. Forestry saved trees, and trees preserved natural beauty. Both kinds of conservation were good, and the editors believed the two approaches should exist in harmony.

However, among the *Garden and Forest* stable of forest writers, who included the most knowledgeable experts in the United States, there were tensions that would one day erupt into conflict. Chief among those writers were Bernhard E. Fernow and Gifford Pinchot. Fernow had been born in 1851 to an aristocratic family in Prussia and entered the forest service at the age of nineteen. After a year, he passed the entrance examination required for enrollment in a famous forestry academy at Muenden in western Prussia. It took him seven years to acquire a forester's license, but at last it seemed that he had a promising future in his field and a huge estate to inherit and run. Then an unforeseen romance with a young American woman pulled him away from that designated role. In 1876, he followed his love, departing from the nation with probably the best forestry system in the world and arriving in a nation where people were still felling trees excessively and wantonly. He settled down in Brooklyn, New York.[10]

When Fernow arrived in the United States in 1876, the nation offered almost no opportunities for a professional forester. However, that year did see Franklin B. Hough appointed a special forestry agent in the US Agriculture Department, and ten years later, in 1886, Fernow became the third chief of the federal Division of Forestry, succeeding Hough and Nathaniel Egleston. He soon became a contributor to *Garden and Forest*. Editor Stiles published forty of Fernow's articles, which discussed the general issues of American forest administration and the relationship between the forest and the natural and social economy. His articles also described the European forestry system and dealt with some more specific forest problems, such as the economic value of white pines, the danger of forest insects, and the planting and thinning of trees. Fernow's view of forest management seemed thoroughly compatible with the magazine's overall goal of promoting conservation among its mainly urban readers.

In one *Garden and Forest* article, Fernow wrote, "We will have to start with a simple, commonsense management, and will have to leave the development of better forestry methods to future years, providing only the opportunity of gaining necessary knowledge and experience for the best results." Despite some conflict between Fernow and Sargent, they agreed that the time was not yet right for the country to develop a real forestry system; the work for their generation was to accumulate knowledge and arouse in later generations public sympathy for forest issues. In a letter to young Gifford Pinchot, Sargent acknowledged the progress they had made on forestry issues and predicted the establishment of a national system, but at the same time, he stated rather cautiously that "whether you and I are going to live to see it is another matter; and, in the meantime, all we can do is to accumulate information and fit ourselves as far as possible for useful work, if the opportunity ever comes to us to do it." This modest goal guided the work of *Garden and Forest* in general. Such information gathering was meant to introduce the concept and practice of forestry as it had developed in European countries and to establish forestry as a profession in the United States.[11]

In Sargent's eyes, Gifford Pinchot was the most gifted forester who could help lead the profession. Born in 1865, Pinchot was equipped with every advantage to become a conservation leader. His family was rich and influential, his strong-minded father was supportive, and his education was impeccable. Personally, Pinchot was shrewd and extremely energetic; he had cultivated a love of nature and outdoor activities since he was a boy, and he put his nation's conservation above everything else. When he was a senior at Yale, Pinchot called upon Fernow, Sargent, and some other important figures advocating forest conservation. Although their view of the promise of the new profession was not optimistic, young Pinchot's determination was not shaken.

After graduating from the forestry school in Nancy, France, Pinchot returned home to the United States to promote the wise use of the nation's important forest resources.[12] Among his supporters was Sargent, who encouraged Pinchot to write for *Garden and Forest*, because it would "have the effect of bringing you to the notice of people in this country interested in forests and forest management, and so perhaps pave the way for something for you in the future." Pinchot, on the other hand, was aware of the significance of *Garden and Forest* among environmental thinkers, for even in Nancy, "as a forester, I studied *Garden and Forest* and the *Mississippi Valley Lumberman*," although the two publications took opposite sides on the issues. Pinchot accepted Sargent's invitation happily and published his first work—a three-part series of articles entitled "The Shilwald" in July 1890, thus introducing the Swiss forestry program to the readers of *Garden and Forest*.[13]

As a fledgling expert, Pinchot thought that Stiles had "uncommon knowledge of what American forestry should mean, and where it ought to be headed. Then and later I gathered much wisdom and encouragement from him, as he . . . let his broad common sense illumine whatever he happened to be talking about. It was a most serious loss when he died and *Garden and Forest* died with him." Although occupied by many other things, Pinchot wrote thirteen articles for *Garden and Forest*, the first in 1890.[14]

In 1895, portions of an address Pinchot gave before a farmers' group were published in *Garden and Forest* as "The Need of Forest Schools of America." In it, he offered a narrow but clear definition of forestry. He saw the purpose of forestry as twofold: first, to maintain the balance of nature's economy, such as soil and rivers, and "to insure a second, and usually a greater, crop of at least equally valuable material. Except in rare instances, to do this is the surest way to secure the preservation of the indirect influences of the forest as they regard water and climate." He added to that general definition what would become a more controversial and dogmatic opinion: "That wise forest-management secures the natural beauty of a region devoted to it is a fortunate accident, but none the less an accident, pure and simple. The purpose of forestry is in a totally different sphere," a utilitarian sphere.[15]

After deserting Sargent on the forest reserve issue, Pinchot replaced Fernow in the Division of Forestry, becoming its fourth chief in 1898. Then in 1905, backed by an equally enthusiastic conservationist, President Theodore Roosevelt, he established the US Forest Service and became its first chief.

Overshadowed by Fernow and Pinchot, both in forestry circles and in the pages of *Garden and Forest*, was another German immigrant, Carl Schenck. He was three years younger than Pinchot and had received his PhD summa cum laude from the University of Giessen. Compared to Pinchot, Schenck paid more attention to the ecological consequences of forestry. For *Garden and Forest*, he wrote a four-part series, "Private Forestry and State Forestry," published in 1897. In those essays, he pointed out that, while primarily financial considerations guided private forestry, public or state forestry had to take into account both the human economy and nature's economy, especially the latter, for it was associated with the long-term prosperity of the commonwealth. In many regions, the value of forests "in the economy of mankind is less than their value in the economy of nature." More than either Fernow or Pinchot, Schenck urged caution in cutting trees. He argued that the "golden rule" of forestry was to "be quick in securing forests, firm in protecting and slow in using them," and he would not "advise, in general, any haste in harvesting tree-growth from the state [i.e., government-owned] forests."[16]

A bigger difference between Pinchot and Schenck, however, was in their understanding of American society. In *Breaking New Ground*, Pinchot complained that Schenck, "being a German with official training, . . . had far less understanding of the mountaineers than he had of the mountains and the woods. He thought of them as peasants. They thought of themselves as independent American citizens—and, of course, they were right." In fact, it did not take long for Schenck to recognize the social differences between democratic America and aristocratic Germany. In one of his essays for *Garden and Forest*, Schenck wrote, "In this country the principle of individual freedom will long prevent the passing of laws similar to the forest laws of Europe. Entailed forest property is still an impossibility." After staying in the United States for almost two decades, he went back to Germany to fight for his homeland during World War I.[17]

Garden and Forest encouraged others, not just forestry experts, to write about forest issues. Partly because Sargent had not been trained as a forester, he had more interest in the noneconomic side of trees and in the forest's ecological functions—and more distrust of politics and politicians. He tried to maintain comprehensiveness in the discussion of forest issues lest the subject become narrowed and dominated by professional foresters. To this end, he recruited various other figures to write on this subject, and most of them were botanists or horticulturists, such as William Beal, Louis Pammel, Robert Douglas from Waukegan, Illinois, and J. D. W. French from Boston, Massachusetts. The most influential nonforester he recruited was Jonathan Baxter Harrison, a Unitarian minister and journalist from Ohio.

Harrison was born in a log cabin in Greene County, Ohio, in 1835. His social and educational background was completely different from that of most contributors to the magazine. In a letter to Charles E. Norton, the prestigious Harvard scholar and educator, he explained, "My father has always been very poor and I have gone to school very little since I was ten years old. From twelve to twenty I worked at clearing land, raising corn, and hiring out by the month much of the time. We lived in the backwoods. When at home I studied some at night by firelight," because his parents could not afford candles. Growing up in this humble environment, Harrison conceived of society in a populist way for the rest of his life.[18]

In 1862, Harrison's articles in *The Students' Responsibility*, a magazine published by a Quaker school for black Americans, captured the attention of

Charles E. Norton, who was then editing *Broadsides* and the *North American Review*. A lifelong friendship and mentor-pupil relationship developed between the elite Bostonian and the Ohio backwoods youth. Norton persuaded Harrison to convert from Methodism to Unitarianism. The youth then moved eastward to be closer to his mentor and to search for financial security. He preached in Unitarian churches in New Jersey and later in Franklin Falls, New Hampshire, where he lived until his death in 1907. Meanwhile, he continued his journalistic career, and his talent in writing was further stimulated by Norton's encouragement and his own experience. In the late 1870s, he published a group of essays on working-class living conditions and environment in the *Atlantic Monthly*. Later, in 1880, Harrison headed toward the South with a mission to observe and report objectively on ordinary southern people's lives and thought. Besides observing social and political aspects of life in the South, Harrison closely recorded the agricultural situation, especially the depletion of the soil by cotton monoculture and the general failure to rotate crops, apply fertilizer, and regularly permit fields to lie fallow, all good agricultural practices.

In 1882, when Norton and Olmsted were collaborating on preserving Niagara Falls, Harrison was recruited to write a series of essays to arouse public sympathy for the famous natural landmark. His articles, which first appeared as eight letters in the *New York Evening Post*, the *New York Tribune*, and the *Boston Daily Advertiser* during the summer of 1882, were considered among the most important reasons for the success of the Niagara campaign. Later, they were compiled into a pamphlet entitled *The Condition of Niagara Falls, and the Measures Needed to Preserve Them*. In these essays, Harrison celebrated the natural beauty of Niagara Falls, denounced the "vandalism" that was defacing them, and lobbied the New York legislature to establish a state reservation to preserve the wildness of this natural miracle for people in the present and future. Both the aesthetic value and the social ideal expressed in these articles were consistent with Olmsted's. Then, in 1885, Harrison and Olmsted became allies in the movement to conserve the Adirondack forest, and the newspaper articles written by the former were later published in the booklet *The Adirondack Forest and the Problem of the Great Natural Waterways of the State of New York*.

Later, Harrison began a survey of various towns along the Massachusetts coastline, trying to identify "to what places on the shore the public had a right to resort and what further provision was needed in this direction." His sponsor was the Trustees of Reservations, and the survey became a seven-part series in *Garden and Forest* from 1891 to 1892. Besides inspecting the situation of public parks, town commons, and other land, he paid close attention to the living conditions of the local people. In one of the essays, he described a town called Mashpee, which had a considerable population of native Americans. He expressed a sympathetic and even admiring attitude toward these aboriginal inhabitants: "Before 1834 there was a reservation here, managed by the commonwealth, and the Indians were oppressed and depressed much as Indians usually have been in this country. But since 1834 the people here have constituted a town, with the same organization and relations to the state which other towns possess. These Indian people are poor, and they appear to have more public spirit than the average white people of this country."[19]

If Stiles was the one Olmsted enlisted to defend urban parks, Harrison became the eloquent spokesman Olmsted enlisted to defend wild natural beauty and resources outside cities.[20] To a great extent, Stiles's and Harrison's lives were very similar. They both had pursued careers in journalism, and both had shown talent and drive in reforming public opinion through the pen. They were both religious and, at the same time, were fascinated with nature's aesthetic and spiritual elements. They were both strong supporters of democracy and devoted to the public good. They both had deep interest in scientific agriculture, horticulture, and forestry and were confident about improving the natural and social environment through the rational use of new tools and techniques. Interestingly, they were both described by their friends as Abraham Lincoln–like figures, probably because of their lanky appearance and, more importantly, their concern for ordinary people. All of these commonalities led to their harmonious cooperation in *Garden and Forest*.

Harrison contributed thirty-two articles to *Garden and Forest*, most of them on national and regional forest issues, with a particular focus on forests in the northeastern states. He knew the issues because he had become secretary of the American Forestry Congress. In these essays, Harrison argued that healthy forests promoted the progress of civilization. Like other contributors to the magazine, he urged the application of scientific knowledge to forests and government control of public land, but he paid particular attention to the relationship between the welfare of farmers and the implementation of forestry.

Reflecting the writings of these influential contributors, *Garden and Forest* tended to emphasize the economic value of forests more than their spiritual or aesthetic significance. Even so enthusiastic an advocate of natural beauty as J. B. Harrison wrote, "Nothing could be more absurd than the notion that trees should never be utilized or removed. Whenever a tree has come to its best [condition] it should be cut down, and its wood applied to some useful purpose, so as to obtain its value, and in order to provide for a succession of generations of trees, and thus for the permanent life of the forest."[21]

In its very first article on forests, the magazine put economics at the center, just as Fernow and Pinchot wanted: "The forests of the United States play an important part in the economy of the nation. Their annual product far exceeds in value any of our great staple crops of the field. The gold and silver mined in the country is insignificant in value compared with the money value of the forest crop. It is difficult to picture the commercial and agricultural ruin which would follow any general disturbance of the productive capacity of our forests."[22] Over the next several years, the magazine pursued this argument persistently, though not exclusively. The "tree crop," the magazine repeatedly showed, was relevant to every corner of industrial society. The ties needed for holding the rails together, the fuel used in factories and mines, the raw materials for houses, furniture, paper, and almost all sorts of industries, in cities and villages, all came from the forests. "The forest primeval," Bernhard Fernow wrote, "is our most valuable inheritance. It is the ready cash of nature's bountiful provision for our future." This value became more significant when it was clear that people could not replace timber with anything else, and if forests were gone, "no other country could supply us with the material we should thus lose."[23]

On 14 September 1894, the constitutional convention of New York State passed an amendment related to the state's forests. "The lands of the state," read the amendment, "now owned or hereafter acquired, constituting the forest-preserve, as now fixed by law, shall be forever kept as wild forest-lands. They shall not be leased, sold or exchanged, or be taken by any corporation, public or private, nor shall the timber thereon be sold, removed or destroyed." Despite having fought assiduously for preserving the forests and their beauty and wildness in New York State since the beginning of the magazine's existence, the editors of *Garden and Forest* did not feel exhilarated after they read those words. They admitted that this amendment demonstrated an increasing interest in forest issues among policy makers in the state capital at Albany, but at the same time they worried that its adoption pushed forest policy in that

state from one extreme to another. According to *Garden and Forest*, the indis-
criminate prohibition on use was the same sort of "actual and reprehensible
waste" as out-and-out abuse.[24]

The editors argued that the amendment demonstrated "a serious miscon-
ception of the true relation of the forest to civilized society," for it not only
denied the value of rational scientific forest management in improving forests
but also underestimated people's capacity to adopt and follow a wise system
of forestry practice. "Under proper management," the editors wrote, "a forest
can yield its products which are indispensable to civilized men, and can even
grow in productiveness every year, while its beneficent influences on soil,
climate and water-supply will remain wholly unimpaired." Under balanced
management the New York forests might become "an object-lesson in forest
economy for the whole country."[25]

Thus, forestry was not a "tree-hugger's" cult but "a branch of agriculture"
in which trees were a crop. Forestry saved forests, but "they must be saved for
use." Landscape architects were not foresters, no matter how familiar they
were with trees. They planted trees for the sake of beauty, while the foresters
planted them "for profit of a more tangible character." The editors summarized
the definition of forestry in two sentences: "Forestry is the art of maintaining
and perpetuating forests. It is successful in proportion as the forest yields the
largest annual income in perpetuity." Using Pinchot's words, trained foresters
regarded the forest as "a great working capital whose function it is to produce interest, and which does not need to be destroyed in the process." By
looking at the forest in this way, Pinchot was convinced that forestry would
be removed "from the anomalous and often illogical position into which the
mistaken zeal of some of its friends has forced it, and [would] ground its roots
in the solid earth of business common sense."[26]

The utilitarian orientation of forestry had been emphasized in *Garden and
Forest* before the nation's top newspapers and magazines began to address the
topic and before Pinchot rose to be a shining star on the nation's political
stage. It is worth noting that this utilitarian attitude focused on the welfare
of the entire nation, not just one individual or one family. The logic behind
it was clear: when the public welfare was secure, the individual profit would
be secure, too. Forestry considered not only the money directly earned from
timber sales but also the indirect revenue that the protection of forests would

generate from agriculture, industry, tourism, and commerce. According to the editors, "The value of mountain forests, and the necessity of maintaining forest-conditions permanently on lands around the sources of mountain streams, are most vital and important features of scientific and practical forestry." Therefore, American forests should not be considered simply money-producing machines.[27]

If forests played a vital part in the regional and national economy, they were especially important for farmers. Yet farmers were seemingly indifferent to that importance and concentrated instead on inflating the money supply as a panacea for all their ills. In an editorial published in 1891, the magazine agreed with Carl Schurz, former secretary of the interior, who argued that the "discussions of tariff and currency and other economic problems might be postponed to some future day, for mistakes in this direction might be rectified by a change of system, and the losses incurred might be retrieved." A more important crisis than the money supply was the disappearance of the nation's forests. Those individuals "who imagine that the free coinage of silver will bring prosperity to them" should see that planting trees offered a more direct and promising remedy for their problems. Thus, the magazine suggested "the diffusion of knowledge and propagation of sound and practical ideas regarding the care of farm woodlands, and the value of timber as a permanent crop, should be a prominent feature of the work of the Granges and other organizations of farmers."[28]

The decline of agriculture across New England had demonstrated that an aggressive harvesting of trees could be profitable only temporarily; in the long run, it would be destructive to the soil and the farmers themselves. "Our agricultural population cannot always continue to go west," the editors warned, and the increasing population sooner or later would have to inhabit the once-abandoned lands east of the Mississippi. Meanwhile, they pointed out that the western states, instead of repeating the mistakes of the East, should learn a lesson from what happened there. In "Farmers and Forestry," the editors stated that "the precepts which should be often repeated to farmers are not that trees produce rain or that trees are sacred objects, which cannot be cut without offense to man and nature." Instead, farmers should be taught to see trees as a crop with money value and to follow the laws of nature for their own benefit. The magazine noted that "wood-lands can only be made profitable when the same care is given to the selection of trees with reference to soil and climate as is bestowed upon the selection of grain and other crops, and that the rules which Nature has established for the perpetuation of forests must be studied and obeyed."[29]

This long-term economic value of forests was not the only lesson for people to learn. The magazine editors wanted readers to see that a living forest had value far beyond a pile of cut trees. What most concerned the editors and contributors of *Garden and Forest* was the relationship between forests and the flow of rivers. They believed this relationship was crucial everywhere but was particularly important in the West, where the supply of water was limited and yet vital to transforming the desert into a productive garden.[30]

In "Mountain Reservoirs and Irrigation," the editors, not immune to visions of human-produced abundance, celebrated the vast changes brought by irrigation. When "an arid and barren waste" was transformed into "a fruitful and populous land" by the magic of water, "vital feelings of delight" were awakened. They exulted in the introduction of irrigation to the arid region as one of the greatest "original creative" powers that human beings had ever exercised. "As the life-giving water invades, conquers and possesses the country," the editors hailed, "its progress is like the march of a triumphant and liberating army, but there is no death or suffering or destruction in the gentle and pervading flow. It brings verdure, beauty and fruitfulness everywhere, and makes the desert to rejoice and blossom as the rose."[31]

This productive garden required the protection of the wild forests in the western mountains. Rivers and streams with their headwaters in the mountains were the major source of artificial irrigation, and the mountain forests constituted "the natural reservoirs for the storage of the water which sustains these rivers with equable flow through the whole year." The forests created a sponge "composed of root-fibers, leaf-mould and decaying vegetable matter," holding the soil and slowing down the process of evaporation. "If the forests which cover the mountains are destroyed the snow will melt more rapidly than it does at present, and the water will seek the valleys, not gradually, but suddenly and rapidly," the editors warned. The rivers would be converted into torrents every spring and summer, and the water needed for irrigation would be "wasted," flushing soil and rocks from high mountain slopes down into valleys, which "sooner or later, will be buried past redemption." "The extinction of the mountain forests," the editors summarized, "results in the destruction of the mountains themselves, and in that of the streams which have their sources in them."[32]

This value of forests as natural reservoirs could not be counted in dollars and cents. "The progress and development of many portions of the Pacific states depends [sic] almost entirely upon their water supply; so much so that a failure of this supply would paralyze all industry and involve the entire section in bankruptcy," the editors wrote. And the fate of mountain forests would "determine the future of vast areas in the western part of our country, whether they shall be fertile, populous and prosperous, or irreclaimably barren, and, in large degree, uninhabitable."[33]

If progress in the West at the time mainly referred to improved agricultural harvests, in the East it connoted the flourishing of industry and the growth of cities. For this region, too, the magazine extolled the value of forests as natural reservoirs. In New England in 1896, when a flood of the Merrimack River swept the valley, jeopardizing a newly repaired dam and "compelling the factories to stop work and leaving six thousand operatives without employment," the editors worried about forest protection in this industrial landscape. They endorsed the words of T. Jefferson Coolidge, treasurer of the Amoskeag Manufacturing Company, that the major cause of the flood and the consequent catastrophe was the denudation of the land at the headwaters of the Pemigewasset and other tributaries of the Merrimack. In an editorial, they directed their readers' attention to an essay written by historian Francis Parkman in 1888 on forests in the White Mountains. "The subject [the relationship of the Merrimack River and the forests] is," Parkman criticized, "one of the last importance to the mill-owners along these rivers," thus implying that mill owners preferred not to think about what effect their industry might have on the river and other elements of the local environment.[34]

Throughout its existence, *Garden and Forest* devoted many pages to the relationship between headwaters and forests in the northeastern part of the nation. In the Adirondacks, the editors claimed, "all other questions regarding the North Woods are unimportant in comparison with that relating to the water supply." This issue had "national importance," for "one of the principal commercial rivers of the world depends upon these forests for its existence." On the New Jersey side of the Delaware River, valleys were in danger of being ruined by floods after forests had been removed. In its pages, *Garden and Forest* listed cold but clear facts about the vital necessity of protecting headwater forests, while carefully describing the desolation and loss that followed forest damage, sympathizing with local people who suffered as a result, but sharply criticizing their ignorance and shortsightedness.[35]

Therefore, the magazine editors believed that, for the sake of the country's general economic growth, there was an urgent need to establish the practice of scientific forestry in the United States. *Garden and Forest* argued that proper forestry required two critical elements. First, the forester must have adequate scientific knowledge of forests and economics, that is, knowledge of how both nature and the economy functioned. People could make forests continuously productive by "adapting natural process to the use of man." By cutting, culling, thinning, sowing, and other related actions, the forester could avoid the waste generated by nature and meet human needs better. Merely possessing knowledge was not enough, however. The forester must be skilled in business as well, for "he has the handling of large capital invested in wood production."[36]

The second prerequisite for proper forestry would be wise foresight. This aspect was the primary concern of the editors and contributors of *Garden and Forest*, for they believed that this quality was in short supply in their nation. The reckless clearing of forests prevalent all over the nation showed no consideration for future generations or the well-being of civilization in the future. In contrast, foresight in forestry, according to Pinchot, rested on two "self-evident truths": "(1) that trees require many years to reach merchantable size; and (2) that a forest-crop cannot be taken every year from the same land." These truths pointed the way to patience and self-discipline.[37]

If these two conditions were met, the editors and contributors of *Garden and Forest* believed there was hope of achieving the ultimate goal of forestry in the United States: the perpetuation and increasing productivity of forests. Because of the lessons they learned from what had occurred in Europe, however, they were aware that without the intervention of government, all their efforts would be in vain. Fernow pointed out that "all European governments, without exception, have felt themselves in duty bound to encourage and aid proper forest management and all efforts at reforestation." Laissez-faire policy might be good in some pursuits, but not in the protection and use of forests, which needed government regulation and legislation. Especially in the United States, the federal government still possessed a vast amount of forestland; thus, it could not shirk its responsibility for managing this national resource. According to Pinchot, "This principle, special to no country or form of government, holds that 'the state is the guardian of all public interests.'"[38]

There were two major reasons for governments, but especially the federal government, to accept responsibility for forest protection. One centered on time, and the other emphasized scope. Compared to the life span of a forest, an individual's life is rather limited. Success in conservation meant not only the permanent growth of forests but also a stable and uninterrupted forestry policy. This permanency, according to *Garden and Forest*, could be sustained only by a relatively unlimited and durable agent like a stable government. Nathaniel Egleston, former chief of the Division of Forestry, wrote, "What is needed in our country, therefore, for the most successful dealing with trees in masses, with forests, is a personality whose life is as lasting as that of the trees themselves. The nation is such a personality." Although actually no form of government would last indefinitely, the state seemed longer lived and more reliable than any individual.[39]

An investment in forestry takes much longer to produce a return than most other types of investment. In the editorial "What Is Forestry?" the editors wrote, "A forest crop may take from one to three centuries to come to maturity. During all this period, if it is to earn a fair return, it must be managed consistently under a plan made before the seeds are sown and intended to cover every operation in the forest, including its regeneration when the original trees have passed to the saw-mill." For most individual owners, a quick profit was what they expected and needed. Neither their financial power nor their self-interest would equip them with enough patience and foresight to prevent them from brandishing the ax when it was not the proper time. The consequence was the ruin of forests. The basic idea was that government was less influenced by financial pressure and thus could more easily maintain a coherent policy on forests.[40]

An equally important reason why government control seemed to promise greater protection for forests was the broad scope of forests in terms of geography and social impact. Geographically, many forests extended across whole states and beyond; thus, the interest and impacts associated with them exceeded the boundaries of cities, counties, and even states. Especially in the West, a vast extent of forestland was officially in the public domain. Western forests were the property of the nation; they "do not belong to the public-land states, nor do they belong to any one section; moreover, they do not belong to any class." The *Garden and Forest* editors summed up the case for government: "In the settlement of this forest-question is the opportunity for the display of broad and enlightened statesmanship; there is no place in it for local jealousies or for the gratification of selfish or sordid ambitions. Its settlement will mean the stability and permanent prosperity of an important section of the country, and, what is of even greater importance, it will mean that the people of the United States have attained to that degree of intelligence and long-sightedness which indicate a high condition of civilization." Thus, a federal forest program should improve the welfare of everyone in the nation at the present and in the future.[41]

The need for responsible protection of forests, presumably by the government, existed in the East as well as the West, although eastern forests had largely become private property. Here, the magazine suggested, state governments should acquire ownership of forests through purchase as soon as possible, and lands the states did not own they could regulate through legislation. The laws should restrain irresponsible acts, like the intrusion of railroads into forest lands or destructive clear-cutting by timber companies.

The Adirondacks, to take one example, could never be safe "unless they are controlled by the state working under a permanent policy." The magazine proposed that New York State should buy the land and establish "a State Park to contain some three million acres, embracing the head waters of all the streams of consequence which take their rise in the wilderness." The editors saw the same necessity in the White Mountains, whose forests were in danger because private corporations had bought them "for the purpose of converting them as quickly and advantageously as possible into money without reference to the future results of their operations." Thus, the editors advised, "the best investment the State of New Hampshire can make would be to buy up all this forest-region and hold it perpetually as a forest-reservation." The core of all these propositions, laws, and purchases, in the West and the East, was "to ensure equal rights and uniform privileges without any discrimination as to localities or industries."[42]

Still, the magazine editors knew that "laws alone cannot save our forests." In "The Future of Our Forests," they wrote, "Americans are impatient of any restraint or interference in the management of their property." Thus, while pushing government to take responsibility, the editors and contributors were aware that a lasting solution required public enlightenment followed by public support: "Americans need important and radical changes in the thought and spirit and character of our people. While the popular feeling about wealth, about bric-a-brac, about the objects of life remains what it is, the destruction of our forests, and of all that depends upon them, is likely to proceed unchecked." The law would be to no avail unless "a general and intelligent appreciation of the value of our forests" was achieved.[43]

Thus, a spirit of public-mindedness was equally necessary to forestry. The editors and contributors of *Garden and Forest* clearly saw that the ideal of individual freedom was almost impossible to shake in their nation, so they felt it was particularly important to arouse a countervailing public spirit. Many essays of the magazine were devoted to this goal; they indicated that the tragedies caused by the devastation of forests endangered not only future generations but also, more pertinently, the present generation. And the careless and ignorant actions of individuals exerted on a forest would not only bring "an injury to themselves, personally, but to the whole community" and to the people whose names they had never even heard. Only if the public spirit was awakened could there be any hope that forestry would be implemented in this nation.[44]

In an editorial discussing the prevention of forest fires, the editors urged the use of a simple solution to stop this most destructive agent: "First, inspire every person with a deeper love for his country. Second, teach him the proper use of fire by showing the danger of its misuse." They went on to indicate that "the sum of the matter is that legislation is ineffective unless supported by the sentiments and the acts of the people." In another essay, one advocating the regulation of fire by individual land owners, the editor wrote, "Freedom is but one side of life in civilized lands. Order and law are quite as necessary, and they subserve the interests of all." Even though the editors did not yet have a well-defined awareness of the modern conclusion that periodic forest fires actually promote the long-term health of the forest ecosystem, they nevertheless promoted the same principles of public self-restraint and care that the later environmental reformers did.[45]

In fact, the producers of *Garden and Forest* thought public education and action would be the appropriate way to tackle all environmental issues. In the editors' view, the public should first cultivate a national identity, breaking the boundary of narrow individualism and regionalism and thus making people care more about public welfare and future generations in a broad sense. The second thing the public needed was some knowledge and sentiment about nature; by having respect for and a connection to nature, people would understand the necessity of protecting forests and would respect the laws of nature. In the United States, the magazine admitted, these two crucial elements were not yet strong enough to forge a better relationship between human beings and nature.

The political implications of the new conservation ethic were profound and involved the core of the American ethos. In his important "Forests and Civilization" series of essays in *Garden and Forest*, Jonathan B. Harrison declared, "A nation should be a vital unity—a population organized for intelligent co-operation for the attainment of worthy practical ideals. The sentiment of nationality, or what is called by that name in our country, is still superficial and indefinite, with little vital relation to the present time, and our national life is in great degree inorganic, made up of scattered nuclei, and without common direction. We are wanting in some of the elements which are necessary to the persistence of national individuality." In *Garden and Forest*'s viewpoint, the lack of a sense of "national individuality" was a moral defect that could doom the nation's forests and its civilization. People usually placed individual and local interest ahead of the national one, and they confined their "public spirit" to their own local community, thus neglecting the national welfare and stifling the federal government.[46]

This was especially true in the West. When politicians and local newspapers from that region jumped to the defense of their forest interests and condemned the tyrannical hand of the East, the editors of *Garden and Forest* reminded them that "the forest reservations cannot be used exclusively for any particular class of the community; they belong as much to the east and to the south as they do to the west. They are part of the public domain, and it is for the interest of the whole country that they should belong to the nation." The magazine reassured readers that no local interest would be injured in practicing forestry. On the contrary, if nothing were done before the national forests vanished, the local inhabitants would be the greatest victims of a national catastrophe.[47]

If on the issue of the urban environment the magazine tended to evoke local pride and attachment among readers, on the issue of national forests it attempted to evoke a more nationalistic spirit. Ultimately, there was no conflict between local and national interests. They were both needed in an urbanized society. A stronger local attachment aimed to restore the lost physical and psychological intimacy between humans and the land under their feet; this type of intimacy emphasized a more aesthetic and spiritual sense. In fact, it was a more universal and inclusive sentiment, not confined to any time, district, class, or race. A patriotic spirit, in contrast, became important when the expanding web of markets and transportation tied all aspects of the nation—industry, agriculture, nature, and culture—closer together. Neither individual persons nor districts could secure their interests when the nation's future was in danger. Developing a patriotic sense of attachment to the nation's natural aspect entailed a more comprehensive type of thinking, which involved politics, economy, class, and nature. If the former (the personal sense of intimacy with nature) was more intuitive, the latter (the patriotic sense) needed to be cultivated.

In addition to believing that the public needed something like moral enlightenment regarding nature, the editors thought that scientific knowledge about trees and their relationship with the soil, water, and climate should be "domesticated," that is, "made at home—in the minds of the people," because "opinions which have no basis of knowledge are of slight value—are, indeed, hardly worthy of the name." People should "think about trees, talk about them, read about them, write about them, until there is a tree-feeling in the air, and such a reverberation of sensible and practical teaching on the subject as will compel general attention." With sufficient general knowledge of forests, the best use of them would be widely practiced, the need of scientific forestry would be felt, and the many values of forests would be appreciated.[48]

The editors foresaw that "when we come as a people to know and appreciate and love trees we shall learn to love forests, too; and once loving them, we shall appreciate their value, and efforts to preserve and maintain them and make them useful and productive for all time will then be a comparatively easy task." Once scientific knowledge combined with affectionate sentiment among the public, especially the children, the editors and contributors of *Garden and Forest* believed, a new age of forest conservation would truly arrive. In this age, they expected that all the values of forests would be emphasized and realized.[49]

WHEN BOTH SCIENTIFIC understanding and love of forests were more fully developed, the value of the forest would not be viewed merely in utilitarian terms. With this more enlightened public perception, the ecological and aesthetic values of the forests would also be secure. Compared to the more divisive conservation program Pinchot later pushed, *Garden and Forest*'s endeavor was the last to incorporate all the values of forests into one broad and unifying scheme. As discussed earlier, Sargent himself was not a professional forester. Even though he was aware of the productive side of the forest and tried hard to apply the novel jargon of the new profession (e.g., phrases like "tree crops"), his perception of the forest essentially followed that of his mentor—George Perkins Marsh, who believed that forests played a complex role in nature's economy, especially in protecting hydrological systems.

Another ecological chain, which emphasized the forest as habitat for diverse fauna, was also discussed in the magazine. As a magazine centered on plants, *Garden and Forest* paid less attention to wildlife, but that silence did not mean it was indifferent to animals. In their discussions of forest values, the magazine editors and contributors saw forests as the irreplaceable home for big and small game and fish. In his essay on the value of mountain forests, Harrison wrote, "As a part of this sanitary function of mountain forests, their value as natural preserves for fish and game deserves far more serious and intelligent attention than it generally receives." Once forests were destroyed, the game and fish would be deprived of their habitats and finally would go extinct, but here again the magazine emphasized the needs of human beings. As a significant part of human recreation, hunting and fishing, if pursued by "civilized and orderly anglers and hunters," was "legitimate and proper."[50]

When it came to the nation's flora, the editors and most of the magazine contributors felt a special sympathy, which sometimes went beyond the anthropocentric perspective. In their articles, the writers discussed thousands of plant species and their environments, some magnificent and rare, some small and ordinary. In many editorials and essays, they deplored the loss of native species and called for preserving the wild flowers of forests and meadows. "The true lover of flowers," the editors wrote, "loves them best when they are appropriately placed and surrounded; and in the case of wild flowers this must usually mean when they are in their own wild home." In many cases, their wild home was a forest or a marsh—places too wild to be left alone in most people's eyes. Thus, in his essay "The Disappearance of Wild Flowers," William Beal lamented that when woodlands, marshes, or ponds no longer remained "unimproved," many native wild species would disappear. This would be a great loss for "a botanist and lover of nature." So he asked people to save these flowers before they were "burned over or plowed under." In another essay, C. L. Allen discerned that the extinction of many native species was due to the clearing of forests, which "has removed the protection that nature afforded them."[51]

Undoubtedly, the magazine editors and contributors knew that many species did not have enough aesthetic appeal to halt the trampling feet of improvement or to melt the apathy of the public. People needed something more attractive to protect than small, nondescript plants—something that could appeal to their national pride. So in their call for sparing the native plant life, *Garden and Forest* mixed in a few patriotic sentiments. The giant sequoias of the Sierra Nevada, the redwood forests of the California coast, and the southern Allegheny deciduous groves were described as "the three most interesting forests in the world." All were "treasures of beauty and sublimity, of majesty and mystery, of grandeur and of grace," and should be safeguarded for posterity. The sequoias, which were the "marvels of the vegetable kingdom" and "probably the oldest living organisms" on the earth, were singled out in particular as worthy of protection at the national level. The magazine editors believed that "every individual [tree] is a monument which should be sacredly preserved for the benefit of future generations. To cut down one of these trees is a crime, and it should be a matter of national humiliation that a considerable part of the Sequoia forest has been allowed to pass from Government control into the hands of lumbermen." As part of the "nation's inheritance," these trees "are worth infinitely more as they stand than they would be when cut down and sawed up."[52]

Stiles, in a letter written in 1890 to Robert Underwood Johnson, expressed his enthusiasm for protecting an endangered stand of those western giants:

Just now, I am more interested in rescuing that grove of Sequoias in Tulare County than in Yosemite or Yellowstone. I have kicked up quite a stir to this end through various newspapers and by getting people to write to [Interior] Secretary [John W.] Noble to keep this bit of Government land withheld from entry. It is the last grove of Sequoias left and probably the very finest of all, being not only a collection of old trees, but having young ones to continue succession forever. I send you last week's GARDEN AND FOREST which

contains an editorial on National Parks, and which was meant to invite
special attention to this Grove.

Stiles also indicated that he was the one who wrote that unsigned editorial
on national parks, which suggests that this New York writer's environmental
imagination extended well beyond the boundaries of Central Park.[53]

For *Garden and Forest*, protecting the integrity and diversity of forests did
not conflict with the idea that forests in general should be harvested for human use. The redwoods in question, for example, constituted only a small
percentage of the vast forest resources of the nation, but their preservation
would show the rest of the world American grandeur and glory. The enshrine-
ment of them was no different from protecting ancient architectural works
in a burgeoning city where older structures were being replaced by modern
ones.

THE ESTABLISHMENT OF national and state parks was a sign that the aesthetic
value of forests was increasingly being recognized and institutionalized. *Garden and Forest* enthusiastically embraced the idea of national parks, although
when the giant sequoia forests were proposed as such a park, Stiles questioned why that wild area was being labeled a "park," a word suggesting "to
most people some attempt at gardening or decoration." He argued that since
this reservation was primarily a forest, "it should be so designated," for "reservation" suggested a wilder and more primeval character. Whatever the ter-
minology chosen, the editors supported the preservation of primitive natural
scenery and warned repeatedly that any efforts to add artificial features to
natural wonders would be incongruous and ridiculous.[54]

The editors and contributors of the magazine celebrated wild natural
beauty in the Adirondacks, the White Mountains, the Sierra Nevada, or wherever there was a forest. Preserving "natural beauty or grandeur" was "a duty
of civilized society." When "the wildness" was chased away by railroads, settlements, and city markets, these places "would still have attractions, but . . .
would no longer be a wilderness. . . . The strangeness and romance would all
vanish, and with them the temptation to tent-life in the presence of untamed
nature." The rugged wilderness might still be attractive but would become
"a commonplace collection of mountains and woods and lakes, with the ordinary conditions of work-day life forever in sight." Preserving wilderness

meant reclaiming the freedom that modern people were losing in the work disciplines and social hierarchies of an industrialized and urbanized world. Once that wildness completely disappeared, the desire among urban people to find freedom in remote places would fade. Just as Thoreau had tried to find freedom in the quiet woods of Concord, these urban reformers also tended to believe that "in wildness is the preservation of the world." Wildness gave people the opportunity to listen to their inner moral compass, escape from authorities and conformity, and elude the unvaryingly toilsome life of cities. The magazine encouraged people to seek, preserve, and explore such wildness.[55]

Just such a primeval forested place still existed on an island along the New England coast. For a very long time, it had been only a name on the map, a name without any attraction—Mount Desert Island. The word *desert* did not refer to an area covered by sand but to a stretch of wild land, much of it heavily forested. Samuel de Champlain, a French explorer, gave the island this name. In 1604, when Champlain first came to this island, he saw several high, craggy peaks standing along the winding coastline. On them grew forests of birches, firs, and pines extending up to the tree line, where huge, bare granite slopes had lain exposed to the sun and wind for thousands of years. For Champlain, this island was dark and depressing, while the aboriginal people, the Abnaki, found it sterile and dreadful. Repelled by the prospect, Champlain named the island Mount Desert, despite the exuberant vitality of plants and creatures dwelling in its ancient forests.

After European colonization of the region, the forests on the island met the same fate as those in other parts of New England. They were felled and burned so that crops could be planted. Then, because the land turned out to be unsuitable for agriculture, the timber business turned out to be one of the major ways local people could make a living. (Another useful resource was the offshore fishery.) In the 1860s, however, people from New York, Boston, and other eastern cities discovered Mount Desert Island. The natural beauty of the island drew them to enjoy the respite it offered from their regular urban life. Many private cottages and hotels for summer vacationers appeared on the island, and the real-estate entrepreneurs started looking for commercial opportunities there. The vacationers' "cottages" were usually incongruous with the wild landscape around them, being too flamboyant with artificial decorations. The cottage owners generally cut down the trees around the houses, transported soil from other places, and planted rose beds, which made the houses look even more out of place among the rugged rocks and gnarled pines. The straight but untidy roads added to the constructed ugliness, contrasting with the natural forests and shores.

In 1889, Edward Lothrop Rand, a Boston lawyer and an amateur botanist, published in *Garden and Forest* his essay "The Woods of Mount Desert Island." He hailed the island as "the crowning glory of the beautiful, countless-harbored coast of Maine" but warned that the destruction of the native vegetation had already left horrible scars. Here, "the character of the soil, the ruggedness of the surface, the stunting influence of the cold sea winds upon its southern shore, all make the question of economic forestry one of secondary importance. That trees must be spared not for the lumber they yield, but for the beauty they may add to the landscape, should be the argument to the mind of the landowners of Mount Desert. Wild beauty means summer visitors as long as the island endures, and such summer residents have, within the last twenty years, made its fame and fortune." Thus, he called for "vigorous public sentiment, and town interference" to save the woods of Mount Desert Island and consequently save the wild beauty for city people to experience.[56]

Rand was among the first to call for the preservation of Mount Desert Island. Although a lawyer, he invested much time in studying and writing on the flora of Mount Desert Island. He produced a report titled "Flora of Mount Desert Island" and served as the corresponding secretary of the New England Botanic Club for twenty-five years. His interest in the island began with a summer trip in 1880, when he was still a student at Harvard College. The person who organized that trip was Charles Eliot, and it was Eliot and Rand who, with others in their group, set up the Champlain Society, devoted to scientific studies on Mount Desert Island, including such disciplines as botany, geology, ornithology, and entomology. The Eliot family built their own cottage on the island in the next year.[57]

Ten years later, Charles Eliot returned to the island, but this time he came as a landscape architect to investigate the place from a more professional perspective. The appalling scenes of devastation he saw led him to take a strong interest in the future of Mount Desert Island and other islands off the coast of Maine. They were all suffering from too much untutored enthusiasm. In "The Coast of Maine," published in 1890 in *Garden and Forest*, Eliot wrote, "The lamentable feature of the situation is the small amount of thought and attention given to considerations of appropriateness and beauty by the builders and inhabitants of the summer colonies of the coast." He went on to warn that "the real danger of the present situation is that this annual flood of humanity, with its permanent structures for shelter, may so completely overflow and occupy the limited stretch of coast which it invades, as to rob it of that flavor of wildness and remoteness which hitherto has hung about it, and which in great measure constitutes its refreshing charm." Already, those who were aware of the real charm of the island were beginning to buy larger amounts of land and to enclose their property to protect its beauty. Yet that remedy, Eliot feared, would leave little open space for public recreation.[58]

Eliot was not filled with despair, however. "Can nothing be done," he asked, "to preserve for the use and enjoyment of the great unorganized body of the common people some fine parts, at least, of this sea-side wilderness of Maine?" He had an answer: a counterpart to the Trustees of Reservations, the Massachusetts association formed to preserve natural scenery through purchase and donation. A similar organization could save Maine: "in many parts of the coast it is full time decisive action was taken, and if the State of Maine should by suitable legislation encourage the formation of associations for the purpose of preserving chosen parts of her coast scenery, she would not only do herself honor, but would secure for the future an important element in her material prosperity."[59]

The material prosperity Eliot had in mind would come from the lucrative business of tourism, an issue often discussed in *Garden and Forest*, however ambivalently. No doubt there were benefits from such business. The magazine editors dared to hope that more tourist travel to the nation's mountains and forests would help refine the public's taste. In addition, the profits acquired from tourism might persuade local governments to preserve their wild spots. The magazine pointed repeatedly to "the close relation between good taste, beautiful scenery and the qualities of an advanced civilization on the one hand, and the means of subsistence on the other."[60]

At the same time, the *Garden and Forest* editors and contributors worried about the adverse impact that the tourism industry might have on the wild landscape. The flood of visitors would make the preservation of wild forests much more difficult: "the undergrowth will be trampled to death; there will be need of drainage to make dry walks, and this will sap the life of some of the trees; the by-paths will be worn wider; the turf in the green roads will be ruined." New roads would be built and new hotels opened. Urban visitors were often thoughtless, and "their carelessness in setting fires and their reck-lessness in barking and destroying trees, are only too well known." But all these problems need not become reasons to discourage the growth of tour-ism. The magazine producers believed that professional landscape architects could solve the problems deriving from the urban influx. And visitors could be educated. With the aid of systematic rules, their thoughtless behaviors could be restricted.[61]

THE SEEMINGLY CONTRADICTORY values of forest lands embraced by *Garden and Forest* emanated from a common underlying spirit—the spirit of an urban age, resting on confidence in science and expertise, belief in government manage-ment, and restraints on individualism. Almost all the magazine's contributors who wrote on forest matters, including Sargent and Harrison, regarded trees managed by forestry as "crops." Yet they also grasped the relation between trees and their natural environment, and they valued forests for more purely spiritual and aesthetic ends.

Different forest enthusiasts emphasized different values. For botanists like Sargent, the primary value of forests lay in their crucial role in maintain-ing the balance of the natural economy and preserving botanical variety. For economic foresters like Pinchot, those values were only a secondary concern, with production values being the primary consideration. And for landscape architects like Charles Eliot, what most drew him to the forest was its wild, rugged beauty. Conflict over diverging values, however, was not yet well de-veloped or entrenched. In the nonsectarian pages of *Garden and Forest*, readers could absorb and share a common vision that brought together different val-ues and ends.

There was wisdom in that inclusive and pragmatic stance that later would become obscured or lost. But what the *Garden and Forest* editors and contrib-utors did not understand well was that government could become as reck-less and destructive toward forests as any private individual or corporation. They also did not see that science was not always as enlightened or benign as they hoped. Historian Paul Hirt points out that after World War II, when the pace of industrialization and urbanization became even faster, demand for timber became voracious. The US Forest Service, politicians, and big industry together carried on "a conspiracy of optimism, asserting that more infusion of technology, labor, and capital would keep artificially high levels of production sustainable and protect forest ecosystems." The lure of economic profit became, even in government hands, the dominant value, and all the other noncommercial values realized in forests were compromised or disregarded. Government science came to serve private interests, and a more simplified and standardized "forest" created by modern technology replaced a diversity of forests nurtured by nature. When a desire for unlimited economic growth and a blind commitment to science were combined, the forest, even under government ownership and control, could suffer.[62]

It would not be fair to blame the editors of and contributors to *Garden and Forest* for that post–World War II "conspiracy of optimism." On the contrary, they cautioned against any such simple-minded fixing of blame. However, even as the magazine articles criticized the ignorance and irresponsibility of private interests, they never questioned the intentions of scientists or doubted the reliability of government stewardship or challenged the pursuit of unlimited growth.

At the same time, nature was far more complicated and fragile than even the editors and writers supposed. Faced with a complexity that could so easily unravel into chaos, science would prove ineffective and reductive at times. Pushed by economic pressures and overconfident about its understanding of nature, scientific forestry would drift further and further away from the comprehensive vision promoted by *Garden and Forest*, until it became trapped in excessive utilitarianism. The notion of forest permanence and sustainability would always be followed by a question mark.

Still, the pioneering efforts undertaken by *Garden and Forest* were not futile. The magazine raised many, perhaps most, of the important questions about environmental ideas and practices that would continue to be relevant throughout the twentieth century. It awakened public interest in lands far away from cities and promoted the establishment of many national and state parks and forests, which today are among the nation's finest achievements.

Nearly two decades after the magazine ceased publication and after the premature death of his talented son the landscape architect, Harvard president Charles W. Eliot wrote "The Need of Conserving the Beauty and Freedom of Nature in Modern Life." The essay may serve as a coda to the magazine and its complex environmental philosophy. The senior Eliot condemned the evils coming in the wake of rising cities and factories and suggested that restoring contact with wild nature could help cure some of the problems. He called on the government to establish a national park in the Northeast, within easy reach of some of the nation's biggest metropolises. That park would be on Mount Desert Island. Five years later, in 1919, it became reality. Later it was renamed Acadia National Park, after the legendary place in Greek mythology where nature and humans coexisted in harmony.[63]

That new national park could trace its origins in part back to *Garden and Forest*. In its pages, this decidedly urban magazine tried hard to transcend the confines of cities and urban spaces, to reach out to the most remote regions, and to redefine a state of harmony between all of nature and all people. It saw the city, the hinterland, and the most distant places as parts of an organic, holistic system connected by natural, economic, and cultural links. The magazine promoted a comprehensive vision that balanced urban and rural needs, natural and local interests, utilitarian and aesthetic values, and professional training and amateur passion and suggested that this vision should guide the nation's environmental reformers. The magazine tried to make Americans realize that without nature, both as a material and a spiritual base, their vaunted civilization would become a true "Mount Desert," a forbidding wasteland for the soul.

CONCLUSION

~~~~~~~~~~~~~~~~~~~~~~~~~~~~~~

A LTHOUGH THE TERM "environmentalism" acquired its current meaning only in the second half of the twentieth century, it traces its intellectual, social, and political origins to a period fifty to one hundred years earlier. Some would say its roots go even deeper—back to early American naturalists or the New England transcendentalists, particularly Henry David Thoreau, in the 1840s and 1850s, all of whom expressed environmental concerns. Those early calls to respect and protect nature did not widely stimulate the public's attention or stir up political reaction. As a national movement, albeit with many local manifestations, environmentalism began in America's Gilded Age and continued into the Progressive Era.

Environmental historians have paid much attention to those roots, but they have not yet given us a full and complete picture of the formative era. They have also tended to set up fierce rivalries and focus on dramatic disagreements. A few individuals—Gifford Pinchot, Theodore Roosevelt, and John Muir in particular—have occupied center stage, and the supposedly bitter confrontation between "conservationists" and "preservationists" has attracted the most attention. Consequently, other figures and their endeavors have been left in relative obscurity, and the movement has been made to seem too narrow and too divided. Furthermore, the story of the late-nineteenth-century environmental movement as narrated by historians is usually set in the vast wilderness and rural areas of the United States, usually in the West. Some environmental historians are not indifferent to cities, but in their works, urban sanitary reforms or pollution management seemed to exist in an independent, artificial world, one that appears different from the broad natural setting and common intellectual context of late-nineteenth-century America.

Garden and Forest magazine exemplifies a more complex and yet unified reality of early environmental reformers. From 1888 to 1897, the magazine undertook a project far larger than turning the United States into a land of efficient resource production or a clean, tidy, but faceless artifact. It sought nothing less than to redefine the relation of people to the natural world in a bold new way. The sense of urgency the magazine editorials and articles expressed was strong, the criticism was sharp, the tone was passionate, and the attitude was optimistic. The magazine tried to promote an integrated landscape, one where nature and culture were seen as one, where cities and countryside were joined in a common effort, and where both gardens and forests were able to thrive in a greener future. In such a landscape, utility and beauty should complement each other, the scientific spirit and aesthetic sentiment should advance together in harmony, and local attachment and national concern, as well as personal experience and collective action, should all work in unison. The magazine brought attention to thousands of wild and domesticated species, shaped several environmental professions, defended various urban, state, and national parks, and helped create a coherent national movement at the grassroots. Above all, it expressed the environmental vision of a more urban age and culture than that of Thomas Jefferson or Henry David Thoreau. That is its significant and lasting contribution.

Had the magazine enterprise endured, it might have helped lay the foundations for a unified, pragmatic environmental movement that would grow stronger and stronger over the decades. Instead, after it ceased publication, the movement fragmented, and that fragmentation would continue right down to the present.

As noted above, *Garden and Forest* emphasized that scientific knowledge and other specialized training would be needed more than ever. It tried to remind people that in the much more complex urban age, humans cannot rely only on their *love* of nature—although it is important to strengthen this love into a deep ethical and spiritual feeling. Knowledge and expertise are also necessary to move beyond empty slogans or ineffectual gestures, to solve practical problems, and to enlist reason to help sort out the choices that have to be made. Such new professions as landscape architecture and forestry, which were established with the support of *Garden and Forest*, would continue to play pivotal roles in reshaping American landscapes.

As professionalization occurred, however, problems in applying expertise became more obvious. These problematic issues arose partly because the professions entered into the service of government, thus creating large and sometimes competing bureaucracies, and partly because of the fragmentation of knowledge into more and more specialized fields. For example, the US Forest Service became an agency in the Department of Agriculture while the National Park Service was set up in the Department of the Interior, and the two agencies began to compete against one another for funds and power. Many urban planning and park commissions appeared, and they too became part of discrete bureaucracies, often working against each other. A unifying and shared vision became harder to find among the new environmental professionals, whatever level of government they joined. Meanwhile, knowledge about nature became more and more specialized, making a holistic understanding harder to achieve. Problems came to be narrowly defined by narrowly trained people, and those experts were often too absorbed and self-confident in their separate spheres to take a more broad-based approach to the natural and human world.

Garden and Forest had been, above all, a magazine for lovers of beauty and grace in the environment, whether urban or rural, and that deeply aesthetic consciousness, grounded in the design arts and natural sciences, was soon overshadowed by more narrowly utilitarian thinking, even among environmentalists. Nature became "resources"; health became a purely medical or hygienic issue. With that change, the professionalism that the magazine had once confidently promoted became a wedge, not a unifying force, among environmental reformers.

Moreover, it became a wedge separating men from women. Professionalization came to mean an assertion of masculine expertise against "feminine amateurishness." In the early twentieth century, a new generation of men appeared who seemed to feel threatened in their manhood, and it might be argued that they used their credentials as "experts" to overcome their inner anxieties. Sargent and Stiles's magazine, in which women and men had worked together and shared a common commitment to practical design, love of nature, and urbanity, became an outmoded voice from a "softer," more inclusive past. The magazine's emphasis on the need for protecting and enhancing the natural beauty of America, integrating it within city boundaries and encouraging city people to care about all aspects of their surroundings, became identified with nonprofessional "feminine" ideals that no longer carried much weight.

The best account of that shift, which so clearly undermined the magazine and its perspective, comes from Adam Rome's important essay, "'Political Hermaphrodites': Gender and Environmental Reform in Progressive America" (2006). Although Rome's principal example of the shift is the fate of the California nature conservationist John Muir, who lost his battle to save the pristine Hetch Hetchy Valley from the construction of a dam to provide San Francisco with a water supply, the magazine *Garden and Forest* might be said to have suffered a similar fate, and with even broader consequences. For with the silencing of the magazine and its message came the decline of the vision of a city natural. That vision, with its emphasis on designing a livable environment for future generations, on safeguarding spiritual as well as physical health, and on bringing natural surroundings into the heart of the city, had been pushed forward by women and men alike. But as Rome shows, by 1910 the vision of a city natural had become identified with women and the divisive politics of women's suffrage. Men who felt threatened by the rising demands of women to take a more active public role retreated into a male bastion of "rational" professionalism. A love of nature, whether pursued in wild places or gardens, was now dismissed as "effeminate."[1]

In its day, *Garden and Forest* had initiated a wide-ranging discussion that foreshadowed many, though not all, of today's environmental concerns. Undoubtedly, those concerns are more complicated today than they were in the nineteenth century. There are certainly new, unforeseen concerns in our age, including such threats as uneven economic growth, global warming, and widespread contamination by toxic wastes. But as the magazine demonstrated, the early environmental movement was not only about saving wild areas or managing forests for sustained yield. In its pages, many persistent environmental issues, such as redesigning the metropolis, restoring natural beauty, using and abusing pesticides, preventing the extinction of species, overcoming pollution, and slowing the depletion of resources and watershed destruction, became matters of concern. And the magazine's broad, integrative point of view offered a basis for unity and coherence, one needed as much today in places like Mexico City, Shanghai, or Lagos as it was in Gilded Age Boston or New York.

Furthermore, the magazine promoted a firm commitment to democratic values and institutions, and that commitment became part of the ethos of the Progressive Era and a persistent feature of modern environmentalism. This commitment has not always been clearly understood. Some historians have been too quick to condemn environmentalists for their elitism. They have charged that, from the late nineteenth century onward, environmental activists assumed too readily that working-class people, new immigrants, and people of color should bow to their authority. Reformers supposedly assumed that everyone should appreciate nature's beauty exactly as they did and that they knew what was best for others. But that is not, on the whole, a fair criticism. The critics are a little too sure that appreciating and wanting nature in one's life are sentiments confined to the wealthy, privileged classes and that those with less education or property did not and do not have the same need or desire.[2]

In their commitment to liberal democracy, American environmentalists, from the late nineteenth century on, gave a new social meaning to an age-old quest. Other philosophies around the world have long searched for harmony between nature and human beings. They include European romanticism, with its celebration of nature's beauty; Chinese Daoism, which has sought to restore a oneness with nature; and Asia's Buddhist religion, which has taught people to avoid killing other animals. But all these philosophies of harmony between human and nature tended to focus on a purely private or individual solution, a strategy of personal enlightenment and awareness. None of them addressed the protection and enhancement of the natural world on a broad political level.

For *Garden and Forest*, the solution to the intertwined human-nature relationships lay in expanding democratic institutions and a democratic ethos. In all its reforms, from street tree planting to urban park building to wilderness preservation to forest protection, the public's convenience, comfort, and interest had to be considered. Like most other progressive entities of its era, the magazine supported a more just distribution of opportunities and resources.

The magazine's call to conserve and manage the nation's forests was to guarantee the material foundation for the development of a democratic society, allowing it to create more permanent wealth in order to enhance the "quality of life" of common people.

Equally important, the magazine advocated that access to the beauty of nature should become a public right and not be limited to the fortunate few. If schools, libraries, museums, and hospitals should be accessible to all citizens, so should natural resources and so should the experience of nature in the form of growing things, clean air and water, and inspiring scenery.

The magazine, however, was not so egalitarian or morally radical as to call for the rights of other species to exist on earth. Others in its day, however, did, and their influence has lasted, unlike the magazine. During the years when the magazine was being published, a lonely walker in the West was thinking and writing about nature. His name was John Muir. As a believer in democracy and a passionate lover of nature, Muir radically broadened the meaning and boundaries of his society's ideals. At the same time, he tried to make people understand that a real democracy should not be limited to the human sphere but should include all creatures and should respect their right to exist. He wanted to persuade people that human beings should occupy only part of the earth.[3]

Compared to Muir, the magazine *Garden and Forest* was more narrowly concerned with the welfare of humans. It offered a more anthropocentric vision of nature. To its credit, however, it did challenge the drive to consume and devour nature in the new urban industrial age. It endeavored to protect nature in and near growing cities, as well as on the far edges of civilization. It sought to reestablish a connection between urban people and the rest of the living world. It called for more wisdom and restraint, as well as better planning and direction, in order to create an environment fit for humans.

Transcending those various issues, the magazine developed a general argument for nature's indispensability in an urban age, an argument that still needs expression in the twenty-first century, as urbanization has come to dominate the whole planet. Those who made the argument originally were not one or two isolated thinkers but rather a collectivity of hundreds who challenged an old American tendency to celebrate the vanquishing of nature by humans or to assume that nature belonged to the nation's past, not its future. This challenge would become stronger and broader in later years, but it has always been at the core of environmentalism, and so it was in the pages of the magazine.

Above all, *Garden and Forest*, one of America's first and most important environmental magazines, was unashamed to promote the need for natural beauty in people's lives. Gardens, flowers, parks, and forests—the whole landscape, from the human-built center of businesslike New York to the remote wilds of New England and beyond—needed nurture and care. That care must be encouraged in the hearts of men and women who had now moved to the city. Thumbing through the faded, crumbling pages of that old magazine might inspire a new generation of citizen-activists to likewise seek beauty in our malnourished spiritual lives.

NOTES

INTRODUCTION

1. Bellamy's utopian novel reflected a wide dissatisfaction with the social problems occurring in concert with urbanization in the late nineteenth century. Historian John Thomas points out that Bellamy, as a reformer, aimed not only to change the political and economic structures but also, or more importantly, to enhance social virtues. Thomas, *Alternative America: Henry George, Edward Bellamy, Henry Demarest Lloyd, and the Adversary Tradition* (Cambridge: Belknap Press of Harvard University Press, 1983).

2. Edward Bellamy, *Looking Backward, 2000–1897* (Boston: William Ticknor, 1888), chap. 3. A digital version is available at http://xroads.virginia.edu/~hyper/BELLAMY/cho3.html.

3. Two years after Bellamy published *Looking Backward*, the British socialist William Morris published an alternative utopia, more pastoral in theme: *News from Nowhere, or, An Epoch of Rest: Being Some Chapters from a Utopian Romance* (London and New York: Longmans, Green, 1891). See Peter Coates, *Nature: Western Attitudes since Ancient Times* (Berkeley: University of California Press, 1998), chap. 8. Bellamy then published *Equality* (New York: D. Appleton, 1897), in which he abandoned his grand-scale city, setting this utopia in village communities and embracing a harmony between humans and nature. Thus, one could argue that Bellamy gave up his hope for cities and converted to Morris-like pastoralism. For a comparison of nature's changing position in Bellamy's two works, see John R. Mullin, "Edward Bellamy's Ambivalence: Can Utopia Be Urban?" *Utopian Studies* 11 (fall 2000): 51–65.

4. William H. Wilson, *The City Beautiful Movement* (Baltimore: Johns Hopkins University Press, 1989). For a discussion of Burnham, his ideas about cities, and his role in the remaking of Chicago, see Carl Smith, *The Plan of Chicago: Daniel Burnham and the Remaking of the American City* (Chicago: University of Chicago Press, 2006). Also see Philip Pregill and Nancy Volkman, *Landscapes in History: Design and Planning in the Eastern and Western Traditions*, 2nd ed. (New York: John Wiley, 1999), 576–97; and Jon A. Peterson, *The Birth of City Planning in the United States, 1840–1917* (Baltimore: Johns Hopkins University Press, 2003), 98–122.

5. Charles Mulford Robinson, *The Improvement of Towns and Cities* (New York and London: G. P. Putnam's Sons, 1901); Robinson, *Modern Civic Art, or, the City Made Beautiful* (New York: G. P. Putman, 1903), 3–39, 287–355.

6. Wilson, *City Beautiful Movement*, 10–35.

7. Sylvester Baxter, "Secretary's Report," *Report of the Board of Metropolitan Park Commissioners, January 1893* (Boston: Wright and Potter, 1893), 2-3.

8. Frank Luther Mott, *A History of American Magazines*, vol. 4, *1885-1905* (Cambridge: Harvard University Press, 1938-68), 16, 342. Mott points out that it is not possible to find accurate circulation numbers for most magazines published before the Audit Bureau of Circulation was established in 1914.

9. For the antebellum origins of conservation, see Richard W. Judd, *The Untilled Garden: Natural History and the Spirit of Conservation in America, 1740-1840* (New York: Cambridge University Press, 2009), which argues that early American naturalists approached the natural world in both aesthetic and scientific ways. The same belief in the integration of scientific spirit and aesthetic love informed *Garden and Forest*. Judd's book is also a good example of how one might write the history of a collective mind.

10. In "Living in Nature: Biography and Environmental History," from *Thinking through the Environment: Green Approaches to Global History*, ed. Timo Myllyntaus (Cambridge: White Horse Press, 2011), 28-39, Donald Worster discusses the question of scale in historical studies. This biography of a magazine would fall toward the micro-end of the scale but represents a wider lens than the biography of a single individual.

11. For a study of a single magazine, see Mark Noonan, *Reading the "Century Illustrated Monthly Magazine": American Literature and Culture, 1870-1893* (Kent: Kent State University Press, 2010). Also see Amy Tucker, *The Illustration of the Master: Henry James and the Magazine Revolution* (Stanford: Stanford University Press, 2010); Cynthia Lee Patterson, *Art for the Middle Classes: America's Illustrated Magazines of the 1840s* (Jackson: University Press of Mississippi, 2010); and Kenneth Price and Susan Smith, eds., *Periodical Literature in Nineteenth-Century America* (Charlottesville: University Press of Virginia, 1995).

12. *Arnoldia* 60, nos. 2 and 3 (2000). Some of these essays may be found in "Historical Essays on *Garden and Forest*," Making of America, Library of Congress, http://www.loc.gov/preservation/about/prd/gardfor/essays/essaysongf.html, which contains the quotations used in the text.

13. Melanie Simo, *Forest and Garden: Traces of Wildness in a Modernizing Land, 1897-1949* (Charlottesville: University of Virginia Press, 2003).

14. Samuel P. Hays, "From Conservation to Environment: Environmental Politics in the United States since World War Two," *Environmental Review* 6 (autumn 1982): 16; Hays, *Beauty, Health, and Permanence: Environmental Politics in the United States, 1955-1985* (New York: Cambridge University Press, 1987).

15. Robert Gottlieb, *Forcing the Spring: The Transformation of the American Environmental Movement* (Washington: Island Press, 1993), 7, 10, 11; Editorial, "The Confiscation of Parks," *Garden and Forest*, 15 March 1889, 229.

16. This split is emphasized in Roderick Nash's *Wilderness and the American Mind* (New Haven: Yale University Press, 1967, and subsequent editions). Some scholars have been aware of this oversimplification and have tried to overcome it. Ben Minteer, for example, in his book *The Landscape of Reform: Civic Pragmatism and Environmental Thought in America* (Cambridge: MIT Press, 2006), offers a "third way" or "pragmatic tradition" to interpret American environmentalism. *Garden and Forest* should be seen as an early expression of pragmatic and inclusive conservation. Related in theme are Richard W. Judd, *Common Lands, Common People: The Origins of Conservation in Northern New England* (Cambridge: Harvard

University Press, 1997); and Ben A. Minteer and Robert E. Manning, eds., *Reconstructing Conservation: Finding Common Ground* (Washington: Island Press, 2003). Another early exception to a dichotomizing perspective on the movement is Donald Worster, ed., *American Environmentalism: The Formative Period, 1860–1915* (New York: John Wiley, 1973).

CHAPTER 1. THE ORIGINS OF ENVIRONMENTAL REFORM

1. Zane Miller and Patricia M. Melvin, *The Urbanization of Modern America: A Brief History*, 2nd ed. (San Diego: Harcourt Brace Jovanovich, 1987), 79. The literature on urbanization and industrialization and their social and environmental consequences in this time period in the United States is rich. An early classic is Howard P. Chudacoff, *The Evolution of American Urban Society* (Englewood Cliffs: Prentice Hall, 1975); see also the seventh edition of that work, by Chudacoff, Judith E. Smith, and Peter C. Baldwin (Upper Saddle River: Prentice Hall, 2010). Also see Stanley K. Schultz, *Constructing Urban Culture: American Cities and City Planning, 1800–1920* (Philadelphia: Temple University Press, 1989). There are also many excellent studies of individual cities, and some of the more recent ones deal with the tension between urbanization and environmental change; examples include Edwin G. Burrows and Mike Wallace, *Gotham: A History of New York City to 1898* (New York: Oxford University Press, 1999); Matthew Gandy, *Concrete and Clay: Remaking Nature in New York City* (Cambridge: MIT Press, 2002); Matthew Klingle, *Emerald City: An Environmental History of Seattle* (New Haven: Yale University Press, 2007); and Michael Rawson, *Eden on the Charles: The Making of Boston* (Cambridge: Harvard University Press, 2010). For the development of railroads and their relationship with American society and landscape, see Richard White, *Railroaded: The Transcontinentals and the Making of Modern America* (New York: Norton, 2011).

2. Leo Marx has examined the intrusion of modern technology into nature and the American literati's reaction to it. He points to the perennial myth of pastoralism in Western and later American literature and political ideals and argues that this myth underlay the search for a "middle landscape," a place that was not too civilized or too wild. This is the place where Jefferson's ideal society dominated by small farmers would flourish. Marx, *The Machine in the Garden: Technology and the Pastoral Ideal in America* (New York: Oxford University Press, 1964).

3. Frederick Law Olmsted, "Public Parks and the Enlargement of Towns," in Olmsted, *Civilizing American Cities: Writings on City Landscape*, ed. S. B. Sutton (New York: Da Capo Press, 1997), 56–57.

4. For the environmental interaction between city and hinterland, see William Cronon, *Nature's Metropolis: Chicago and the Great West* (New York: Norton, 1991). For the story of how specially trained professionals secured a place of authority at the city level between 1870 and 1900, see Jon C. Teaford, *The Unheralded Triumph: City Government in America, 1870–1900* (Baltimore: Johns Hopkins University Press, 1984), chap. 6. For the rising role of experts in managing nature and the role of government in regulating it, see Samuel P. Hays's groundbreaking work, *Conservation and the Gospel of Efficiency: The Progressive Conservation Movement, 1890–1920* (Cambridge: Harvard University Press, 1959). For the relationship between expertise and the shaping of urban environments, see Wilson, *City Beautiful Movement*; Lawrence W. Kennedy, *Planning the City upon a Hill: Boston since 1630* (Amherst: University of Massachusetts Press, 1992); Peterson, *Birth of City Planning in the United States*; and Mona Domosh, *Invented Cities: The Creation of Landscape in Nineteenth-Century*

New York & Boston (New Haven: Yale University Press, 1996). A classic work on the changing relationship between humans and nature is Peter Schmitt, *Back to Nature: The Arcadian Myth in Urban America* (New York: Oxford University Press, 1969; repr., Baltimore: Johns Hopkins University Press, 1990).

5. For scholarship on social problems associated with nineteenth-century American cities, see Paul Boyer, *Urban Masses and Moral Order in America* (Cambridge: Harvard University Press, 1978); and John M. Levy, *Urban America: Processes and Problems* (Upper Saddle River: Prentice Hall, 2000). For the confrontation between labor and capital, see James R. Green, *Death in the Haymarket: A Story of Chicago, the First Labor Movement and the Bombing That Divided Gilded Age America* (New York: Pantheon Books, 2006). For a good case study on social and demographic changes and the political and economic conflict in their wake, see Stephan Thernstrom, *The Other Bostonians: Poverty and Progress in the American Metropolis, 1880–1970* (Cambridge: Harvard University Press, 1973); and Thomas H. O'Connor, *The Hub: Boston Past and Present* (Boston: Northeastern University Press, 2001), chaps. 7 and 8. For urban environmental problems of the period, see Martin V. Melosi, *Garbage in the Cities: Refuse, Reform, and the Environment, 1880–1980* (College Station: Texas A&M University Press, 1981); Andrew Hurley, "Creating Ecological Wastelands: Oil Pollution in New York City, 1870–1900," *Journal of Urban History* 20 (May 1994): 340–64; and William A. Newman and Wilfred E. Holton, *Boston's Back Bay: The Story of America's Greatest Nineteenth-Century Landfill Project* (Boston: Northeastern University Press, 2006).

6. Schmitt, *Back to Nature*, 4.

7. T. J. Jackson Lears, *No Place of Grace: Antimodernism and the Transformation of American Culture, 1880–1920* (1981; repr., Chicago: University of Chicago Press, 1994), 7. Lears argues that antimodernism was not simply escapism; often it was ambivalently mixed with enthusiasm for material progress. As an unintended consequence, it helped ease the adaption to modern culture. See ibid., 4, 5, xv, xvii. For an antiurban tradition in the United States, see Morton White and Lucia White, *The Intellectual versus the City: From Thomas Jefferson to Frank Lloyd Wright* (Cambridge: Harvard University Press, 1962). Unlike the Whites, other historians tell a more complicated story about intellectuals' reception of the urban age. Thomas Bender, for example, argues that an urban vision "developed out of the interplay of a New England version of early American agrarian ideals and the modernizing forces associated with the industrial city. It sought to bring city and country, and the values they respectively stand for, into a contrapuntal relationship." Bender, *Toward an Urban Vision: Ideas and Institutions in Nineteenth-Century America* (Lexington: University Press of Kentucky, 1975), x. Also see Andrew Lees, *Cities Perceived: Urban Society in European and American Thought, 1820–1940* (Manchester: Manchester University Press, 1985) for a comparative perspective.

8. The progressive reformers have attracted historians' attention for a long time. Classical works include Richard Hofstadter, *Age of Reform: From Bryan to F. D. R.* (New York: Knopf, 1955); and Robert Wiebe, *The Search for Order, 1877–1920* (New York: Hill and Wang, 1967). Daniel Rodgers's *Atlantic Crossings: Social Politics in a Progressive Age* (Cambridge: Harvard University Press, 1998) locates those reformers in an international context. Also see Norman K. Risjord, *Populists and Progressives* (Lanham: Rowman & Littlefield, 2005); Steven L. Piott, *American Reformers, 1870–1920: Progressives in Word and Deed* (Lanham: Rowman & Littlefield, 2006); and Kristofer Allerfeldt, ed., *The Progressive Era in the USA, 1890–1921* (Aldershot and Burlington: Ashgate, 2007). For the settlement house movement, racial and

ethnic conflicts, and women's role in reform, see Allen F. Davis, *Spearheads for Reform: The Social Settlements and the Progressive Movement, 1890–1914* (New York: Oxford University Press, 1967); Paul McBride, *Culture Clash: Immigrants and Reformers, 1880–1920* (San Francisco: R and E Research Associates, 1975); Elisabeth Lasch-Quinn, *Black Neighbors: Race and the Limits of Reform in the American Settlement House Movement, 1890–1945* (Chapel Hill: University of North Carolina Press, 1993); and Daphne Spain, *How Women Saved the City* (Minneapolis: University of Minnesota Press, 2001).

9. The conservation movement is one of the major subjects in American environmental history. Besides Hays's *Conservation and the Gospel of Efficiency*, Nash's *Wilderness and the American Mind* has been influential. For collected readings, see Roderick Nash, ed., *American Environmentalism: Readings in Conservation History*, 3rd ed. (New York: McGraw-Hill, 1990); and Worster, *American Environmentalism*. The latter tries to tie the conservation movement, whether wilderness preservation or natural resource conservation, to urban sanitary reforms, parks, and planning. More recently, Richard Judd has emphasized grassroots activism in his *Common Lands, Common People*. Karl Jacoby and Louis Warren, in contrast, criticize the movement for its class bias; see Jacoby, *Crimes against Nature: Squatters, Poachers, Thieves, and the Hidden History of American Conservation* (Berkeley: University of California Press, 2001); and Warren, *The Hunter's Game: Poachers and Conservationists in Twentieth-Century America* (New Haven: Yale University Press, 1997). Important biographies of conservation figures include Donald Worster, *A River Running West: A Life of John Wesley Powell* (New York: Oxford University Press, 2001); Worster, *A Passion for Nature: The Life of John Muir* (New York: Oxford University Press, 2009); David Lowenthal, *George Perkins Marsh, Prophet of Conservation* (Seattle: University of Washington Press, 2000); Char Miller, *Gifford Pinchot and the Making of Modern Environmentalism* (Washington: Island Press/Shearwater Books, 2001); Madelyn Holmes, *American Women Conservationists: Twelve Profiles* (Jefferson: McFarland, 2004); and Timothy Egan, *The Big Burn: Teddy Roosevelt and the Fire That Saved America* (Boston: Houghton Mifflin Harcourt, 2009).

10. The establishment and management of American national parks is one of the oldest and best researched subjects in environmental history. For a comprehensive survey, see Alfred Runte, *National Parks: The American Experience*, 3rd ed. (Lincoln: University of Nebraska Press, 1997); Richard Sellars, *Preserving Nature in the National Parks: A History* (New Haven: Yale University Press, 1997); and Dayton Duncan, *The National Parks: America's Best Idea; An Illustrated History* (New York: Knopf, 2009). More narrowly focused are Polly Welts Kaufman, *National Parks and the Woman's Voice: A History* (Albuquerque: University of New Mexico Press, 2006); and Scott Herring, *Lines on the Land: Writers, Art, and the National Parks* (Charlottesville: University of Virginia Press, 2004). For provocative studies of individual parks, see Harvey Meyerson, *Nature's Army: When Soldiers Fought for Yosemite* (Lawrence: University Press of Kansas, 2001); Anne Whiston Spirn, "Constructing Nature: The Legacy of Frederick Law Olmsted," in *Uncommon Ground: Rethinking the Human Place in Nature*, ed. William Cronon (New York: Norton, 1996), 91–113; Mark Spence, "Dispossessing the Wilderness: Yosemite Indians and the National Parks Ideal, 1864–1930," *Pacific Historical Review* 61 (February 1996): 27–59; and David Stradling, *Making Mountains: New York City and the Catskills* (Seattle: University of Washington Press, 2007).

A comprehensive study of nineteenth-century urban parks is David Schuyler, *The New Urban Landscape: The Redefinition of City Form in the Nineteenth Century* (Baltimore: Johns

Hopkins University Press, 1986). Also see Galen Cranz, *The Politics of Park Design: A History of Urban Parks in America* (Cambridge: MIT Press, 1982); Albert Fein, *Frederick Law Olmsted and the American Environmental Tradition* (New York: G. Braziller, 1972); Francis R. Kowsky, *Country, Park, and City: The Architecture and Life of Calvert Vaux, 1824–1895* (New York: Oxford University Press, 1997); Roy Rosenzweig and Elizabeth Blackmar, *The Park and the People: A History of Central Park* (Ithaca: Cornell University Press, 1992); Terence Young, *Building San Francisco's Parks, 1850–1930* (Baltimore: Johns Hopkins University Press, 2004); and Craig E. Colten, "Reintroducing Nature to the City: Wetlands in New Orleans." *Environmental History 7* (April 2002): 226–46.

11. George B. Emerson, *A Report on the Trees and Shrubs Growing Naturally in the Forests of Massachusetts* (Boston: Commonwealth of Massachusetts, 1846), 2. This Emerson was one of the crucial figures in founding the Arnold Arboretum, whose first director, Charles Sargent, established *Garden and Forest*. As a trustee of the Arnold Fund (named after James Arnold), he first proposed the establishment of an arboretum for native and exotic trees. See Ida Hay, *Science in the Pleasure Ground: A History of the Arnold Arboretum* (Boston: Northeastern University Press, 1994).

For Marsh's American predecessors, see Judd, *Untilled Garden*, which argues that naturalists and explorers laid the foundations for the conservation movement and for American attitudes toward nature. The basic themes of the conservation movement—commercial utility, romantic attraction, and ecological necessity—all had their origins among the pre-Darwinian naturalists.

12. Emerson, *Report on the Trees and Shrubs*, 2. On the fear of the so-called forest famine, see Donald Pisani, "Forests and Conservation, 1865–1890," in *American Forests: Nature, Culture, and Politics*, ed. Char Miller (Lawrence: University Press of Kansas, 1997), 16–19. The most comprehensive history of American forests and their exploitation is Michael Williams's *Americans and Their Forests: A Historical Geography* (New York: Cambridge University Press, 1989). Williams argues that forest protection started in the last three decades of the nineteenth century, but its advocates were conflicted over who should own the forests and how they should be managed. Also see Andrew Denny Rodgers III, *Bernhard Eduard Fernow: A Story of North American Forestry* (Princeton: Princeton University Press, 1951); Samuel P. Hays, *The American People & the National Forests: The First Century of the U.S. Forest Service* (Pittsburgh: University of Pittsburgh Press, 2009); Nancy Langston, *Forest Dreams, Forest Nightmares: The Paradox of Old Growth in the Inland West* (Seattle: University of Washington Press, 1995); and Brian Balogh, "Scientific Forestry and the Roots of the Modern American State: Gifford Pinchot's Path to Progressive Reform," *Environmental History 7* (April 2002): 198–225.

13. Urban sanitary reforms in the nineteenth century were an important aspect of progressive environmental reforms. Urban environmental historians have paid particular attention to this subject. On efforts to improve urban sanitation and combat pollution, see Martin V. Melosi, *The Sanitary City: Urban Infrastructure in America from Colonial Times to the Present* (Baltimore: Johns Hopkins University Press, 2000), esp. 103–16; and Joel A. Tarr, *The Search for the Ultimate Sink: Urban Pollution in Historical Perspective* (Akron: University of Akron Press, 1996); Andrew Hurley, ed., *Common Fields: An Environmental History of St. Louis* (Saint Louis: Missouri Historical Society Press, 1997); David Stradling, *Smokestacks and Progressives: Environmentalists, Engineers and Air Quality in America, 1881–1951* (Baltimore: Johns

Hopkins University Press, 1999); Daniel Eli Burnstein, *Next to Godliness: Confronting Dirt and Despair in Progressive Era New York City* (Urbana: University of Illinois Press, 2006); and Frank Uekoetter, *The Age of Smoke: Environmental Policy in Germany and the United States, 1880–1970* (Pittsburgh: University of Pittsburgh Press, 2009).

14. Nathaniel Hillyer Egleston, *Arbor Day Leaves* (New York: American Book Company, 1893), 5. For more details on the founding of Arbor Day and the American celebration of trees, see Shaul E. Cohen, *Planting Nature: Trees and the Manipulation of Environmental Stewardship in America* (Berkeley: University of California Press, 2004), chap. 3; and Kevin Armitage, *The Nature Study Movement: The Forgotten Popularizer of America's Conservation Ethic* (Lawrence: University Press of Kansas, 2009), 180–81.

15. In 1930, *Forest and Stream* became *Field and Stream*. Daniel J. Philippon examines the Boone and Crockett Club and the Audubon Society groups as case studies of how literature influenced social activism in his *Conserving Words: How American Nature Writers Shaped the Environmental Movement* (Athens: University of Georgia Press, 2004), chaps. 1 and 2. On Grinnell, see Gerald A. Diettert, *Grinnell's Glacier: George Bird Grinnell and Glacier National Park* (Missoula: Mountain Press, 1992); and Michael Punke, *Last Stand: George Bird Grinnell, the Battle to Save the Buffalo, and the Birth of the New West* (New York: Smithsonian Books/Collins, 2007).

16. George Bird Grinnell, *American Big Game in Its Haunts: The Book of the Boone and Crockett Club* (New York: Forest and Stream Publishing, 1904), 487. See also John Reiger, *American Sportsmen and the Origins of Conservation*, 3rd ed. (Corvallis: Oregon State University Press, 2001); and Thomas Dunlap, "Sport Hunting and Conservation, 1880–1920," *Environmental Review* 12 (spring 1988): 51–60.

17. Jennifer Price, in *Flight Maps: Adventures with Nature in Modern America* (New York: Basic Books, 1999), chap. 2, tells an engaging story about establishing the Audubon Society and challenging women's fashions.

18. John Muir, *The Mountains of California* (New York: Century Company 1894), 4.

There are many biographies and studies of Muir, the celebrated nature lover and advocate of national parks. Earlier ones include Linnie Marsh Wolfe, *Son of the Wilderness: The Life of John Muir* (New York: Knopf, 1945); and Stephen R. Fox, *John Muir and His Legacy: The American Conservation Movement* (Boston: Little, Brown, 1981). The surpassing study is Worster, *Passion for Nature*.

19. Donald Worster, *Nature's Economy: A History of Ecological Ideas* (New York: Cambridge University Press, 1994), 58, 103. For the romantic perception of nature, see Marjorie Hope Nicolson, *Mountain Gloom and Mountain Glory: The Development of the Aesthetics of the Infinite* (Seattle: University of Washington Press, 1997). For the influence of the European naturalistic tradition on nineteenth-century America, see Aaron Sachs, *The Humboldt Current: Nineteenth-Century Exploration and the Roots of American Environmentalism* (New York: Viking, 2006). Also important are Robert Richardson's two biographies: *Henry Thoreau: A Life of the Mind* (Berkeley: University of California Press, 1986); and *Emerson: The Mind on Fire: A Biography* (Berkeley: University of California Press, 1995). For the transcendental tradition and the rise of American environmentalism, see Lawrence Buell, *The Environmental Imagination: Thoreau, Nature Writing, and the Formation of American Culture* (Cambridge: Belknap Press of Harvard University Press, 1995).

20. Astonishingly, neither Marsh nor Olmsted appears anywhere in the index to

Gottlieb's *Forcing the Spring*, while figures as tangential as Friedrich Engels, Eugene Debs, and Herbert Marcuse do.

21. See Lowenthal, *George Perkins Marsh.*

22. George Perkins Marsh, "Address Delivered before the Agricultural Society of Rutland County," 30 September 1847, 18–19, Evolution of American Conservation Movement, 1850–1920, American Memory Project, Library of Congress.

23. Ibid., 1–2.

24. Ibid., 18–19.

25. Ibid., 6 (first quote); George Perkins Marsh, *Man and Nature*, ed. David Lowenthal (Cambridge: Harvard University Press, 1965), 40 (second quote).

26. Marsh, *Man and Nature*, 38, 46.

27. There is an extensive literature on Frederick Law Olmsted and his environmental vision. The most comprehensive biography is by Laura Wood Roper, *FLO: A Biography of Frederick Law Olmsted* (Baltimore: Johns Hopkins University Press, 1973). Also see Elizabeth Stevenson, *Park Maker: A Life of Frederick Law Olmsted* (New Brunswick: Transaction Publishers, 2000); Witold Rybczynski, *A Clearing in the Distance: Frederick Law Olmsted and America in the Nineteenth Century* (New York: Scribner, 1999); Melvin Kalfus, *Frederick Law Olmsted: The Passion of a Public Artist* (New York: New York University Press, 1990); and Lee Hall, *Olmsted's America: An "Unpractical" Man and His Vision of Civilization* (Boston: Little, Brown, 1995). Most of the works, however, do not pay enough attention to Olmsted's connection with the broader environmental reforms occurring in urban and wilderness areas in the late nineteenth century.

28. The biographical details about Olmsted are from Roper, *FLO*, if not otherwise noted.

29. Frederick Law Olmsted, *Walks and Talks of an American Farmer in England*, 2 vols. (New York: G. P. Putnam, 1852), 1:79, 81.

30. Judith Major suggests that Downing transferred his fascination with European aesthetic traditions, especially England's huge landscaped estates, to an affection for and admiration of America's simple rural farmsteads. She argues that, in this process, Downing "offered men and women a message of moderation and simplicity, encouraging them to practice economy, to use America's rich natural resources wisely yet artificially—to be content with a little cottage and a few fine native trees. Downing ultimately accommodated a republican as opposed to an aristocratic rural art." Major, *To Live in the New World: A. J. Downing and American Landscape Gardening* (Cambridge: MIT Press, 1997), 5. Also see David Schuyler, *Apostle of Taste: Andrew Jackson Downing, 1815–1852* (Baltimore: Johns Hopkins University Press, 1996).

31. Andrew Jackson Downing, "The New-York Park," *The Horticulturist and Journal of Rural Art and Rural Taste* 6, no. 8 (1851): 346.

32. Olmsted, "Public Parks and the Enlargement of Towns," 64–65.

33. Ibid., 75.

34. Olmsted, "Preliminary Report upon the Yosemite and Big Tree Grove," in *The Papers of Frederick Law Olmsted*, vol. 5, *The California Frontier, 1863–1865*, ed. Victoria Post Ranney (Baltimore: Johns Hopkins University Press, 1990), 502.

35. Ibid., 505.

CHAPTER 2. TWO MINDS, ONE MAGAZINE

1. Stiles to Olmsted, 26 December 1887, Olmsted Papers, Library of Congress, Washington.

2. Stiles to Olmsted, 25, 27, 30 December 1887, Olmsted Papers.

3. Stiles to Olmsted, 28 December 1887, Olmsted Papers.

4. In the late nineteenth century, there were many magazines published in the field of horticulture, including *The Gardeners' Monthly and Horticulturist, Devoted to Horticulture, Arboriculture and Rural Affairs* (1876–88); *Meehan's Monthly* (1892–1901), edited by Thomas Meehan in Philadelphia; *Gardening* (1892–1925), edited by William Falconer in Chicago; and *The Farm and Garden* (1881–88), also published in Philadelphia. These journals focused solely on issues related to horticulture and agriculture, paying little attention to either the relationship between nature and city or broader social issues.

5. *Garden and Forest*, 29 December 1897, 518.

6. William Trelease, "Biographical Memoir of Charles Sprague Sargent," *National Academy of Science of the United States of America: Biographical Memoirs* 12, no. 9 (1929): 247.

7. Ernest H. Wilson, "Charles Sprague Sargent," *Harvard Graduates' Magazine* 35, no. 140 (June 1927): 605. For Sargent's life, see S. B. Sutton, *Charles Sprague Sargent and the Arnold Arboretum* (Cambridge: Harvard University Press, 1970); Charles Sprague Sargent Papers, Archives of the Arnold Arboretum Library, Harvard University, Boston; and Ida Hay's *Science in the Pleasure Ground.*

8. Major, *To Live in the New World.*

9. Besides his monumental achievement in history, Francis Parkman was also a renowned horticulturist. He began to practice horticulture in the early 1850s and won no less than 326 horticultural awards from 1859 to 1884. He was closely associated with the Massachusetts Horticultural Society and served as its president from 1875 to 1878. He was appointed professor of horticulture at the Bussey Institution in early 1871, but the death of his mother and a brother in that year ruined his persistently weak health, so he resigned at the end of the academic year. Charles Haight Farnham, *A Life of Francis Parkman* (Boston: Little, Brown, 1900), 29–34; Walter M. Whitehill, "Francis Parkman as Horticulturist," *Arnoldia* 33, no. 3 (1973): 177.

10. S. B. Sutton speculates that Hunnewell might have made the appointment possible, for he was a rich benefactor of Harvard botanical research. Sutton, *Charles Sprague Sargent and the Arnold Arboretum*, 29. Walter M. Whitehill suggests that Francis Parkman "must have played a crucial part in the selection of his successor." Whitehill, "Francis Parkman as Horticulturist," 177.

11. Sutton, *Charles Sprague Sargent and the Arnold Arboretum*, 20–21.

12. Stiles to Olmsted, 26 December 1887, Olmsted Papers.

13. Editorial, "Asa Gray," *Garden and Forest*, 29 February 1888, 1.

14. Sargent to Robert Johnson, 25 November 1908, Sargent Papers.

15. Ibid.

16. Ibid.

17. Sargent, "The Protection of Forests," *North American Review* 135, no. 311 (1882): 386.

18. "The Protection of Forests," *New York Times*, 18 September 1882, 4.

19. Sargent, *Nation* 37 (September 1883): 201.

20. Sutton, *Charles Sprague Sargent*, 96.

21. Donald Worster, "John Muir and the Modern Passion for Nature," *Environmental History* 10 (January 2005): 8–19.

22. Sargent, "The Report of the Forestry Commission," State of New York Assembly, no. 36, January 1885: 16.

23. Sutton, *Charles Sprague Sargent*, 63. For a detailed discussion on the construction of the Boston park system, see Cynthia Zaitzevsky, *Frederick Law Olmsted and the Boston Park System* (Cambridge: Belknap Press, 1982).

24. For the physical changes in Jamaica Plain in the second half of the nineteenth century and the relationship between the building of the Arnold Arboretum as a public park and the local expectation, see Alexander von Hoffman, *Local Attachments: The Making of an American Urban Neighborhood, 1850 to 1920* (Baltimore: Johns Hopkins University Press, 1994), chap. 3.

25. Most biographic information on Stiles, if not specially noted, is from "William A. Stiles, a Sketch of His Life," *New York Daily Tribune*, 7 October 1897, 7; Editorial, "William A. Stiles," *Garden and Forest*, 13 October 1897, 399; and "William A. Stiles Is Dead," *New York Times*, 7 October 1897, 5.

26. "William A. Stiles Is Dead," *New York Times*, 7 October 1897, 5.

27. Ibid.

28. "William A. Stiles, a Sketch of His Life," *New York Daily Tribune*, 7 October 1897, 7.

29. "William A. Stiles, a Sketch of His Life," *New York Daily Tribune*, 7 October 1897, 7. Samuel Parsons Jr., another contemporary landscape architect, recorded the story of how Stiles was hired to be an editorial writer for the *New York Daily Tribune*. Parsons also appreciated Stiles's writing style, saying that, "in addition to facts, Stiles had that literary touch, the penetrative, imaginative quality that no horticulturist had whom I have ever known." Mabel Parsons, ed., *Memories of Samuel Parsons* (New York: Putnam's, 1926), 127, quoted in Phyllis Andersen, "'Master of a Felicitous English Style': William Augustus Stiles, Editor of *Garden and Forest*," Historical Essays on *Garden and Forest*, The Nineteenth Century in Print: Periodicals, Library of Congress, http://www.loc.gov/preservation/about/prd/gardfor/essays/andersen.html; "William A. Stiles Is Dead," *New York Times*, 7 October 1897, 5.

30. Stiles to Olmsted, 25 December 1885, Olmsted Papers.

31. Stiles to Olmsted, 7 December 1885, Olmsted Papers.

32. Stiles to Olmsted, 12 June 1887, Olmsted Papers.

33. "New Park Commissioners," *New York Times*, 10 November 1895, 16; Stiles to Olmsted, 12 June 1887, Olmsted Papers.

34. Trelease, "Biographical Memoir of Charles Sprague Sargent," 248; Ernest Wilson, "Charles Sprague Sargent," 610; Editorial, "William A. Stiles," *New York Daily Tribune*, 7 October 1897, 6.

35. Editorial, "William A. Stiles," *Garden and Forest*, 13 October 1897, 399.

36. Ibid.; "William A. Stiles, a Funeral," *New York Daily Tribune*, 9 October 1897, 6.

37. "William A. Stiles, a Park Name Petition," *New York Daily Tribune*, 16 December 1897, 9.

38. Editorial, "William A. Stiles," *Garden and Forest*, 13 October 1897, 399; W. A. Stiles, "Orchids," *Scribner's Magazine*, February 1894, 190–205.

39. Stiles to Olmsted, 7 January 1888, Olmsted Papers.

40. Due to a fire that destroyed Sargent's house, there is no surviving correspondence between Sargent and Stiles, but Stiles's letters to other contributors, such as Olmsted and Pinchot, suggested that he wrote to Sargent regularly. Sometimes, Sargent went to New York or Stiles went to Holm Lea.

41. Stiles to Gray Herbarium, 29 September, 14 October, 15 November 1892, Semi-Historic Letters, Archives of the Gray Herbarium, Harvard University Herbaria Library, Harvard University, Cambridge.

42. Sargent, *Annual Report of the Arnold Arboretum* (1918), published by the library of the Arnold Arboretum.

43. "The Prospectus of *Garden and Forest*," *Garden and Forest*, 29 February 1888, ii; Editorial, "Public Gardens," *Garden and Forest*, 11 November 1894, 529.

44. "The Prospectus of *Garden and Forest*," *Garden and Forest*, 29 February 1888, ii; Editorial, "The Organization of the Trustees of Public Reservations," *Garden and Forest*, 15 July 1891, 326; "The Future of American Forest," *Garden and Forest*, 14 March 1888, 25.

45. Editorial, "Organized Protection for Parks," *Garden and Forest*, 1 January 1890, 1.

46. Editorial, "The Adirondack Forests in Danger," *Garden and Forest*, 28 March 1888, 49; J. B. Harrison, "The Forest, Forest Interests in Pennsylvania, II," *Garden and Forest*, 26 June 1889, 310; Editorial, "Forests and Civilization," *Garden and Forest*, 19 December 1888, 505.

47. "New Park Commissioners," *New York Times*, 10 November 1895, 16.

48. Ibid., 16.

49. There were also others responsible for putting out the magazine. In 1887, Sargent recruited not only Stiles as editor but also David A. Munro as business manager. Munro had come to the United States from Scotland in 1872, when he was twenty-eight years old. He had been working at the publishing house of Harper Brothers before he joined the staff of *Garden and Forest*. Stiles described him as "a capital man—bright—square—straightforward—has been brought up at Harpers." He toiled with Stiles to raise money for the publication when Sargent was sick and managed to sell the first advertisement page to Harper for the full rate. Munro did not write anything for the magazine, though, and he left *Garden and Forest* after his two-year contract ended. "Obituary of David A. Munro," *New York Times*, 10 March 1910, 9; "Mr. Munro Surprised," *New York Times*, 21 November 1887, 12.

50. "Talented Woman Summoned by Death; Mrs. M. B. Coulston, Secretary of the Park Committee, Died Suddenly in Oakland; Remains to Be Cremated Today; a Useful Life," *San Diego Union and Daily Bee*, 19 July 1904.

51. After *Garden and Forest* ceased publication, Coulston went to Cornell to study horticulture, forestry, and other nature-related subjects. There, she likely met the influential environmental thinker Liberty Hyde Bailey, who had been an important contributor to the magazine. In 1902, she settled in San Diego, where she served as secretary of the park commission and wrote a number of articles for local newspapers on the need for and functions of urban parks; these articles, in their style and views, revealed her training by Stiles. She was also an active force in bringing Samuel Parsons, a renowned New York landscape architect and a follower of park designers Frederick Law Olmsted and Calvert Vaux, to be the designer of the new Balboa Park in San Diego. Thus, Coulston's later career reflected the legacy of *Garden and Forest*. What Coulston chose to do after she left New York was what Stiles had been doing all along—combining words with practical

actions in promoting and defending urban parks. See Richard W. Amero, "Samuel Parsons Finds Xanadu in San Diego," *Journal of San Diego History* 44, no. 1 (1998). See also http://www.sandiegohistory.org/journal/98winter/parsons.htm (accessed 10 June 2010).

52. "A Park Name Petition," *New York Daily Tribune*, 16 December 1897, 9; "A Park Name Petition, Mitchell E. Opposes," *New York Daily Tribune*, 30 December 1897, 6.

53. Editorial, "William A. Stiles," *Garden and Forest*, 13 October 1897, 399.

54. Sargent to John Muir, 24 December 1897, frame 2375, reel 9, John Muir Papers, Holt-Atherton Library, University of the Pacific, Stockton.

CHAPTER 3. SHAPING NEW PROFESSIONS

1. Editorial, "Thinning Plantations," *Garden and Forest*, 26 June 1889, 30. For the relationship between the establishment of early professions and journal publication, see Dana F. White, *The Urbanists, 1865–1915* (New York: Greenwood Press, 1989), 35–36.

2. The data exclude contributors whose surnames and given names were indicated only by initials.

3. At least two contributors were from Japan. Inaso Nitobe and H. Yoshida introduced Japanese plant species to American readers.

4. For example, *Garden and Forest* published two series of articles by William Botting Hemley on his botanical explorations of China and eastern Burma in 1889 and 1891, respectively, while Edward L. Greene introduced the flora of California in a series from 1889 to 1892. Cyrus G. Pringle reported his expeditions into Mexico in different series throughout the publication of *Garden and Forest*. Elisha N. Plank's investigation of Texas flora appeared in *Garden and Forest* in a series of twenty-five pieces from November 1892 to May 1895, and another series comprising five parts appeared in 1896. John G. Jack's "Notes from the Arnold Arboretum" recorded the botanical discoveries of the Arnold Arboretum from all over the world, and reports from Sargent's flora expedition to Japan were published by *Garden and Forest* in a series of twenty-eight segments in 1893.

5. Andrew Denny Rodgers III, *American Botany, 1873–1892: Decades of Transition* (Princeton: Princeton University Press, 1944), 199.

6. Ibid., 129, 278.

7. William A. Farlow, "The Change from the Old to the New Botany in the United States," *Science* 37 (17 January 1913): 85.

8. Rodgers, *American Botany*, 277.

9. Edward Greene, who believed that species were immutable, was probably the only one who could challenge Gray's authority among botanists.

10. Sutton, *Charles Sprague Sargent*, 44, 45. It is hard to know the state of the relationship between Sargent and Cyrus G. Pringle during the publication of *Garden and Forest*. Pringle had been Sargent's collector in the West when, in 1882, Sargent was in charge of a botanical exhibition of the Natural History Museum of New York City. Sargent's bossy attitude and unjustified criticism infuriated Pringle, and their cooperation ended. Sargent's reputation among collectors, according to Sutton, never fully recovered from this break.

11. Editorial, "Professor Goodale's Botanical Articles," *Garden and Forest*, 2 January 1889, 2; George Goodale, "Principles of Physiological Botany, XX," *Garden and Forest*, 22 May 1889, 250.

12. Worster, *Nature's Economy*, 204.

13. Charles Bessey, "Are the Trees Receding from the Nebraska Plains?" *Garden and Forest*, 17 November 1897, 456, 457; Worster, *Nature's Economy*, 202. Undoubtedly, Bessey greatly inspired his talented student, Frederic Clements, who became one of the world's pioneering ecologists.

14. William J. Beal, "Methods of Botanical Study," *Garden and Forest*, 9 April 1890, 175; "Forestry at the Michigan Agricultural College," *Garden and Forest*, 10 April 1895, 149.

15. Editorial, "Horticultural Novelty," *Garden and Forest*, 14 February 1894, 61.

16. Francis Parkman, "The Presidential Address to the Massachusetts Horticultural Society," 1875, quoted in Farnham, *Life of Francis Parkman*, 33–34.

17. Parkman's interest in forest conservation issues was shown in his review of Sargent's forest census report. He extolled the value of Sargent's work and agreed with his concerns about the forest situation in the United States; he emphasized the indispensability of forests for the prosperity of the nation, criticized wanton felling, overgrazing, and fire, and urged federal and state government to take action to protect forests. Francis Parkman, "The Forest and the Census," *Atlantic Monthly* 55 (June 1885): 835–39. For a more detailed analysis of Parkman's view of nature, see Wilbur R. Jacobs, "Francis Parkman: Naturalist-Environmental Savant," *Pacific Historical Review* 61, no. 3 (May 1992): 341–56.

18. Editorial, "Botany in the Agriculture Colleges," *Garden and Forest*, 19 October 1892, 493.

19. Allan Carlson, *The New Agrarian Mind: The Movement toward Decentralist Thought in Twentieth Century America* (New Brunswick: Transaction Publishers, 2000), 8. For Bailey's contribution to the conservation movement, also see Minteer, *Landscape of Reform*, chap. 2. Minteer treats Bailey as a model for his own pragmatic conservation.

20. For a detailed discussion of Bailey's role in the nature-study movement, see Armitage, *Nature Study Movement*, chap. 7.

21. Carlson, *New Agrarian Mind*, 5.

22. Liberty Hyde Bailey, *The Holy Earth* (New York: Charles Scribner's Sons, 1915), 22, 16.

23. Henry Sargent Codman, "The National School of Horticulture at Versailles," *Garden and Forest*, 16 January 1889, 27; Editorial, "Schools of Horticulture," *Garden and Forest*, 16 January 1889, 25; Editorial, "Horticulture and Health," *Garden and Forest*, 21 October 1896, 431.

24. E. S. Goff, "Plant-breeding at the Experiment Stations," *Garden and Forest*, 24 July 1895, 292; Liberty H. Bailey, "Correspondence," *Garden and Forest*, 7 August 1895, 318–19; E. S. Goff, "Plant-breeding Once More"; and Luther Burbank, "Plant-Breeding," both in *Garden and Forest*, 28 August 1895, 349.

25. For further discussion of the relationship between horticulture and urban society, see chap. 5.

26. Robert F. Becker, "Henderson, Peter," in *Pioneers of American Landscape Design*, ed. Charles A. Birnbaum and Robin Karson (New York: McGraw-Hill, 2000), 170; Peter Henderson, "Floriculture in the United States," *Garden and Forest*, 28 February 1888, 3.

27. Watson wrote approximately 340 pieces for *Garden and Forest*, and most of them were published in the foreign correspondence section. In these essays, Watson discussed botanical and horticultural research and discoveries at Kew Gardens, the flower and fruit market in London, and the activities of other botanical and horticultural organizations in England.

28. George Thurber contributed an essay to *Garden and Forest* on poisonous primrose in 1890, the year in which he died.

29. Mildred Selfridge Orpet, "E. O. Orpet, Horticulturist," *Journal of the California Horticultural Society* 13, no. 2 (April 1952): 43.

30. Editorials, "The Society of American Florists," *Garden and Forest*, 22 August 1888, 301; "The Florist," *Garden and Forest*, 29 August 1888, 313.

31. Editorials, "The Responsibilities of Florists and Nurserymen," *Garden and Forest*, 12 September 1888, 337; "Street-Trees," *Garden and Forest*, 19 March 1890, 137; "Tree-planting in Cities," *Garden and Forest*, 29 April 1891, 193.

32. Editorials, "Street Trees," *Garden and Forest*, 11 April 1888, 74; "Street Trees," *Garden and Forest*, 27 December 1893, 532.

33. One of the contentious questions for these new professionals and their advocates was the most appropriate label for this new profession. Olmsted accepted the term "landscape architecture" reluctantly, as did Charles Eliot. In his letter to Mary C. Robbins in 1896, Eliot wrote, "I confess that 'landscape architecture' is a barbarous expression, and I feel it as much as Mr. Sargent does, but your [Robbins's] own phrase 'the art of public (and private) improvement' is certainly long, and is not convertible into any descriptive noun like 'landscape architect,' so until somebody invents a better phrase, I think we shall have to stick to the term 'landscape architect.'" Charles Eliot to Mary Caroline Robbins, 2 and 5 December 1896, Charles Eliot Papers, Frances Loeb Library, Harvard Graduate School of Design, Cambridge.

Mariana Van Rensselaer was inclined to use the phrase "landscape gardening," because she thought that landscape architects did their work using the same material as nature did. See more details in Judith Major, "Mariana Griswold Van Rensselaer's Landscape Gardening Manifesto in *Garden and Forest*," *Landscape Journal* 26, no. 2 (2007): 183–200. Likewise, the *Garden and Forest* editors used "landscape gardening" most often, but sometimes they referred to "landscape architecture" or "landscape art." Throughout, I adopt the modern, standard phrase "landscape architecture," except for the sentences quoted.

34. Warren Manning wrote one essay for *Garden and Forest* on horticultural nomenclature. He was hired to work in Olmsted's office in 1888 as a specialist in horticulture and planting design, and he opened his own office in 1896. Manning was one of the first to advocate establishing a professional organization for landscape architects.

35. Codman was one of Olmsted's most promising protégés. He became the partner of Olmsted and John C. Olmsted (Olmsted's stepson and nephew) in 1889. He wrote only four essays for the magazine. Later, he was Olmsted's major assistant in his design of the Chicago world's fair in 1893, but he died suddenly in January before the project was finished, when he was only twenty-nine years old.

36. Peter Walker and Melanie Simo, *Invisible Gardens: The Search for Modernism in the American Landscape* (Cambridge: MIT Press, 1994), 19.

37. Wilhelm Miller was the founder of the prairie school of landscape architecture, which emphasized including native prairie flora and imitating the form of prairie landscapes in landscape design. Frank Waugh was famous for the so-called "natural" style in landscape architecture. The difference between that style and the "naturalistic" style advocated by A. J. Downing was the plant material applied in their design. Waugh advocated the use of native species to create a natural scene, while the naturalistic style

imitated only the form of nature, not specific species. Even more importantly, Waugh introduced an ecological approach in landscape architecture, which paid primary attention to the association between the plants placed by the landscape architect and the natural environment around them, such as soil, moisture, and other plant and animal species.

38. Editorial, "Art and Nature in Landscape-gardening," *Garden and Forest*, 19 May 1897, 192.

39. Editorial, "The Administration of Public Parks," *Garden and Forest*, 6 February 1889, 61–62.

40. Ibid.

41. Stiles's editorials in *Garden and Forest* played the crucial role in fighting against the proposed racetrack in Central Park, for he believed it would destroy the entire landscape designed by Olmsted and Vaux.

42. Vaux's name also appeared in the list of those who promised contributions to the magazine, but he did not write a word for *Garden and Forest*, perhaps because he was distracted by financial and personal problems. His body was found in the water of Gravesend Bay, Brooklyn, on 17 November 1895, and no one could say whether it was a case of suicide or due to an accident because of heavy fog. He did not die a rich man; his total assets were valued at only twenty-five hundred dollars. In her biography *FLO*, Roper discusses in more detail the relationship between Vaux and Olmsted and Olmsted's supportive attitude in the Harlem Speedway issue.

43. Editorials, "City Engineers and Public Parks," *Garden and Forest*, 6 March 1895, 91–92; "The Harlem River Speedway," *Garden and Forest*, 8 August 1894, 311.

44. Editorial, "Park Lands and Their Boundaries," *Garden and Forest*, 21 October 1996, 421.

45. Cynthia D. Kinnard suggests that Van Rensselaer met Olmsted through Henry Adams or Richardson in 1882. Her father made acquaintance with Olmsted during the Civil War, but Kinnard doubts that Van Rensselaer had any personal contact with Olmsted that early. They never corresponded until after Richardson's death. Cynthia D. Kinnard, "The Life and Works of Mariana Griswold Van Rensselaer, American Art Critic" (PhD diss., Johns Hopkins University, 1977). Sargent and Olmsted collaborated to get Van Rensselaer's work on Richardson published, but it is hard to know when Sargent and Van Rensselaer got to know each other.

46. Stiles to Olmsted, 7 January 1888, Olmsted Papers.

47. Mariana Van Rensselaer, "Landscape Gardening: A Definition," *Garden and Forest*, 28 February 1888, 2; Van Rensselaer, "Landscape Gardening: A Definition," *Garden and Forest*, 4 April 1888, 64. Van Rensselaer later compiled this series of essays, along with others written for *Garden and Forest*, into *Art Out-of-Doors: Hints on Good Taste in Gardening*, published by Charles Scribner's Sons in 1893. This book has been regarded as one of the classics in landscape architecture theory and was widely adopted in professional courses of landscape architecture.

48. Olmsted to Van Rensselaer, 9 April 1888, Olmsted Papers.

49. Judith Major suggests that Van Rensselaer deserves credit for some of the unsigned editorials in the magazine, those she incorporated into her book *Art Out-of-Doors*, and others clearly linked to her experience, such as the editorial comparing landscape architects and painters. Major, "Mariana Griswold Van Rensselaer's Landscape Gardening Manifesto in *Garden and Forest*."

50. Mary C. Robbins, "How We Renewed an Old Place, I," *Garden and Forest*, 1 April 1891, 146; Robbins, "How We Renewed an Old Place, III," *Garden and Forest*, 15 April 1891, 170.

51. In some articles, there were only the initials "M.C.R." Presumably, articles bearing these initials had been written by Robbins, for their style was identical to those published with her full name.

52. Kinnard, "Life and Works of Mariana Griswold Van Rensselaer," 280; Mariana Van Rensselaer, "The Waste of Women's Intelligence," *Forum* 13, no. 25 (July 1892): 620; Kinnard, "Life and Works of Mariana Griswold Van Rensselaer," 283.

53. Kinnard, "Life and Works of Mariana Griswold Van Rensselaer," 280–81; Mariana Van Rensselaer, "Thoughts on Women Suffrage, IV," *World* (New York), 19 May 1894, 4, quoted in Kinnard, "Life and Works of Mariana Griswold Van Rensselaer," 283.

54. Editorial, "Taste Indoors and Out," *Garden and Forest*, 10 August 1892, 373, 374.

55. Mary C. Robbins, "Correspondence: Some Questions about Taste," *Garden and Forest*, 24 August 1892, 405; Editorial, "Taste Indoors and Out," *Garden and Forest*, 14 September 1892, 433.

56. Jones refused to use the term "landscape architecture" and stuck to "landscape gardening."

57. Olmsted added, "I ought to have excepted Stiles, but I suppose that I did not feel that regular hack newspaper work should count. Stiles does well but he has not half your advantages." Olmsted to Charles Eliot, 28 October 1886, Olmsted Papers.

58. Charles Eliot, "The Landscape Gardeners," *Garden and Forest*, 13 February 1889, 74.

59. For more detailed discussion on the history of the Trustees of Reservations, see Gordon Abbott Jr., *Saving Special Places: A Centennial History of the Trustees of Reservations; Pioneers of the Land Trust Movement* (Ipswich: Ipswich Press, 1993). Abbott argues that Eliot should receive most of the credit for its founding. Also see Richard Brewer, *Conservancy: The Land Trust Movement in America* (Lebanon: Dartmouth College Press, 2004), 13–24.

60. Editorial, "The Waverly Oaks," *Garden and Forest*, 19 February 1890, 85; Charles Eliot, "Correspondence: The Waverly Oaks," *Garden and Forest*, 5 March 1890, 117, 118.

61. Charles W. Eliot, *Charles Eliot, Landscape Architect: A Lover of Nature and of His Kind, Who Trained Himself for a New Profession, Practised It Happily and through It Wrought Much Good* (Boston: Houghton Mifflin, 1902), 381.

62. Cynthia Zaitzevsky, "Baxter, Sylvester," in *Pioneers of American Landscape Design*, ed. Birnbaum and Karson.

63. Sylvester Baxter, "The German Way of Making Better Cities," *Atlantic Monthly*, 104 (July 1909): 72.

64. Curtis M. Hinsley and David R. Wilcox, eds., *The Southwest in the American Imagination: The Writings of Sylvester Baxter, 1881–1889* (Tucson: University of Arizona Press, 1996).

65. Sylvester Baxter, "Correspondence: The Lynn Public Forest," *Garden and Forest*, 30 October 1889, 527. The Boston Metropolitan Park System—its comprehensive scale, democratic spirit, natural character, and professional management—to a great extent fulfilled Baxter's hopes. From 1892 to 1893, he served as secretary of the park system's preliminary commission, while Eliot was its landscape architect.

66. Charles Eliot, "The Necessity of Planning," *Garden and Forest*, 26 August 1896, 342.

67. Eliot to Robbins, 2 and 5 December 1896, Eliot Papers.

68. In 1900, after Eliot's untimely death in 1897, his father, the president of Harvard,

established the first independent program in landscape architecture at the university, and Olmsted Jr. was invited to teach in it. From this beginning, the profession of regional planning emerged.

69. "*Garden and Forest* for 1891," *Garden and Forest*, all issues of April 1891, vi. Later, Pinchot criticized Sargent's egotism: "It throws an interesting sidelight on Sargent that the name of its editor, William A. Stiles, who had far more to do with its usefulness than Sargent himself, appeared nowhere in the publication." Gifford Pinchot, *Breaking New Ground* (New York: Harcourt, Brace, 1947), 91.

70. Rodgers, *Bernhard Eduard Fernow*, 17. Besides *Garden and Forest*, another important magazine covering forest issues was *Forest and Stream*. While it advocated protecting wild animal habitats, it did not provide a systematic introduction to forestry or pay much attention to the economic, aesthetic, and ecological functions of forests. In 1895, John Clayton Gifford edited *American Forests* (aka *The Forester*), which had an affiliation with the American Forestry Association. It was the first magazine in the country to focus on the profession. Before *American Forests* appeared, *Garden and Forest* served as the major forum for forestry and forest issues.

71. J. B. Harrison, "The Pennsylvania Forestry Association," *Garden and Forest*, 23 March 1888, 155.

72. Simo, *Forest and Garden*, xii.

CHAPTER 4. NATURE AND CIVILIZATION

1. Editorial, "The Desolation of Central Tunis: Was It Caused by the Destruction of Forests?" *Garden and Forest*, 22 November 1893, 481–82. The report being reviewed was Paul Bourde, *Rapport sur les cultures fruitières et en particulier sur la culture de l'olivier dans le centre de la Tunisie*.

2. Editorial, "Desolation of Central Tunis," 481–82.

3. J. B. Harrison, "Forests and Civilization: The North Woods, VII," *Garden and Forest*, 11 September 1889, 441.

4. Mariana Van Rensselaer, "Landscape Gardening, V," *Garden and Forest*, 28 March 1888, 51.

5. Editorial, "Attacks on Civilization," *Garden and Forest*, 23 October 1889, 505.

6. Editorial, "The Soil and National Development," *Garden and Forest*, 13 February 1889, 73.

7. Editorial, "Arbor Day Tree-planting," *Garden and Forest*, 23 January 1889, 37.

8. Scholars in various disciplines continue to debate the meaning of nature. Within the field of environmental history, a representative work is Cronon's edited volume, *Uncommon Ground*. The basic argument in that book is that "nature is a human idea, with a long and complicated cultural history which has led different human beings to conceive of the natural world in very different ways." Ibid., 20. Thus, the volume contributors all emphasize nature as a creation of human imagination, not nature as a physical world consisting of organic and inorganic objects. Both meanings are possible.

9. "Book Review," *Garden and Forest*, 12 December 1894, 499–500.

10. Editorial, "The Tree as a Schoolmaster," *Garden and Forest*, 24 February 1892, 85.

11. Sylvester Baxter, "A 'Massachusetts Forest,'" *Garden and Forest*, 5 August 1891, 362.

12. Editorial, "Formal Gardening: Does It Conflict with the Natural Style?" *Garden and Forest*, 15 March 1893, 119; 22 March 1893, 129.

13. Van Rensselaer, "Landscape Gardening, V," *Garden and Forest*, 28 March 1888, 51.

14. Editorial, "The Beautiful in the Surroundings of Life," *Garden and Forest*, 9 November 1892, 529.

15. Editorial, "Some Uses of Flowers," *Garden and Forest*, 23 March 1892, 133.

16. Editorial, "The Love of Nature," *Garden and Forest*, 20 July 1892, 337.

17. "A Quote," *Garden and Forest*, 8 July 1891, 314.

18. Editorials, "The Defacement of Natural Scenery," *Garden and Forest*, 7 December 1892, 577; "The Defacement of Scenery," *Garden and Forest*, 27 February 1895, 81.

19. Editorials, "The Defacement of Natural Scenery," *Garden and Forest*, 7 December 1892, 577; "The Defacement of Scenery," *Garden and Forest*, 27 February 1895, 81; "The Beautiful in the Surroundings of Life," *Garden and Forest*, 9 November 1892, 530.

20. Editorials, "Protection of the Yellowstone Park," *Garden and Forest*, 10 December 1890, 593; "The Defacement of Scenery," *Garden and Forest*, 27 February 1895, 81; "Formal Gardening," *Garden and Forest*, 20 September 1893, 205.

21. Editorial, "Nature and American Literature," *Garden and Forest*, 8 May 1895, 181–82.

22. "Book Review," *Garden and Forest*, 25 December 1889, 623.

23. Editorial, "Botany for Young People," *Garden and Forest*, 26 February 1890, 97.

24. Editorial, "Botany for Young People," *Garden and Forest*, 26 February 1890, 97.

25. W. G. R., "The Study of Botany," *Garden and Forest*, 30 April 1890, 218; Editorials, "Elementary Botany for Young People," *Garden and Forest*, 31 December 1890, 629; "The Summer Vacation," *Garden and Forest*, 12 August 1891, 373.

26. Editorial, "The Future of American Gardening," *Garden and Forest*, 7 March 1888, 13; Mariana Van Rensselaer, "The Art of Gardening: A Historical Sketch, I," *Garden and Forest*, 20 March 1889, 134; Editorial, "The Love of Nature, I," *Garden and Forest*, 20 April 1892, 193.

27. Editorials, "The Love of Nature," *Garden and Forest*, 20 July 1892, 337; "The Love of Nature, I," *Garden and Forest*, 20 April 1892, 194.

28. Editorial, "The Love of Nature, III," *Garden and Forest*, 11 May 1892, 218.

29. Editorial, "The Love of Nature," *Garden and Forest*, 4 May 1892, 205.

30. J. B. Harrison, "Correspondence: Forests and Civilization," *Garden and Forest*, 17 July 1889, 345.

31. Charles Eliot, "The Coast of Maine," *Garden and Forest*, 5 March 1890, 86; Editorial, "Horticulture in England and America," *Garden and Forest*, 11 July 1894, 271.

32. Editorial, "Art and Nature," *Garden and Forest*, 4 July 1894, 261; Mariana Van Rensselaer, "Landscape Gardening: A Definition, II," *Garden and Forest*, 7 March 1888, 14.

33. Editorial, "The Rapid Settlement of Our Arable Lands," *Garden and Forest*, 18 June 1890, 293.

34. Editorials, "The Arid West and Irrigation," *Garden and Forest*, 25 July 1888, 253; "Rainfall on the Great Plains," *Garden and Forest*, 4 April 1888, 62. In the latter article, the editor, despite ridiculing the myth of increased rainfall, was still confident about the power of the plow to add "to the value of the rainfall." The belief was that, by breaking up the soil and covering the ground with crops, more moisture would be retained in the soil.

35. Donald Worster points out that Powell never advocated cutting down all the headwater forests. However, climate and landscape were very different in the West, so

theories originating in and applicable to the East could not be easily transferred to the West. In the arid West, Powell argued, forests were not always effective in maximizing stream flow. Still, Powell had more trust than Sargent in the capability of technology to improve nature to better serve humans. See Worster, *River Running West*, 483–90.

36. Editorial, "Mountain Reservoirs and Irrigation," *Garden and Forest*, 3 July 1889, 313. See also Editorials, "The Influence of Mountain Forests," *Garden and Forest*, 2 January 1889, 1; "The Danger from Mountain Reservoirs," *Garden and Forest*, 19 June 1889, 289.

37. J. B. Harrison, "Forest Interests in Pennsylvania, III," *Garden and Forest*, 3 July 1889, 321; Editorials, "The Bursting of the Walnut Grove Dam," *Garden and Forest*, 5 March 1890, 110; "Mountain Forests and Mountain Stream," *Garden and Forest*, 9 December 1891, 577.

38. Mary Robbins, "How We Renewed an Old Place, X," *Garden and Forest*, 24 June 1891, 292.

39. T. H. Hoskins, "The Abuse of Insecticides," *Garden and Forest*, 27 May 1891, 247.

40. Byron D. Halsted, "Are Fungicides Abused"? *Garden and Forest*, 29 July, 1891, 359; T. H. Hoskins, "Insecticides and Fungicides in the Orchard," *Garden and Forest*, 1 June 1892, 261.

41. Liberty H. Bailey, "Is Spraying Overdone?" *Garden and Forest*, 29 June 1892, 310; T. H. Hoskins, "Orchard Spraying," *Garden and Forest*, 3 August 1892, 370.

42. Rachel Carson, *Silent Spring* (Boston: Houghton Mifflin, 1962), 297.

43. Editorial, "Arbor Day Tree-planting," *Garden and Forest*, 23 January 1889, 37; J. B. Harrison, "Correspondence: Forests and Civilization," *Garden and Forest*, 17 July 1889, 345.

44. Editorials, "Sentimentalism and Tree-felling," *Garden and Forest*, 26 July 1893, 311; "Natural Beauty and the Landscape Gardener," *Garden and Forest*, 5 December 1888, 481; Mariana Van Rensselaer, "Landscape Gardening," *Garden and Forest*, 4 April 1888, 63; Van Rensselaer, "A Glimpse of Nantucket," *Garden and Forest*, 14 November 1888, 447.

45. William Buckhout, "The Forest: The Need of a Forest Policy in Pennsylvania," *Garden and Forest*, 19 February 1890, 93; Buckhout, "The Forest: Suggestions for Restoring Wasted Forests," *Garden and Forest*, 20 August 1890, 410; B. E. Fernow, "The Forest: Its Significance as a National Resource," *Garden and Forest*, 29 July 1891, 357; Gifford Pinchot, "The Forest: Forestry in Prussia," *Garden and Forest*, 17 August 1892, 393; Editorial, "The Timber-supply of the United States," *Garden and Forest*, 26 April 1893, 181.

46. Mariana Van Rensselaer, "Landscape Gardening: A Definition, I–VII," *Garden and Forest*, 29 February–11 April 1888.

47. Editorials, "Do Not Spare the Axe," *Garden and Forest*, 7 November 1888, 433; "The Judicious and Systematic Thinning of Trees," *Garden and Forest*, 22 March 1889, 241.

48. Editorial, "The Key-note in Landscape-gardening," *Garden and Forest*, 27 December 1893, 531. See also "Natural Beauty and the Landscape Gardener," *Garden and Forest*, 5 December 1888, 481.

49. Editorial, "Art and Nature in Landscape-gardening," *Garden and Forest*, 19 May 1897, 192. See also "The Yosemite Valley," *Garden and Forest*, 2 January 1889, 1; "The Preservation of Natural Scenery," *Garden and Forest*, 28 March 1890, 257; and "National Parks," *Garden and Forest*, 6 August 1890, 377.

50. Editorial, "Arbor Day Tree-planting," *Garden and Forest*, 23 January 1889, 37; Van Rensselaer, "Landscape Gardening: A Definition," *Garden and Forest*, 14 March 1888, 27.

51. Gen. 1:28 (authorized King James version).

52. John Winthrop, *A Model of Christian Charity* (Boston: Collections of the Massachusetts Historical Society, 1838, 3rd series 7), 47–48. The spelling has been modernized.

53. John Locke, *Two Treatises of Government*, ed. Peter Laslett (Cambridge: Cambridge University Press, 1960).

54. J. B. Harrison, "Correspondence: Forests and Civilization," *Garden and Forest*, 10 July 1889, 333.

55. Sylvester Baxter, "Private Grounds and Enclosures in Cities and Towns, I," *Garden and Forest*, 10 December 1890, 594.

CHAPTER 5. DESIGN WITH NATURE

1. In *The Country and the City* (London: Chatto & Windus, 1973), Raymond Williams examines how British urban and pastoral ideas have changed, co-evolved, and intermingled. Also see Keith Thomas, *Man and the Natural World: Changing Attitudes in England, 1500–1800* (London: Allen Lane, 1983). According to one author, "The belief that eastern cities were not overcivilized but undercivilized already was prominent before the Civil War." James L. Machor, *Pastoral Cities: Urban Ideals and the Symbolic Landscape of America* (Madison: University of Wisconsin Press, 1987), 150.

2. Editorial, "Park Work near Boston," *Garden and Forest*, 29 April 1896, 171.

3. "The Prospectus of *Garden and Forest*," *Garden and Forest*, 29 February 1888, ii.

4. Editorial, "The Decline of the Country Gentleman," *Garden and Forest*, 13 May 1891, 217.

5. Editorial, "The Confiscation of Parks," *Garden and Forest*, 15 March 1889, 229.

6. Peterson, *Birth of City Planning in the United States*, 22.

7. For more discussion of Olmsted and Charles Eliot's influence on city planning, see Irving D. Fisher, *Frederick Law Olmsted and the City Planning Movement in the United States* (Ann Arbor: UMI Research Press, 1986); Peterson, *Birth of City Planning*; Karl Haglund, "Emerald Metropolis," *Arnoldia* 53 (fall 1993): 2–17; Keith N. Morgan, "Charles Eliot, Landscape Architect: An Introduction to His Life and Work," *Arnoldia* 59 (summer 1999): 3–21; and Karl Haglund, *Inventing the Charles River* (Cambridge: MIT Press, 2003).

8. Editorials, "Parks for Growing Cities," *Garden and Forest*, 10 February 1892, 61; "Park Work near Boston," *Garden and Forest*, 29 April 1896, 171.

9. For the development of small-scale gardens and the growing interest in gardening, see Walter T. Punch, ed., and the Massachusetts Horticultural Society, *Keeping Eden: A History of Gardening in America* (Boston: Bulfinch Press, 1992); M. Christine Klim Doell, *Gardens of the Gilded Age: Nineteenth-Century Gardens and Homegrounds of New York State* (Syracuse: Syracuse University Press, 1986); and Mac Griswold and Eleanor Weller, *The Golden Age of American Gardens: Proud Owners, Private Estates, 1890–1940* (New York: H. N. Abrams with the Garden Club of America, 1991). Also see an engaging story about African American women's gardening interest in Dianne D. Glave, "'A Garden So Brilliant with Colors, So Original in Its Design': Rural African American Women, Gardening, Progressive Reform, and the Foundation of an African American Environmental Perspective," *Environmental History* 8 (July 2003): 395–411.

10. Editorial, "Water Lilies," *Garden and Forest*, 18 July 1888, 241.

11. Peter Henderson, "Floriculture in the United States," *Garden and Forest*, 29 February 1888, 2–3; Editorial, "Cut Flowers and Growing Plants," *Garden and Forest*, 2 May 1888, 110.

12. E. P. Powell, "Housetop Gardens," *Garden and Forest*, 16 March 1892, 125–26.

13. Editorial, "Why We Do Not Buy Growing Plants," *Garden and Forest*, 9 May 1888, 121–22.

14. Tamara Plakins Thornton, "Horticulture and American Character," in *Keeping Eden*, ed. Punch and Massachusetts Horticultural Society, 189, 200. Also see Tamara Plakins Thornton, *Cultivating Gentlemen: The Meaning of Country Life among the Boston Elite, 1785–1860* (New Haven: Yale University Press, 1989).

15. J. D. W. French, "Window Gardening," *Garden and Forest*, 18 July 1888, 243. French was citing *The Life of the Earl of Shaftesbury*, by Edwin Hodder, who praised his subject for promoting gardening among workers in England.

16. Mary C. Robbins, "Gardening: A Good Outlet for American Vitality," *Garden and Forest*, 30 January 1895, 42–44.

17. Ibid., 43; Editorial, "The Effect of Gardening upon the Mind," *Garden and Forest*, 28 October 1891, 505.

18. Armitage, *Nature Study Movement*, 1–14.

19. Editorial, "Natural Beauty in Urban Parks," *Garden and Forest*, 30 June 1897, 251.

20. Editorials, "The Speedroad in Central Park," *Garden and Forest*, 30 March 1892, 145; "Preserving Natural Scenery," *Garden and Forest*, 2 July 1890, 317; "Street-trees," *Garden and Forest*, 5 June 1895, 221; "The Railroad in Horticulture," *Garden and Forest*, 13 March 1889, 121; "The Improvement of School Grounds," *Garden and Forest*, 16 May 1888, 133; "Good Taste in Our Cemeteries," *Garden and Forest*, 1 June 1892, 253. On the development of the American cemetery, see Thomas Bender, "The Rural Cemetery Movement: Urban Travail and the Appeal of Nature," *New England Quarterly* 47, no. 2 (1974): 196–211; and Aaron Sachs, "American Arcadia: Mount Auburn Cemetery and the Nineteenth-Century Landscape Tradition," *Environmental History* 15 (April 2010): 206–35.

21. Editorial, "The True Function of City Parks," *Garden and Forest*, 7 July 1897, 261.

22. For the debate between park and playground advocates, see Roy Rosenzweig, *Eight Hours for What We Will: Workers and Leisure in an Industrial City, 1870–1920* (New York: Cambridge University Press, 1983), chap. 5. Rosenzweig argues that the central issue of the debate was whether working-class people should be active in urban parks (e.g., participate in sports or attend concerts) or accept the much quieter and meditative way of behaving defined by Olmsted and his followers.

23. Galen Cranz dates the conflict between the park and playground advocates to the early twentieth century, but in the pages of *Garden and Forest*, it exploded a decade earlier. Cranz, *Politics of Park Design*, 63–65, 85–87.

24. Peter Schmitt points out that psychologists helped change the concept of urban parks: "Play was no longer a means of exercise but an end in itself, a science conforming to the needs of an urban culture. The rural image of informal outdoor exercise gave way to an urban ideal for town and country alike." Schmitt, *Back to Nature*, 75.

25. Editorial, "Playgrounds and Parks," *Garden and Forest*, 6 June 1894, 221–22.

26. Editorials, "Keep Off the Grass," *Garden and Forest*, 25 July 1894, 291; "The Deface-ment of City Parks," 12 June 1895, 232, 231, respectively.

27. Editorials, "A Proposed Invasion of Central Park," *Garden and Forest*, 20 March 1889, 133; "Park Works near Boston," *Garden and Forest*, 29 April 1896, 171.

28. Editorial, "Natural Beauty in Urban Parks," *Garden and Forest*, 30 June 1897, 251.

29. Roy Rosenzweig and Elizabeth Blackmar, in *The Park and the People*, chaps. 1–3,

accuse Olmsted of imposing his ethnic bias for picturesque gardens on others—a view that this author does not share. Also see Gandy, *Concrete and Clay*, chap. 2; and Rawson, *Eden on the Charles*, chap. 5.

30. Peterson argues that there were three major forms of system design in progressive urban reforms, all requiring scientific expertise: water supply, sewerage, and urban parks. Peterson, *Birth of City Planning in the United States*, 22.

31. Theodore Steinberg describes an "organic city" that was too messy and dirty for urban reformers, although it "had a certain social and environmental logic." He argues that "city dwellers and their animals were largely integrated into the regional soil cycle, supplying it with the nutrients for growing food that was then trucked back into town. Thus did life proceed in the organic city, with vegetables and hay flowing one way and waste the other." Steinberg, *Down to Earth: Nature's Role in American History* (New York: Oxford University Press, 2002), 159.

32. Editorials, "The Proper Use of Public Parks," *Garden and Forest*, 25 September 1889, 457; "The Use of City Parks," *Garden and Forest*, 29 July 1891, 349–50.

33. Donald Worster, "The Wilderness of History," *Viewpoint* 7, no. 3 (1997): 12–13.

34. Editorial, "Small Parks for New York," *Garden and Forest*, 5 June 1895, 222; Lewis Mumford, *The Brown Decades: A Study of the Arts in America, 1865–1895* (New York: Harcourt, Brace, 1931). David Schuyler argues that Olmsted and his followers sought "a naturalistic landscape that in its very rusticity was the antithesis of the urban environment," but this is not how Olmsted himself understood what he was doing, especially in his later years. Schuyler, *New Urban Landscape*, 146.

35. Sylvester Baxter, "Boston's New Metropolitan Parks," *Garden and Forest*, 17 January 1894, 22; Editorial, "The Metropolitan Parks of Boston," *Garden and Forest*, 1 May 1895, 171. Rawson, *Eden on the Charles*, chap. 5, suggests that the park system represented Boston Brahmins' efforts to preserve traditional values that were losing out to the rising power of new immigrants. Perhaps so, but then one must ask why cities all over the world today are trying to preserve their surrounding natural beauty and finding inspiration in Boston's achievement. Also see James C. O'Connell, "How Metropolitan Parks Shaped Greater Boston, 1893–1945," in *Remaking Boston: An Environmental History of the City and Its Surroundings*, ed. Anthony N. Penna and Conrad Edick Wright (Pittsburgh: University of Pittsburgh Press, 2009), 168–97.

36. Editorials, "Park Work near Boston," *Garden and Forest*, 29 April 1896, 171; "The Park System of Greater Boston," *Garden and Forest*, 23 June 1897, 241–42.

37. Charles Eliot, "Parks and Squares of United States Cities," *Garden and Forest*, 24 October 1888, 412; Editorial, "The Debt of America to A. J. Downing," *Garden and Forest*, 29 May 1895, 211.

38. Editorial, "The Proper Use of Public Parks," *Garden and Forest*, 25 September 1889, 457–58.

39. Bender, *Toward an Urban Vision*, 181–87, points out that an emphasis on spontaneity and naturalness, along with sensitivity to local character, distinguished Olmsted's ideal of the suburb from the bland and unnatural conformity of many modern suburbs. Rawson, *Eden on the Charles*, 263–64, grants that the Boston Metropolitan Park System was the first effort to curtail the environmental damage done by suburban sprawl.

40. Eliot's essays on the Maine coast and the Waverly Oaks were published in

Garden and Forest in 1889 and 1890, respectively. Harrison's series, "In the Shore Towns of Massachusetts," was published in 1891. In general, see Kenneth Jackson, *Crabgrass Frontier: The Suburbanization of the United States* (New York: Oxford University Press, 1985); and John R. Stilgoe, *Borderland: Origins of the American Suburb, 1820–1939* (New Haven: Yale University Press, 1988). For more particular case studies, see Henry C. Binfor, *The First Suburbs: Residential Communities on the Boston Periphery, 1815–1860* (Chicago: University of Chicago Press, 1985); Hoffman, *Local Attachments*; and David Contosta, *Suburb in the City: Chestnut Hill, Philadelphia, 1850–1990* (Columbus: Ohio State University Press, 1992).

41. On the environmental damage and problems created by the postwar mass housing industry, see Adam Rome, *The Bulldozer in the Countryside: Suburban Sprawl and the Rise of American Environmentalism* (New York: Cambridge University Press, 2001).

42. For an account of the populist movement, see Charles Postel, *The Populist Vision* (New York: Oxford University Press, 2007).

43. Editorial, "The Decline of the Country Gentleman," *Garden and Forest*, 13 May 1891, 217.

44. Bailey, *Holy Earth*, 51.

45. Richard Ross Cloues argues that village improvement "paralleled but did not imitate nor derive" from the urban park movement; see Cloues, "Where Art Is Combined with Nature: Village Improvement in Nineteenth-Century New England" (PhD diss., Cornell University, 1987), 82. See also Editorial, "The Improvement of Villages," *Garden and Forest*, 27 March 1889, 145. For village improvement in Stockbridge, Massachusetts, and its intellectual roots and influence, see Kirin Makker, "Building Main Street: Village Improvement and the Small Town Ideal" (PhD diss., University of Massachusetts Amherst, 2010).

46. Charles Mulford Robinson, *The Improvement of Towns and Cities or The Practical Basis of Civic Aesthetics* (New York: G. P. Putman's Sons, 1901), 262. Richard Cloues, "Where Art Is Combined with Nature," chap. 7, argues that the urban-based civic movement differed from village improvement "in terms of its national perspective, its uniform standards, its professionalism, and its bureaucracy." One movement regarded the village as the ideal place to live while the other embraced cities as the new "paradise." True, but there was much overlap and interaction between the two. Makker, "Building Main Street," shows that the village improvement movement advocated a middle-landscape ideal, just as the urban park planners did, and moved to embrace a similar ideal of comprehensive professional planning. Editorial, "The City Improvement Societies," *Garden and Forest*, 20 August 1890, 401.

47. Editorial, "Rural Improvement Societies," *Garden and Forest*, 23 May 1888, 145. According to one scholar, American intellectuals came to believe that rural virtues, traditional values, rural landscapes, and the simple way of living were inadequate for the modern world while they also believed that urbanism alone, with its advanced technology, prosperous market economy, and cultural diversity, could not make life complete, healthy, and harmonious. The best landscape, most observers believed, was "the urban-pastoral vision [that] conceives of an alternate 'middle' realm in which the city blends harmoniously with the countryside or contains within its own boundaries urbanity, complexity, and sophistication combined with the physical or social attributes of simple rusticity." Machor, *Pastoral Cities*, 12.

48. Editorials, "The Improvement of Villages," *Garden and Forest*, 27 March 1889, 145; "The Money Value of Rural Improvements," *Garden and Forest*, 22 January 1890, 37.

49. Notes, *Garden and Forest*, 22 September 1897, 378.

50. Editorial, "County Parks," *Garden and Forest*, 3 June 1896, 221.

51. Ibid.

CHAPTER 6. DISTANT FORESTS

1. Editorial, "The Future of Our Forests," *Garden and Forest*, 14 March 1888, 25–26.

2. Editorials, "The Nation's Forests," *Garden and Forest*, 30 January 1889, 49; "The Care of the National Forest-reservations," *Garden and Forest*, 23 August 1893, 351. Sargent's proposal stirred up a debate among the country's major conservationists. In 1895, *Century* magazine organized a forum about it, and thirteen leading conservationists—Edward A. Bowers, B. E. Fernow, Frederick Law Olmsted, J. F. Rothrock, Verplanck Colvin, Theodore Roosevelt, Gifford Pinchot, N. S. Shaler, D. M. Riordan, John Muir, Cleveland Abbe, William J. Palmer, and George S. Anderson—joined the discussion. They divided into two camps: Muir and Roosevelt led those who supported Sargent's plan of army protection, while Fernow and Bowers opposed it. Olmsted was more conciliatory, but he warned that the army "ought not to be a Jack-of-all-trades." Pinchot suggested using military personnel to guard forest reserves while training professional foresters to do the administrative work. "Comments on Professor Charles S. Sargent's Scheme of Forest Preservation by Military Control," *Century* 49 (February 1895): 626–34. Earlier, in 1889, *Century* also published an editorial introducing and discussing *Garden and Forest*'s plan for forests. See "Topics of the Time: How to Preserve the Forests," *Century* 38 (June 1889): 312–13.

3. Editorials, "A Mountain Meadow," *Garden and Forest*, 3 July 1889, 314; "National Parks," *Garden and Forest*, 6 August 1890, 377. On the relationship between Sargent and Muir, see Worster, *Passion for Nature*, chaps. 12 and 13.

4. Editorial, "The Mountains of California," *Garden and Forest*, 26 February 1896, 81.

5. On this expedition, the tension between Sargent and Pinchot, and its consequences, see Sutton, *Charles Sprague Sargent and the Arnold Arboretum*, 159–70; Miller, *Gifford Pinchot and the Making of Modern Environmentalism*, chap. 6; and Worster, *Passion for Nature*, chap. 12.

6. Editorials, "The New Forest Reserves," *Garden and Forest*, 3 March 1897, 81; "Congress and the Forest Reservations," *Garden and Forest*, 17 March 1897, 101.

7. Sargent to Johnson, 25 November 1908, Sargent Papers.

8. Sargent to Pinchot, 20 April 1998, Gifford Pinchot Papers, Library of Congress, Washington. In his letter to Sargent on 16 April, Pinchot had defended his acceptance of the appointment from the Department of Interior by arguing that forest commission members Arnold Hague and William Brewer both supported him. Pinchot to Sargent, 16 April 1898, Pinchot Papers.

9. Editorial, "Protection of the National Forests," *Garden and Forest*, 15 December 1897, 490; Sargent to Muir, 24 December 1897, frame 2375, reel 9, Muir Papers.

10. Rodgers, *Bernhard Eduard Fernow*, 17.

11. Ibid., 627; Editorial, "Management of the National Forest Reservations," *Garden and Forest*, 13 January 1892, 20; Sargent to Pinchot, 1 March 1890, Pinchot Papers. The conflict between Sargent and Fernow started in 1884, when both of them were serving on the

committee charged with investigating ways to preserve the Adirondack forests. Fernow disagreed with Sargent's bill proposing to establish an unpaid forest commission that had no practical power to manage the forest.

12. Pinchot's mentor in Europe was Dietrich Brandis, the influential German forester who had worked in British India and developed the forestry system there. Brandis published twenty-five essays in *Garden and Forest*, including a series entitled "The Burma Teak Forest." See S. S. Negi, *Sir Dietrich Brandis: Father of Tropical Forestry* (Dehra Dun: Bishen Singh Mahendra Pal Singh, 1991); and "Sir Dietrich Brandis, F. R. S.," *Geographical Journal* 30 (July 1907): 97.

13. Pinchot, *Breaking New Ground*, 14–15.

14. Ibid., 33.

15. Gifford Pinchot, "The Need of Forest Schools in America," *Garden and Forest*, 24 July 1895, 298.

16. Carl A. Schenck, "Private Forestry and State Forestry, II," *Garden and Forest*, 23 June 1897, 242; Schenck, "Private Forestry and State Forestry, IV," *Garden and Forest*, 7 July 1897, 262.

17. Pinchot, *Breaking New Ground*, 65; Schenck, "Private Forestry and State Forestry, I," *Garden and Forest*, 16 June 1897, 233.

18. J. B. Harrison to Charles E. Norton, 15 October 1863, Charles Eliot Norton Papers, Houghton Library, Harvard College Library, Cambridge. See also Timothy J. Crimmins, "Frederick Law Olmsted and Jonathan Baxter Harrison: Two Generations of Social Critics of the American South," in *Olmsted South: Old South Critic/New South Planner*, ed. Dana F. White and Victor A. Kramer (Westport: Greenwood Press, 1979), 138.

19. J. B. Harrison, "Correspondence: In the Shore Towns of Massachusetts," *Garden and Forest*, 10 February 1892, 69.

20. Stiles's and Harrison's interests overlapped. While Stiles promoted the "big tree" sequoias in California and the national parks, Harrison advocated for Central Park. See Harrison's report, coauthored with Olmsted, *Observations on the Treatment of Public Plantations, More Especially Relating to the Use of the Axe* (Boston: T. R. Marvin, Printers, 1889).

21. J. B. Harrison, "Correspondence: Forests and Civilization," *Garden and Forest*, 17 July 1889, 345; Harrison, "The Forest: Forestry in New England," *Garden and Forest*, 20 February 1889, 92.

22. Editorial, "The Future of Our Forests," *Garden and Forest*, 14 March 1888, 25–26.

23. Bernhard Fernow, "The Forest: Its Significance as a National Resource," *Garden and Forest*, 29 July 1891, 357–58.

24. Editorials, "The Constitutional Amendment Relating to State Forest-lands" *Garden and Forest*, 19 September 1894, 372; "Forestry in the Constitution of the State of New York," *Garden and Forest*, 12 September 1894, 361–62. Roderick Nash remarks that, in the Adirondack Park issue, "the rationale for wilderness preservation was gradually catching up with the ideology of appreciation." Nash, *Wilderness and the American Mind*, 121. On the preservation of the Adirondacks, see Frank Graham, *The Adirondack Park: A Political History* (New York: Knopf, 1978); and Paul Schneider, *The Adirondacks: A History of America's First Wilderness* (New York: Henry Holt, 1997).

25. Editorials, "The Constitutional Amendment Relating to State Forest-lands," *Garden*

and Forest, 19 September 1894, 372; "Forestry in the Constitution of the State of New York," *Garden and Forest*, 12 September 1894, 361–62; "Proposed Change in Forestry Practice in New York," *Garden and Forest*, 10 February 1897, 52.

26. Editorials, "What Is Forestry?" *Garden and Forest*, 9 January 1896, 11; "The Cascade Range Forest Reservation in Danger," *Garden and Forest*, 18 March 1896, 111; Gifford Pinchot, "The Forest: Forestry for the Farmer," *Garden and Forest*, 2 March 1892, 104.

27. Editorial, "Our Forest Interests," *Garden and Forest*, 18 December 1889, 601.

28. Editorials, "Congress and the National Forests," *Garden and Forest*, 11 February 1891, 61–62; "Our Forest Interests," *Garden and Forest*, 18 December 1889, 601.

29. Editorial, "Farmers and Forestry," *Garden and Forest*, 11 July 1888, 229.

30. Bernhard Fernow, "Effect of Forest-Mismanagement on Orchards," *Garden and Forest*, 24 September 1890, 462–63.

31. Editorial, "Mountain Reservoirs and Irrigation," *Garden and Forest*, 3 July 1889, 313.

32. Ibid.; Editorial, "The Forests of California," *Garden and Forest*, 26 September 1888, 361.

33. Editorials, "Forests of California," *Garden and Forest*, 15 January 1890, 25–26; "Our Forest Interests," *Garden and Forest*, 18 December 1889, 601.

34. Editorial, "Forests and Floods," *Garden and Forest*, 4 November 1896, 441; Francis Parkman, "The Forests of the White Mountains," *Garden and Forest*, 29 February 1888, 2. The Merrimack River valley, covering five thousand square miles of water and land in New Hampshire and Massachusetts, was one of the first and the most heavily industrialized regions in the United States. In the 1820s, a group of industrialists known as the Boston Associates moved their textile manufacturing from the low-power Charles River to the Merrimack River and began to exploit its energy. They established the Waltham-Lowell system—a new labor and production mode—and several industrial cities along the river. Urban capital managed to turn flowing rivers into a commodity that could make money. Forests throughout the valley disappeared, especially in the period 1860 to 1880. See Theodore Steinberg, *Nature Incorporated: Industrialization and the Water of New England* (New York: Cambridge University Press, 1991).

35. Editorials, "Legislation for the Adirondacks," *Garden and Forest*, 12 March 1890, 121; "The Adirondack Forests in Danger," *Garden and Forest*, 28 March 1888, 49; J. B. Harrison, "The Forest: The Forests and Woodland of New Jersey, III," *Garden and Forest*, 30 January 1889, 57.

36. Editorials, "Lumberman and Forester," *Garden and Forest*, 21 March 1894, 111; "An American School of Forestry," *Garden and Forest*, 18 April 1888, 86.

37. Gifford Pinchot, "The Forest: Forest-policy Abroad," *Garden and Forest*, 7 January 1891, 8.

38. Bernhard Fernow, "The Forest: European State Forestry," *Garden and Forest*, 12 September 1888, 345; Gifford Pinchot, "The Forest: Forest-policy Abroad," *Garden and Forest*, 7 January 1891, 8.

39. N. H. Egleston, "The Forest: Preserving Small Forests," *Garden and Forest*, 24 September 1890, 470.

40. Editorial, "What Is Forestry?" *Garden and Forest*, 9 January 1896, 11.

41. Editorials, "The Latest Forest Legislation," *Garden and Forest*, 9 June 1897, 221–22; "Care of the National Forests," *Garden and Forest*, 23 March 1894, 201.

42. Editorials, "Legislation for the Adirondacks," *Garden and Forest*, 12 March 1890, 121;

"Legislation for the Adirondacks," *Garden and Forest*, 30 April 1890, 209; "The Value of the White Mountain Forests and the Dangers Which Threaten Them," *Garden and Forest*, 8 February 1893, 62; "The Forests of the White Mountains in Danger," *Garden and Forest*, 12 December 1888, 493–94; "Protection of Public Forests," *Garden and Forest*, 10 February 1892, 62.

43. J. B. Harrison, "Laws Alone Cannot Save Our Forests," *Garden and Forest*, 14 March 1888, 26; Editorial, "The Future of Our Forests," *Garden and Forest*, 14 March 1888, 25; C. A. Schenck, "Private Forestry and State Forestry, I," *Garden and Forest*, 16 June 1897, 233; Editorial, "The Forestry Meeting at Philadelphia," *Garden and Forest*, 16 October 1889, 493; J. B. Harrison, "The Forest: The Pennsylvania Forestry Association," *Garden and Forest*, 23 May 1888, 154. Harrison gave the address at the annual meeting of the Pennsylvania Forestry Association.

44. Editorial, "Forestry Commissions," *Garden and Forest*, 10 October 1888, 385.

45. Editorials, "Forest Fires—How to Stop Them," *Garden and Forest*, 2 May 1894, 172; "The Regulation of Brush Fires," *Garden and Forest*, 22 January 1890, 38.

46. J. B. Harrison, "Forests and Civilization," *Garden and Forest*, 10 July 1889, 333.

47. Editorial, "Congress and the Forest Reservations," *Garden and Forest*, 17 March 1897, 101.

48. Editorial, "Forests and Civilization," *Garden and Forest*, 19 December 1888, 505; J. B. Harrison, "The Forest: Forestry in New England," *Garden and Forest*, 20 February 1889, 92–93.

49. Editorials, "Portable Saw-mills," *Garden and Forest*, 17 July 1891, 277; "The Love of Trees," *Garden and Forest*, 18 May 1892, 230.

50. J. B. Harrison, "The Forest: Value of Mountain Forests—II," *Garden and Forest*, 24 December 1890, 625.

51. Editorial, "Spare the Wild Flowers," *Garden and Forest*, 9 October 1889, 481; W. J. Beal, "The Disappearance of Wild Flowers," *Garden and Forest*, 30 October 1889, 527; C. L. Allen, "The Disappearance of Wild Flowers," *Garden and Forest*, 25 December 1889, 623.

52. Editorials, "A Scheme of Californian Lumbermen," *Garden and Forest*, 6 October 1897, 390; "National Parks," *Garden and Forest*, 6 August 1890, 377; "A Suggestion," *Garden and Forest*, 13 July 1892, 325–26; "The Sequoia Reservation," *Garden and Forest*, 27 April 1892, 193.

53. Stiles to Robert Underwood Johnson, 13 August 1890, Yosemite National Park Correspondence, Century Company Records, Manuscripts and Archives Division, New York Public Library, New York.

54. Editorial, "National Parks," *Garden and Forest*, 6 August 1890, 377.

55. Editorials, "Save the Big Trees," *Garden and Forest*, 30 July 1890, 366; "Railroads in the Adirondacks," *Garden and Forest*, 10 June 1891, 266.

56. Edward L. Rand, "The Woods of Mount Desert Island," *Garden and Forest*, 9 October 1889, 483.

57. B. L. Robinson, "Edward Lothrop Rand," *Rhodora: Journal of the New England Botanic Club* 27 (February 1925): 17–27; Eliot, *Charles Eliot, Landscape Architect*, 20–27.

58. Charles Eliot, "The Coast of Maine," *Garden and Forest*, 19 February 1890, 86–87.

59. Ibid., 87.

60. J. B. Harrison, "Correspondence: Forestry Matters in New Hampshire," *Garden and Forest*, 12 February 1890, 81.

61. Editorials, "Epping Forest," *Garden and Forest*, 29 July 1896, 301–2; "The Adirondack Forests in Danger," *Garden and Forest*, 28 March 1888, 49. On the relationship between landscape architects and the national parks, see Ethan Carr, *Wilderness by Design: Landscape Architecture and the National Park Service* (Lincoln: University of Nebraska Press, 1998).

62. Paul W. Hirt, *A Conspiracy of Optimism: Management of the National Forests since World War Two* (Lincoln: University of Nebraska Press, 1994), 293–94.

63. Charles W. Eliot, "The Need of Conserving the Beauty and Freedom of Nature in Modern Life," *National Geographic Magazine* 26 (July 1914): 67–74.

CONCLUSION

1. Adam Rome, "'Political Hermaphrodites': Gender and Environmental Reform in Progressive America," *Environmental History* 11 (July 2006): 440–63. The article includes a cartoon from 1913 that expressed rather well *Garden and Forest*'s urban vision: on one side of the picture is a dark and dangerous city, where nature has been replaced by tall gloomy buildings, while on the other side the buildings have shrunk in scale and a river, trees, sunshine, and human sociability now dominate the landscape. Between the two cities, a slender hand places a card reading, "Women's Vote." Suffrage, that is, must be the means to realize the city natural.

2. See, for example, historians Roy Rosenzweig and Elizabeth Blackmar's criticism in *The Park and the People* that, since the beginning of its construction, Central Park has involved a sacrifice of poor people's interests. Before the construction of the park, the site contained the scattered housing of Seneca Village, where many impoverished New Yorkers lived. In *Crimes against Nature*, Karl Jacoby has made the similar argument that the Adirondacks, Yellowstone, and Grand Canyon parks all coopted the homes of poor and marginalized people. That injustices were committed by environmentalists is undoubtedly true, but one could also argue that these "injustices" were justified because they enhanced the lives of many more people, rich and poor, majority or minority.

3. See Worster, *Passion for Nature*, esp. 3–12.

BIBLIOGRAPHY

Primary Sources

ARCHIVAL MATERIAL

Archives of the Arnold Arboretum Library, Arnold Arboretum of Harvard University, Boston
    Charles Sprague Sargent Papers, 1893–1927 (inclusive)
    Arnold Arboretum Correspondence
Archives of the Gray Herbarium, Harvard University Herbaria Library, Harvard University, Cambridge
    Asa Gray Papers, 1810–1888
    Historic Letters, 1830–1888
    Semi-Historic Letters, 1890–1955
Francis Loeb Library, Graduate School of Design, Harvard University, Cambridge
    Charles Eliot Papers, 1859–1897, Special Collection
Holt-Atherton Library, University of the Pacific, Stockton
    John Muir Papers, reel 9
Houghton Library, Harvard College Library, Cambridge
    Charles Eliot Norton Papers, 1827–1908
Library of Congress, Washington
    Frederick Law Olmsted Papers, Correspondence, 1838–1928
    Gifford Pinchot Papers, Correspondence, 1870–1946
New York City Department of Parks & Recreation, Parks Library, New York
    Minutes and Annual Reports of the Park Board of Commissioners, 1895–1897
New York Public Library, Manuscripts and Archives Division, New York
    Century Company Records, 1871–1924
        General Correspondence
        Yosemite National Park Correspondence

MAGAZINES AND NEWSPAPERS

Garden and Forest: A Journal of Horticulture, Landscape Art, and Forestry, 1888–97
Atlantic Monthly (1880–1900 issues)

Century (1880–1900 issues)
Scribner's Magazine, 1887–96
New York Times (1880–1900 issues)
New York Tribune (1880–1900 issues)

BOOKS

Bailey, Liberty Hyde. *The Country Life Movement in the United States.* New York: Macmillan, 1911.
———. *Cyclopedia of American Horticulture: Comprising Suggestions for Cultivation of Horticultural Plants, Descriptions of the Species of Fruits, Vegetables, Flowers, and Ornamental Plants Sold in the United States and Canada, Together with Geographical and Biographical Sketches and a Synopsis of the Vegetable Kingdom.* New York: Gordon Press, 1975.
———. *The Holy Earth.* New York: Charles Scribner's Sons, 1915.
———. *The Nature-Study Idea; Being an Interpretation of the New School-Movement to Put the Child in Sympathy with Nature.* New York: Doubleday, Page, 1903.
Bellamy, Edward. *Equality.* New York: D. Appleton, 1897.
———. *Looking Backward, 2000–1897.* Boston: William Ticknor, 1888.
Chuang Tzu. *The Complete Works of Chuang Tzu.* Translated by Burton Watson. New York: Columbia University Press, 1968.
Egleston, Nathaniel Hillyer. *Arbor Day Leaves.* New York: American Book Company, 1893.
Eliot, Charles W. *Charles Eliot, Landscape Architect: A Lover of Nature and of His Kind, Who Trained Himself for a New Profession, Practised It Happily and through It Wrought Much Good.* Boston and New York: Houghton Mifflin, 1902.
Emerson, George B. *A Report on the Trees and Shrubs Growing Naturally in the Forests of Massachusetts.* Boston: Commonwealth of Massachusetts, 1846.
Farnham, Charles Haight. *A Life of Francis Parkman.* Boston: Little, Brown, 1900.
Fernow, Bernhard E. *Economics of Forestry: A Reference Book for Students of Political Economy and Professional and Lay Students of Forestry.* New York: T. Y. Crowell, 1902.
Grinnell, George Bird. *American Big Game in Its Haunts: The Book of the Boone and Crockett Club.* New York: Forest and Stream Publishing, 1904.
Marsh, George Perkins. *Man and Nature.* Edited by David Lowenthal. Cambridge: Harvard University Press, 1965. Reprint, Seattle: University of Washington Press, 2003.
Morris, William. *News from Nowhere, or, An Epoch of Rest: Being Some Chapters from a Utopian Romance.* London and New York: Longmans, Green, 1891.
Muir, John. *The Mountains of California.* New York: Century Company, 1894.
Olmsted, Frederick L. *Civilizing American Cities: Writing on City Landscapes.* Edited by S. B. Sutton. New York: Da Capo Press, 1997.
———. *Journeys and Explorations in the Cotton Kingdom of America: A Traveller's Observations on Cotton and Slavery in the American Slave States, Based upon Three Former Volumes of Journeys and Investigations by the Same Author.* 2 vols. London: Sampson Low, Son and Company, 1861.
———. *The Papers of Frederick Law Olmsted.* 6 vols. and supplementary vol. 1. Edited by Charles Capen McLaughlin, Charles E. Beveridge, David Schuyler, Jane Turner Censer, and Victoria Post Ranney. Baltimore: Johns Hopkins University Press, 1977–97.
———. *Walks and Talks of an American Farmer in England.* 2 vols. New York: G. P. Putnam, 1852.
Pinchot, Gifford. *Breaking New Ground.* New York: Harcourt, Brace, 1947.

Robbins, Mary Caroline. *The Rescue of an Old Place*. Boston and New York: Houghton, Mifflin, 1892.

Robinson, Charles Mulford. *The Improvement of Towns and Cities or The Practical Basis of Civic Aesthetics*. New York: G. P. Putman's Sons, 1901.

——. *Modern Civic Art, or, the City Made Beautiful*. New York: G. P. Putman, 1903.

Sargent, Charles Sprague. *Report on the Forests of North America (Exclusive of Mexico)*. Washington: Government Printing Office, 1884.

——. *The Silva of North America: A Description of the Trees Which Grow Naturally in North America Exclusive of Mexico*. 14 vols. Boston and New York: Houghton, Mifflin, 1890–1902.

Van Rensselaer, Mariana Schuyler. *Art Out-of-Doors: Hints on Good Taste in Gardening*. New York: Scribner's Sons, 1893.

Whitehill, Walter Muir. *A Life of Francis Parkman*. Boston: Little, Brown, 1901.

SECONDARY SOURCES

ARTICLES

Andersen, Phyllis. "'Master of a Felicitous English Style: William Augustus Stiles, Editor of *Garden and Forest*." *Arnoldia* 60, no. 2 (2000): 39–43.

Balogh, Brian. "Scientific Forestry and the Roots of the Modern American State: Gifford Pinchot's Path to Progressive Reform." *Environmental History* 7 (April 2002): 198–225.

Bender, Thomas. "The 'Rural' Cemetery Movement: Urban Travel and the Appeal to Nature." *New England Quarterly* 47, no. 2 (1974): 196–211.

Carr, Ethan. "*Garden and Forest* and 'Landscape Art.'" *Arnoldia* 60, no. 3 (2000): 5–8.

Colten, Craig E. "Reintroducing Nature to the City: Wetlands in New Orleans." *Environmental History* 7 (April 2002): 226–46.

Dunlap, Thomas. "Sport Hunting and Conservation, 1880–1920." *Environmental Review* 12 (spring 1988): 51–60.

Glave, Dianne D. "'A Garden So Brilliant with Colors, So Original in Its Design': Rural African American Women, Gardening, Progressive Reform, and the Foundation of an African American Environmental Perspective." *Environmental History* 8 (July 2003): 395–411.

Griswold, Mac. "The Influence of *Garden and Forest* on the Development of Horticulture." *Arnoldia* 60, no. 3 (2000): 29–32.

Haglund, Karl. "Emerald Metropolis." *Arnoldia* 53 (fall 1993): 2–17.

Hays, Samuel P. "From Conservation to Environment: Environmental Politics in the United States since World War Two." *Environmental Review* 6 (autumn 1982): 16.

Hurley, Andrew. "Creating Ecological Wastelands: Oil Pollution in New York City, 1870–1900." *Journal of Urban History* 20 (May 1994): 340–64.

Hyland, Howard L. "History of U.S. Plant Introduction." *Environmental Review* no. 4 (1977): 26–33.

Kowsky, Francis R. "Municipal Parks and City Planning: Frederick Law Olmsted's Buffalo Park and Parkway System." *Journal of the Society of Architectural Historians* 46 (March 1987): 49–64.

Jacobs, Wilbur R. "Francis Parkman: Naturalist-Environmental Savant." *Pacific Historical Review* 61 (May 1992): 341–56.

Judd, Richard W. "A 'Wonderful Order and Balance': Natural History and the Beginnings of Forest Conservation in America." *Environmental History* 11 (January 2006): 8–36.

Major, Judith. "Mariana Griswold Van Rensselaer's Landscape Gardening Manifesto in *Garden and Forest.*" *Landscape Journal* 26, no. 2 (2007): 183–200.

Miller, Char. "A High Grade Paper: *Garden and Forest* and Nineteenth-Century American Forestry." *Arnoldia* 60, no. 2 (2000): 19–22.

——, and James G. Lewis. "A Contested Past: Forestry Education in the United States, 1898–1998." *Journal of Forestry* 97 (1999): 38–43.

Morgan, Keith N. "Charles Eliot, Landscape Architect: An Introduction to His Life and Work." *Arnoldia* 59 (summer 1999): 3–21.

Mullin, John R. "Edward Bellamy's Ambivalence: Can Utopia Be Urban?" *Utopian Studies* 11 (fall 2000): 51–65.

Orpet, Mildred S. "E. O. Orpet, Horticulturist." *Journal of the California Horticultural Society* 13, no. 2 (April 1952): 39–52.

Rome, Adam. "'Political Hermaphrodites': Gender and Environmental Reform in Progressive America." *Environmental History* 11 (July 2006): 440–63.

Rudolph, Emanuel D. "One Hundred Years of the Missouri Botanical Garden." *Annals of the Missouri Botanical Garden* 78, no. 1 (1991): 1–18.

Rybczynski, Witold. "Why We Need Olmsted Again." *Wilson Quarterly* 23 (summer 1999): 15–21.

Sachs, Aaron. "American Arcadia: Mount Auburn Cemetery and the Nineteenth-Century Landscape Tradition." *Environmental History* 15 (April 2010): 206–35.

Spence, Mark. "Dispossessing the Wilderness: Yosemite Indians and the National Parks Ideal, 1864–1930." *Pacific Historical Review* 61 (February 1996): 27–59.

Spongberg, Stephen A. "*Garden and Forest:* The Botanical Basis of It All." *Arnoldia* 60, no. 2 (2000): 7–9.

Terrie, Philip G. "'Imperishable Freshness': Culture, Conservation, and the Adirondack Park." *Forest and Conservation History* 37, no. 3 (1993): 132–41.

Thornton, Tamara Plakins. "The Moral Dimension of Horticulture in Antebellum America." *New England Quarterly* 57 (March 1984): 3–24.

Whitehill, Walter M. "Francis Parkman as Horticulturist." *Arnoldia* 33, no. 3 (1973): 177.

Worster, Donald. "John Muir and the Modern Passion for Nature." *Environmental History* 10 (January 2005): 8–20.

——. "Living in Nature: Biography and Environmental History." In *Thinking through the Environment: Green Approaches to Global History,* edited by Timo Myllyntaus, 28–39. Cambridge: White Horse Press, 2011.

——. "The Wilderness of History." *Wild Earth* 7, no. 3 (1997): 9–13.

BOOKS AND DISSERTATIONS

Abbott, Gordon. *Saving Special Places: A Centennial History of the Trustees of Reservations; Pioneers of the Land Trust Movement.* Ipswich: Ipswich Press, 1993.

Allerfeldt, Kristofer, ed. *The Progressive Era in the USA, 1890–1921.* Aldershot and Burlington: Ashgate, 2007.

Armitage, Kevin. *The Nature Study Movement: The Forgotten Popularizer of America's Conservation Ethic.* Lawrence: University Press of Kansas, 2009.

Bender, Thomas. *Toward an Urban Vision: Ideas and Institutions in Nineteenth-Century America*. Lexington: University Press of Kentucky, 1975.

Binfor, Henry C. *The First Suburbs: Residential Communities on the Boston Periphery, 1815–1860*. Chicago: University of Chicago Press, 1985.

Birnbaum, Charles A., and Robin Karson, eds. *Pioneers of American Landscape Design*. New York: McGraw-Hill, 2000.

Boyer, Paul. *Urban Masses and Moral Order in America*. Cambridge: Harvard University Press, 1978.

Brewer, Richard. *Conservancy: The Land Trust Movement in America*. Lebanon: Dartmouth College Press, 2004.

Buell, Lawrence. *The Environmental Imagination: Thoreau, Nature Writing, and the Formation of American Culture*. Cambridge: Belknap Press of Harvard University Press, 1995.

Burnstein, Daniel Eli. *Next to Godliness: Confronting Dirt and Despair in Progressive Era New York City*. Urbana: University of Illinois Press, 2006.

Burrows, Edwin, and Mike Wallace. *Gotham: A History of New York City to 1898*. New York: Oxford University Press, 1999.

Carlson, Allan. *The New Agrarian Mind: The Movement toward Decentralist Thought in Twentieth Century America*. New Brunswick: Transaction, 2000.

Carr, Ethan. *Wilderness by Design: Landscape Architecture and the National Park Service*. Lincoln: University of Nebraska Press, 1998.

Carson, Rachel. *Silent Spring*. Boston: Houghton Mifflin, 1962.

Chudacoff, Howard. *The Evolution of American Urban Society*. Englewood Cliffs: Prentice Hall, 1975.

———, Judith E. Smith, and Peter C. Baldwin. *The Evolution of American Urban Society*. 7th ed. Upper Saddle River: Prentice Hall, 2010.

Clouse, Richard R. "Where Art Is Combined with Nature: Village Improvement in Nineteenth-Century New England." PhD dissertation, Cornell University, 1987.

Coates, Peter. *American Perceptions of Immigrant and Invasive Species: Strangers on the Land*. Berkeley: University of California Press, 2006.

———. *Nature: Western Attitudes since Ancient Times*. Berkeley: University of California Press, 1998.

Cohen, Shaul E. *Planting Nature: Trees and the Manipulation of Environmental Stewardship in America*. Berkeley: University of California Press, 2004.

Contosta, David. *Suburb in the City: Chestnut Hill, Philadelphia, 1850–1990*. Columbus: Ohio State University Press, 1992.

Cranz, Galen. *The Politics of Park Design: A History of Urban Parks in America*. Cambridge: MIT Press, 1982.

Cronon, William. *Nature's Metropolis: Chicago and the Great West*. New York: Norton, 1991.

———, ed. *Uncommon Ground: Rethinking the Human Place in Nature*. New York: Norton, 1996.

Davis, Allen F. *Spearheads for Reform: The Social Settlements and the Progressive Movement, 1890–1914*. New York: Oxford University Press, 1967.

Diettert, Gerald A. *Grinnell's Glacier: George Bird Grinnell and Glacier National Park*. Missoula: Mountain Press, 1992.

Doell, M. Christine Klim. *Gardens of the Gilded Age: Nineteenth-Century Gardens and Homegrounds of New York State*. Syracuse: Syracuse University Press, 1986.

Domosh, Mona. *Invented Cities: The Creation of Landscape in Nineteenth-Century New York & Boston.* New Haven: Yale University Press, 1996.

Duncan, Dayton. *The National Parks: America's Best Idea; An Illustrated History.* New York: Knopf, 2009.

Egan, Timothy. *The Big Burn: Teddy Roosevelt and the Fire That Saved America.* Boston: Houghton Mifflin Harcourt, 2009.

Fein, Albert. *Frederick Law Olmsted and the American Environmental Tradition.* New York: G. Braziller, 1972.

Fisher, Irving D. *Frederick Law Olmsted and the City Planning Movement in the United States.* Ann Arbor: UMI Research Press, 1986.

Flader, Susan. *Thinking Like a Mountain: Aldo Leopold and the Evolution of an Ecological Attitude toward Deer, Wolves, and Forests.* Columbia: University of Missouri Press, 1974.

Fox, Stephen R. *John Muir and His Legacy: The American Conservation Movement.* Boston: Little, Brown, 1981.

Fraser, Derek, and Anthony Sutcliffe, eds. *The Pursuit of Urban History.* London: Edward Arnold, 1983.

Gandy, Matthew. *Concrete and Clay: Remaking Nature in New York City.* Cambridge: MIT Press, 2002.

Gottlieb, Robert. *Forcing the Spring: The Transformation of the American Environmental Movement.* Washington: Island Press, 1993.

Graham, Frank. *The Adirondack Park: A Political History.* New York: Knopf, 1978.

Green, James R. *Death in the Haymarket: A Story of Chicago, the First Labor Movement and the Bombing that Divided Gilded Age America.* New York: Pantheon Books, 2006.

Griswold, Mac, and Eleanor Weller. *The Golden Age of American Gardens: Proud Owners, Private Estates, 1890–1940.* New York: H. N. Abrams with the Garden Club of America, 1991.

Grove, Carol. "Aesthetics, Horticulture and the Gardenesque: Victorian Sensibilities at Tower Grove Park." PhD dissertation, University of Missouri, 1998.

Grove, Richard H. *Green Imperialism: Colonial Expansion, Tropical Island Edens and the Origin of Environmentalism, 1600–1860.* New York: Cambridge University Press, 1995.

Haglund, Karl. *Inventing the Charles River.* Cambridge: MIT Press, 2003.

Hall, Lee. *Olmsted's America: An "Unpractical" Man and His Vision of Civilization.* Boston: Little, Brown, 1995.

Havlick, Spenser W. *The Urban Organism: The City's Natural Resources from an Environmental Perspective.* New York: Macmillan, 1974.

Hay, Ida. *Science in the Pleasure Ground: A History of the Arnold Arboretum.* Boston: Northeastern University Press, 1994.

Hays, Samuel P. *The American People & the National Forests: The First Century of the U.S. Forest Service.* Pittsburgh: University of Pittsburgh Press, 2009.

———. *Beauty, Health, and Permanence: Environmental Politics in the United States, 1955–1985.* New York: Cambridge University Press, 1987.

———. *Conservation and the Gospel of Efficiency: The Progressive Conservation Movement, 1890–1920.* Cambridge: Harvard University Press, 1959.

Herring, Scott. *Lines on the Land: Writers, Art, and the National Parks.* Charlottesville: University of Virginia Press, 2004.

Hinsley, Curtis M., and David R. Wilcox, eds. *The Southwest in the American Imagination: The Writings of Sylvester Baxter, 1881–1889.* Tucson: University of Arizona Press, 1996.

Hirt, Paul W. *A Conspiracy of Optimism: Management of the National Forests since World War Two.* Lincoln: University of Nebraska Press, 1994.

Hofstadter, Richard. *Age of Reform: From Bryan to F. D. R.* New York: Knopf, 1955.

Holmes, Madelyn. *American Women Conservationists: Twelve Profiles.* Jefferson: McFarland, 2004.

Hurley, Andrew, ed. *Common Fields: An Environmental History of St. Louis.* Saint Louis: Missouri Historical Society Press, 1997.

Irland, Lloyd. *The Northeast's Changing Forests.* Hanover: University of New England Press, 1999.

Jackson, Kenneth. *Crabgrass Frontier: The Suburbanization of the United States.* New York: Oxford University Press, 1985.

Jacoby, Karl. *Crimes against Nature: Squatters, Poachers, Thieves, and the Hidden History of American Conservation.* Berkeley: University of California Press, 2001.

Judd, Richard W. *Common Lands, Common People: The Origins of Conservation in Northern New England.* Cambridge: Harvard University Press, 1997.

———. *The Untilled Garden: Natural History and the Spirit of Conservation in America, 1740–1840.* New York: Cambridge University Press, 2009.

Kalfus, Melvin. *Frederick Law Olmsted: The Passion of a Public Artist.* New York: New York University Press, 1990.

Kaufman, Polly Welts. *National Parks and the Woman's Voice: A History.* Albuquerque: University of New Mexico Press, 2006.

Kennedy, Lawrence W. *Planning the City upon a Hill: Boston since 1630.* Amherst: University of Massachusetts Press, 1992.

Kinnard, Cynthia D. "The Life and Works of Mariana Griswold Van Rensselaer, American Art Critic." PhD dissertation, Johns Hopkins University, 1977.

Klingle, Matthew. *Emerald City: An Environmental History of Seattle.* New Haven: Yale University Press, 2007.

Kowsky, Francis R. *Country, Park, and City: The Architecture and Life of Calvert Vaux, 1824–1895.* New York: Oxford University Press, 1997.

Langston, Nancy. *Forest Dreams, Forest Nightmares: The Paradox of Old Growth in the Inland West.* Seattle: University of Washington Press, 1995.

Lasch-Quinn, Elisabeth. *Black Neighbors: Race and the Limits of Reform in the American Settlement House Movement, 1890–1945.* Chapel Hill: University of North Carolina Press, 1993.

Lears, T. J. Jackson. *No Place of Grace: Antimodernism and the Transformation of American Culture, 1880–1920.* New York: Pantheon Books, 1981. Reprint, Chicago: University of Chicago Press, 1994.

Lees, Andrew. *Cities Perceived: Urban Society in European and American Thought, 1820–1940.* Manchester: Manchester University Press, 1985.

Leopold, Aldo. *A Sand County Almanac: With Other Essays on Conservation from Round River.* New York: Oxford University Press, 1966.

Levy, John M. *Urban America: Processes and Problems.* Upper Saddle River: Prentice Hall, 2000.

Liner, Marc, and Lawrence S. Zacharias. *Of Cabbages and Kings County: Agriculture and the Formation of Modern Brooklyn.* Iowa City: University of Iowa Press, 1999.

Lowenthal, David. *George Perkins Marsh: Prophet of Conservation*. Seattle: University of Washington Press, 2000.

Machor, James L. *Pastoral Cities: Urban Ideals and the Symbolic Landscape of America*. Madison: University of Wisconsin Press, 1987.

Makker, Kirin. "Building Main Street: Village Improvement and the Small Town Ideal." PhD dissertation, University of Massachusetts Amherst, 2010.

Major, Judith K. *To Live in the New World: A. J. Downing and American Landscape Gardening*. Cambridge: MIT Press, 1997.

Marx, Leo. *The Machine in the Garden: Technology and the Pastoral Ideal in America*. New York: Oxford University Press, 1964.

McBride, Paul. *Culture Clash: Immigrants and Reformers, 1880–1920*. San Francisco: R and E Research Associates, 1975.

McClelland, Linda F. *Building the National Parks: Historic Landscape Design and Construction*. Baltimore: Johns Hopkins University Press, 1998.

Melosi, Martin V. *Garbage in the Cities: Refuse, Reform, and the Environment, 1880–1980*. College Station: Texas A&M University Press, 1981.

———. *The Sanitary City: Urban Infrastructure in America from Colonial Times to the Present*. Baltimore: Johns Hopkins University Press, 2000.

Merchant, Carolyn. *Reinventing Eden: The Fate of Nature in Western Culture*. New York: Routledge, 2003.

Meyers, Amy R., ed. *Art and Science in America: Issues of Representation*. San Marino: Huntington Library Press, 1998.

Meyerson, Harvey. *Nature's Army: When Soldiers Fought for Yosemite*. Lawrence: University Press of Kansas, 2001.

Miller, Char, ed. *American Forests: Nature, Culture, and Politics*. Lawrence: University Press of Kansas, 1997.

———. *Gifford Pinchot and the Making of Modern Environmentalism*. Washington: Island Press/ Shearwater Books, 2001.

———, and Hal Rothman, eds. *Out of the Woods: Essays in Environmental History*. Pittsburgh: University of Pittsburgh Press, 1997.

Miller, Zane, and Patricia M. Melvin. *The Urbanization of Modern America: A Brief History*. 2nd ed. San Diego: Harcourt Brace Jovanovich, 1987.

Minteer, Ben. *The Landscape of Reform: Civic Pragmatism and Environmental Thought in America*. Cambridge: MIT Press, 2006.

———, and Robert E. Manning, eds. *Reconstructing Conservation: Finding Common Ground*. Washington: Island Press, 2003.

Mott, Frank Luther. *A History of American Magazines*, vol. 4, *1885–1905*. Cambridge: Harvard University Press, 1938–68.

Mumford, Lewis. *The Brown Decades: The Study of the Arts in America, 1865–1895*. New York: Harcourt, Brace, 1931.

———. *The City in History: Its Origins, Its Transformations, and Its Prospects*. New York: Harcourt, Brace, and World, 1961.

Nash, Roderick, ed. *American Environmentalism: Readings in Conservation History*. 3rd ed. New York: McGraw-Hill, 1990.

———. *Wilderness and the American Mind*. New Haven: Yale University Press, 1967, and subsequent editions.

Negi, S. S. *Sir Dietrich Brandis: Father of Tropical Forestry*. Dehra Dun: Bishen Singh Mahendra Pal Singh, 1991.

Newman, William A., and Wilfred E. Holton. *Boston's Back Bay: The Story of America's Greatest Nineteenth-Century Landfill Project*. Boston: Northeastern University Press, 2006.

Nicolson, Marjorie Hope. *Mountain Gloom and Mountain Glory: The Development of the Aesthetics of the Infinite*. Seattle: University of Washington Press, 1997.

Noonan, Mark. *Reading the "Century Illustrated Monthly Magazine": American Literature and Culture, 1870–1893*. Kent: Kent State University Press, 2010.

O'Connor, Thomas H. *The Hub: Boston Past and Present*. Boston: Northeastern University Press, 2001.

Patterson, Cynthia Lee. *Art for the Middle Classes: America's Illustrated Magazines of the 1840s*. Jackson: University Press of Mississippi, 2010.

Penna, Anthony N., and Conrad Edick Wright, eds. *Remaking Boston: An Environmental History of the City and Its Surroundings*. Pittsburgh: University of Pittsburgh Press, 2009.

Peterson, Jon A. *The Birth of City Planning in the United States, 1840–1917*. Baltimore: Johns Hopkins University Press, 2003.

Philippon, Daniel J. *Conserving Words: How American Nature Writers Shaped the Environmental Movement*. Athens: University of Georgia Press, 2004.

Piott, Steven L. *American Reformers, 1870–1920: Progressives in Word and Deed*. Lanham: Rowman & Littlefield, 2006.

Postel, Charles. *The Populist Vision*. New York: Oxford University Press, 2007.

Pregill, Philip, and Nancy Volkman. *Landscapes in History: Design and Planning in the Eastern and Western Traditions*. 2nd ed. New York: John Wiley, 1999.

Price, Jennifer. *Flight Maps: Adventures with Nature in Modern America*. New York: Basic Books, 1999.

Price, Kenneth, and Susan Smith, eds. *Periodical Literature in Nineteenth-Century America*. Charlottesville: University of Virginia Press, 1995.

Punch, Walter T., ed., and the Massachusetts Horticultural Society. *Keeping Eden: A History of Gardening in America*. Boston: Bulfinch Press, 1992.

Punke, Michael. *Last Stand: George Bird Grinnell, the Battle to Save the Buffalo, and the Birth of the New West*. New York: Smithsonian Books/Collins, 2007.

Rawson, Michael. *Eden on the Charles: The Making of Boston*. Cambridge: Harvard University Press, 2010.

Reiger, John. *American Sportsmen and the Origins of Conservation*. 3rd ed. Corvallis: Oregon State University Press, 2001.

Richardson, Robert. *Emerson: The Mind on Fire: A Biography*. Berkeley: University of California Press, 1995.

———. *Henry Thoreau: A Life of the Mind*. Berkeley: University of California Press, 1986.

Risjord, Norman K. *Populists and Progressives*. Lanham: Rowman & Littlefield, 2005.

Rodgers, Andrew Denny, III. *American Botany, 1873–1892: Decades of Transition*. Princeton: Princeton University Press, 1944.

———. *Bernhard Eduard Fernow: A Story of North American Forestry*. Princeton: Princeton University Press, 1951.

———. *Liberty Hyde Bailey: A Story of American Plant Sciences*. Princeton: Princeton University Press, 1949.

Rodgers, Daniel. *Atlantic Crossings: Social Politics in a Progressive Age*. Cambridge: Harvard University Press, 1998.

Rome, Adam. *The Bulldozer in the Countryside: Suburban Sprawl and the Rise of American Environmentalism*. New York: Cambridge University Press, 2001.

Roper, Laura Wood. *FLO: A Biography of Frederick Law Olmsted*. Baltimore: Johns Hopkins University Press, 1973.

Rosenzweig, Roy. *Eight Hours for What We Will: Workers and Leisure in an Industrial City, 1870–1920*. New York: Cambridge University Press, 1983.

———, and Elizabeth Blackmar. *The Park and the People: A History of Central Park*. Ithaca: Cornell University Press, 1992.

Runte, Alfred. *National Parks: The American Experience*. 3rd ed. Lincoln: University of Nebraska Press, 1997.

Rybczynski, Witold. *A Clearing in the Distance: Frederick Law Olmsted and America in the Nineteenth Century*. New York: Scribner, 1999.

Sachs, Aaron. *The Humboldt Current: Nineteenth-Century Exploration and the Roots of American Environmentalism*. New York: Viking, 2006.

Scheese, Don. *Nature Writing: The Pastoral Impulse in America*. New York: Twayne, 1996.

Schmitt, Peter J. *Back to Nature: The Arcadian Myth in Urban America*. New York: Oxford University Press, 1969. Reprint, Baltimore: Johns Hopkins University Press, 1990.

Schneider, Paul. *The Adirondacks: A History of America's First Wilderness*. New York: Henry Holt, 1997.

Schultz, Stanley K. *Constructing Urban Culture: American Cities and City Planning, 1800–1920*. Philadelphia: Temple University Press, 1989.

Schuyler, David. *Apostle of Taste: Andrew Jackson Downing, 1815–1852*. Baltimore: Johns Hopkins University Press, 1996.

———. *The New Urban Landscape: The Redefinition of City Form in Nineteenth-Century America*. Baltimore: Johns Hopkins University Press, 1986.

Scott, James C. *Seeing Like a State: How Certain Schemes to Improve the Human Condition Have Failed*. New Haven: Yale University Press, 1998.

Seasholes, Nancy S. *Gaining Ground: A History of Landmaking in Boston*. Cambridge: MIT Press, 2003.

Sellars, Richard. *Preserving Nature in the National Parks: A History*. New Haven: Yale University Press, 1997.

Simo, Melanie. *Forest and Garden: Traces of Wildness in a Modernizing Land, 1897–1949*. Charlottesville: University of Virginia Press, 2003.

Smith, Carl. *The Plan of Chicago: Daniel Burnham and the Remaking of the American City*. Chicago: University of Chicago Press, 2006.

Smith, Daniel S. "The Discipline of Nature: A History of Environmental Discourse in the Northern Forest of New England and New York." PhD dissertation, Yale University, 2003.

Spain, Daphne. *How Women Saved the City*. Minneapolis: University of Minnesota Press, 2001.

Spongberg, Stephen A. *A Reunion of Trees: The Discovery of Exotic Plants and Their Introduction into North American and European Landscapes*. Cambridge: Harvard University Press, 1990.

Steinberg, Theodore. *Down to Earth: Nature's Role in American History.* New York: Oxford University Press, 2002.

———. *Nature Incorporated: Industrialization and the Waters of New England.* New York: Cambridge University Press, 1991.

Stevenson, Elizabeth. *Park Maker: A Life of Frederick Law Olmsted.* New Brunswick: Transaction, 2000.

Stilgoe, John R. *Borderland: Origins of the American Suburb, 1820–1939.* New Haven: Yale University Press, 1988.

Stradling, David. *Making Mountains: New York City and the Catskills.* Seattle: University of Washington Press, 2007.

———. *Smokestacks and Progressives: Environmentalists, Engineers and Air Quality in America, 1881–1951.* Baltimore: Johns Hopkins University Press, 1999.

Stroud, Ellen Frances. "The Return of the Forest: Urbanization and Reforestation in the Northeastern United States." PhD dissertation, Columbia University, 2001.

Sutton, S. B. *Charles Sprague Sargent and the Arnold Arboretum.* Cambridge: Harvard University Press, 1970.

Tarr, Joel A. *The Search for the Ultimate Sink: Urban Pollution in Historical Perspective.* Akron: University of Akron Press, 1996.

Teaford, Jon C. *The Unheralded Triumph: City Government in America, 1870–1900.* Baltimore: Johns Hopkins University Press, 1984.

Thernstrom, Stephan. *The Other Bostonians: Poverty and Progress in the American Metropolis, 1880–1970.* Cambridge: Harvard University Press, 1973.

Thomas, John. *Alternative America: Henry George, Edward Bellamy, Henry Demarest Lloyd, and the Adversary Tradition.* Cambridge: Belknap Press of Harvard University Press, 1983.

Thomas, Keith. *Man and the Natural World: Changing Attitudes in England, 1500–1800.* London: Allen Lane, 1983.

Thornton, Tamara Plakins. *Cultivating Gentlemen: The Meaning of Country Life among the Boston Elite, 1785–1860.* New Haven: Yale University Press, 1989.

Tucker, Amy. *The Illustration of the Master: Henry James and the Magazine Revolution.* Stanford: Stanford University Press, 2010.

Turner, Frederick. *The Frontier in American History.* New York: Henry Holt, 1920.

Uekoetter, Frank. *The Age of Smoke: Environmental Policy in Germany and the United States, 1880–1970.* Pittsburgh: University of Pittsburgh Press, 2009.

von Hoffman, Alexander. *Local Attachments: The Making of an American Urban Neighborhood, 1850 to 1920.* Baltimore: Johns Hopkins University Press, 1994.

Walker, Peter, and Melanie Simo. *Invisible Gardens: The Search for Modernism in the American Landscape.* Cambridge: MIT Press, 1994.

Warren, Louis. *The Hunter's Game: Poachers and Conservationists in Twentieth-Century America.* New Haven: Yale University Press, 1997.

White, Dana F. *The Urbanists, 1865–1915.* New York: Greenwood Press, 1989.

———, and Victor A. Kramer, eds. *Olmsted South: Old South Critic/New South Planner.* Westport: Greenwood Press, 1979.

White, Morton, and Lucia White. *The Intellectual versus the City: From Thomas Jefferson to Frank Lloyd Wright.* Cambridge: Harvard University Press, 1962.

White, Richard. *Railroaded: The Transcontinentals and the Making of Modern America*. New York: Norton, 2011.

Wiebe, Robert H. *The Search for Order, 1877–1920*. New York: Hill and Wang, 1967.

Williams, Michael. *Americans and Their Forests: A Historical Geography*. New York: Cambridge University Press, 1989.

Williams, Raymond. *The Country and the City*. London: Chatto & Windus, 1973.

Wilson, William H. *The City Beautiful Movement*. Baltimore: Johns Hopkins University Press, 1989.

Wolfe, Linnie Marsh. *Son of the Wilderness: The Life of John Muir*. New York: Knopf, 1945.

Worster, Donald, ed. *American Environmentalism: The Formative Period, 1860–1915*. New York: John Wiley, 1973.

——. *Nature's Economy: A History of Ecological Ideas*. 2nd ed. New York: Cambridge University Press, 1994.

——. *A Passion for Nature: The Life of John Muir*. New York: Oxford University Press, 2009.

——. *A River Running West: The Life of John Wesley Powell*. New York: Oxford University Press, 2001.

——. *The Wealth of Nature: Environmental History and the Ecological Imagination*. New York: Oxford University Press, 1993.

Young, Terence. *Building San Francisco's Parks, 1850–1930*. Baltimore: Johns Hopkins University Press, 2004.

Zaitzevsky, Cynthia. *Frederick Law Olmsted and the Boston Park System*. Cambridge: Belknap Press, 1982.

INDEX

Note: page numbers appearing in italic refer to illustrations.